What Others Say About the Impact of the Last Edition

"I've used the *Ultimate Guide to Google AdWords* since the first edition. Transforming a client's unprofitable AdWords account into a cash cow—churning out $30 to $35k profits every month. Just scratching the surface of the book's contents.

"This is the best book on AdWords, period. Plus, it's a dang good book on internet marketing. Not only can you use it to tap Google's huge traffic stream, you'll also convert the thundering hordes of traffic into buyers and profits in your pocket. Do what I do—don't just buy and use it yourself; buy copies for your friends!"

—Roy Furr, Editor, *Breakthrough Marketing Secrets*, Direct Marketing Consultant

"I'm often asked by peers in my niche how I manage to rank so well in search engines and not go broke using Google AdWords. There are a couple of reasons—I've been subscribing to Perry Marshall's newsletters since 2003; I've read every one of his books; I listen in on all the conference calls he organizes; and finally, I IMPLEMENT his strategies and tactics.

"The *Ultimate Guide to Google AdWords* lists for $24.95. Only a fool would continue to run Google AdWords campaigns and NOT invest in, study, and implement the ideas in it. And no, you'll not find an affiliate link to Amazon here. Just get the book!"

—Jer Ayles-Ayler, AdWords User, Trihouse Enterprises, Inc.

"I bought this book to learn how to get better results from AdWords for my clients. The advice given is easy to follow, and following up on the results of your campaign is exciting. I've already seen a huge increase in clickthrough rates for the different customers and campaigns I run. I get far better results for less money.

"I would recommend reading *Ultimate Guide to Google AdWords* to anyone interested in starting AdWords marketing, or tuning their current campaigns for better results. On the other hand, I'd like to keep what's in here a secret."

—Henrik Hedberg, AdWords User

"Naming this the Ultimate Guide is not a fluke. I have been tweaking the hell out of the ads I'm using to lead searchers into my funnel. Over the past few weeks, I've managed to get one of my ads up to just over 7% CTR from a previous 1 to 2%!"

—Bill Perry, AdWords User

"I thought I knew it all. I set up an AdWords account and a couple of days later I came back to check if I was rich yet. Unfortunately, the only thing that happened was Google enjoyed free access to my bank account. Luckily the traffic was not that high so it was just a couple hundred dollars. And I made no money.

"Frustrated, I went online and did some research. Every forum, article, and blog seemed to be talking about Perry Marshall, so I decided to get *Ultimate Guide to Google AdWords*. 30 minutes into reading my mind was blown away.

"Next, my Quality Score went up from an average of two and three to a six and nine for various keywords. At the same time, my cost-per-click went down from over $4 to about $0.50.

"The rest is history. Seriously, if you don't know the stuff in this book don't even think of AdWords. This is THE guide."

—Jean Paul Essiam, AdWords User

"An exemplary Google AdWords manual that could easily prevent costly mistakes and help boost profits."

—Kirkus Reviews

[Editor's Note] These testimonials are in reference to the previous version of this book, which was titled using the former name for what is now known as Google Ads: Google AdWords.

Entrepreneur MAGAZINE'S
ULTIMATE
GUIDE TO

Google
Ads

Sixth Edition

- Access more than 1 billion people in 10 minutes
- **Double your website traffic overnight**
- Build a profitable ad campaign today—from scratch

PERRY MARSHALL   BRYAN TODD   MIKE RHODES

Entrepreneur Press®

This publication is designed to provide accurate and authoritative information in regard to the subject matter covered. It is sold with the understanding that the publisher is not engaged in rendering legal, accounting, or other professional services. If legal advice or other expert assistance is required, the services of a competent professional person should be sought.

Entrepreneur Press® is a registered trademark of Entrepreneur Media, Inc.

Library of Congress Cataloging-in-Publication Data

An application to register this book for cataloging has been submitted to the Library of Congress.

ISBN 978-1-59918-673-3 (paperback) | ISBN 978-1-61308-430-4 (ebook)

Printed in the United States of America

25 24 23 22 21   10 9 8 7 6 5 4 3 2 1

Contents

CHAPTER 13

How to Get Your Ads on Millions of Websites with Google's Display Network

CHAPTER 14

Remarketing: The Single Most Profitable Online Advertising Strategy

CHAPTER 15

Google Shopping Campaigns: A Huge ROI Boost for Ecommerce

Wait!
Before You Read
This Book . . .

If you're brand-new to Google Ads and you're just getting started, you MUST read this short section first.

And if you've got years of Ads experience under your belt or you already own an earlier edition of this book, we'll give you shortcuts and page numbers for the advanced, new material in the book at the end of this preface.

The first thing you need to do is go get your online bonus material at www.perrymarshall.com/supplement. There, you'll also find a collection of supplemental material that I consider *vital* to this book (because Google is constantly fussing with things), and you'll get in line for a series of updates you'll need as Google's system changes.

OK, now that you've done that, let me tell you *how* to go about learning Google Ads.

IF YOU'RE A RANK BEGINNER . . .

There's an old saying: "You can't learn to ride a bicycle at a seminar," and it definitely applies to Ads. Google Ads and, really, everything you do in direct marketing is hands-on. It's not theory. It's the real world. It's the school of hard knocks.

About that last part: When Google Ads (formerly Google AdWords) was brand-new, there were many inexpensive clicks available, and you could find your way by making lots of cheap mistakes.

Those days are over. Today, that strategy will get you slaughtered.

When you open a Google Ads account, go ahead and enter your keywords, write some ads, and set some bid prices. It's OK if you don't really know what you're doing at this point. The first few chapters of this book will show you exactly how to do it. But here's the most important thing of all:

Set a low daily budget, say $5 or $10 per day, to make absolutely sure that your first experience with Google Ads is a GOOD one—not a painful one. The worst thing you can do in your new career as a Google advertiser is accidentally run up $2,500 of clicks that you don't know how to pay for. All advertisers have to go through some trial and error before things really come together. Google will make many assumptions about how to set up your account that are wrong, and if you blindly follow its menus, you'll make some costly mistakes.

Another giant mistake advertisers make is assuming that Google is "benevolent." *Not true!* If I had a dollar for every person who told me, "The Google rep called me with some friendly suggestions and . . . well, I lost thousands of dollars," I'd be a good deal richer. Google does have a Green Beret team of crackerjack reps who know what they're doing, but only huge advertisers and premium agencies get those guys. Everybody else gets reps who are hustling to meet their sales quota. Most Google reps have never spent a single dollar of their own money buying Google Ads, let alone been required to make a profit and meet payroll. And once they have your money, you will never get it back. Sleep with one eye open.

The best thing you can do is enjoy the process of watching those clicks come in and seeing your handiwork produce results. If you're hands-on from the word "go," everything you read in this book will make ten times more sense.

So go ahead and get started. Create your Google Ads account, roll up your sleeves, and jump in. We recommend you read the first two chapters to get a good overview of Google Ads, direct marketing, and all the strategy behind it.

If you're just starting out, or you want a refresher, we cover the fundamentals in Chapters 3 through 7. They'll give you a fantastic grounding.

Then, when you're ready to dive into the more advanced material, Chapters 8 to 28 will cover every technique you need to get into the top 1 percent of all Google Ads practitioners.

As you go from one chapter to the next, make changes to your account. You'll literally be able to see the performance difference in a few hours.

But before you even spend $10 on Google clicks, please make sure you're using this book as your guide. If you don't, you'll make a slew of common mistakes and blow a lot of cash you could have used to grow your business. Also make sure you access the special reports and the audios and videos in the Book Bonus members' area. They're at www.perrymarshall.com/supplement.

IF YOU'RE A VETERAN PAY-PER-CLICK MARKETER . . .

This is the sixth edition of the *Ultimate Guide to Google Ads*. We've added new chapters and sections that reflect the sharpest and most current Google strategies, including:

- Getting started with your initial market research
- Planning and goal setting
- Campaign types
- Using "discovery" campaigns
- Targeting audiences for search and Shopping
- Mastering your tracking
- Mastering optimization

Plus, we've got significant updates on:

- Building your first campaign
- Bidding and budgets
- Keywords
- Landing pages
- Shopping
- Automating and using Google's AI
- Analytics and attribution

Whether you're a seasoned veteran, you've read the previous editions of this book, or you're already a pay-per-click ninja, I bet you've never seen these before.

ADVANCED MATERIAL FOR GO-GETTER GOOGLE ADVERTISERS

I've added new, advanced material at www.perrymarshall.com/supplement for aggressive marketers, including extended reports and videos for all the strategies I just named: YouTube advertising, advanced campaign types, and improved Display Network techniques, as well as USP, "bionic" Google ads, and savvy market selection.

Once you've registered for the bonus material, you'll also receive the regular updates we send out about Google's ever-changing system.

One last thing: I mince no words. Google is THE benchmark for advertisers and information providers worldwide. In fact, from the standpoint of ordinary people getting things done every single day, Google is the most trusted brand on the web. If you're up to Google's standards, you're world-class.

So don't bring a knife to a gunfight. I'm not saying it's easy. It is not. But I do promise—it IS rewarding.

THE WINNING METHOD THE WORLD'S SMARTEST MARKETERS STOLE FROM THE WRIGHT BROTHERS

The boneyard of modern civilization is littered with "great" marketing ideas that never got off the ground.

Think of the trillions of dollars companies have spent developing products, only to find out that their products weren't what people wanted in the first place.

Let's *not* assume you're a corporation with billions of dollars to spend. Instead, let's assume you're a regular person who quit a cushy job to pursue an entrepreneurial vision. As you calculate it, you've got to start making a profit in six to nine months before you run out of money.

If that's you, then you can't afford to make a mistake. You can't spend three months developing a product and then find out in month six that it has to be totally redesigned. That'll kill your business and send you back to the J.O.B. with your tail between your legs.

Let's make sure this never happens to you.

How can you prevent it? By testing your product idea and even your website on the cheap, using Google, *before* you've spent a lot of money. With the internet, you can find out if a product idea will succeed or fail for a few hundred to a few thousand dollars.

If you do this, you can be sure that the product you develop will be well-received.

HOW THE WRIGHT BROTHERS' SAVVY TESTING METHOD MADE THEM "FIRST IN FLIGHT"

The year: 1903. The place: a houseboat on the Potomac River, USA.

Just weeks before Wilbur and Orville Wright flew the world's first airplane at Kitty Hawk, North Carolina, Samuel Pierpont Langley (seen in Figure P–1 on page xvii), a well-

FIGURE P–1. Samuel Pierpont Langley

funded engineer and inventor, was attempting to launch an airplane of his own—with the assistance of an entire staff.

Langley's assumption: Put a big enough engine on the thing, and it would fly. He focused all his effort on that one project: creating an engine powerful enough for a plane to go airborne. On October 7, 1903, Langley tested his model for the very first time.

The plane crashed immediately after leaving the launch pad, badly damaging the front wing.

Two months later, just eight days before the Wright brothers' successful flight, Langley made a second attempt. This time the tail and rear wing collapsed completely during launch.

Langley was ridiculed by the press and criticized by members of Congress for throwing away taxpayer dollars on his failed projects. (Can you imagine the cynicism? I'm sure many sneering reporters believed that nobody could or would ever fly.) Disillusioned by the public response, Langley abandoned his vision.

Wilbur and Orville Wright, meanwhile, had a completely different approach: build a glider (which you can see in Figure P-2 on page xviii) that would glide from a hilltop with no engine at all. They focused on balance and steering. Power was almost an afterthought. Only after the glider worked by itself would they try to put an engine on it.

After three years of tedious experimentation, the glider was working well, so they commissioned bicycle shop machinist Charlie Taylor to build them an engine. It was the smallest engine he could design—a 12-horsepower unit that weighed 180 pounds.

And on December 17, 1903, at Kitty Hawk, North Carolina, Wilbur and Orville Wright made history.

FIGURE P–2. The Wright Brothers' Test Glider

The Wright brothers changed the world and earned lasting fame, while few have ever heard of Samuel Langley. Their approach of making the plane fly *before* applying power was the winning idea.

Langley . . . had spent most of four years building an extraordinary engine to lift their heavy flying machine. The Wrights had spent most of four years building a flying machine so artfully designed that it could be propelled into the air by a fairly ordinary internal combustion engine.

—Smithsonian, April 2003

Skill comes by the constant repetition of familiar feats rather than by a few overbold attempts at feats for which the performer is yet poorly prepared.

—Wilbur Wright

Samuel Pierpont Langley died in 1906, a broken and disappointed man.

PEOPLE WHO TEST, FLY. PEOPLE WHO RELY ON BRUTE FORCE, DIE

You don't want to die a broken and disappointed person. You want to die rich and famous. Or at least rich, right?

Then there is a direct comparison between the Wright brothers and your career as an internet marketer.

The search engine is the motor. Your website is the glider.

A motor without a good set of wings does you no good. When you put an engine on a glider, you have a plane. When you feed traffic to a website that can "fly," you have a business.

And as smart marketers like Claude Hopkins have known for more than a century, you get the wings to work through careful, systematic testing.

This is not a new concept. For more than 100 years, smart, savvy marketers have followed these principles of proven good sense and made their advertising dollars go many times further.

In 1923, Claude Hopkins wrote:

> [A]dvertising and merchandising become exact sciences. Every course is charted. The compass of accurate knowledge directs the shortest, safest, cheapest course to any destination.
>
> We learn the principles and prove them by repeated tests. . . . We compare one way with many others, backward and forward, and record the results. . . .
>
> [A]dvertising is traced down to the fraction of a penny. The cost per reply and cost per dollar of sale show up with utter exactness.
>
> One ad is compared with another, one method with another. Headlines, settings, sizes, arguments, and pictures are compared. To reduce the cost of results even 1 percent means much. . . .
>
> So no guesswork is permitted. One must know what is best.

Building a business online doesn't have to be guesswork. It's not a crapshoot. It's a *science*. Wise men and women before us have taken the risks, tested the limits, learned the hard lessons, and laid down a clear path for us that we can follow with confidence.

Whether your business is entirely online or only partly so, the foundation remains the same: Start small, test carefully, make modest improvements, get deeper insights into your market, and then test some more, and you'll *know* that your business is going to grow.

This well-worn path builds a sales process that works. And when you have a persuasive website, you have a glider—just like the Wright brothers. All you need to do is put a lightweight engine on it, and you can fly.

Add Google traffic the smart way, and you'll have a business that soars. Google Ads can bring you a lot of traffic, and that traffic is valuable to the extent that your website can convert it to leads and sales.

When you're getting started, Google is like a lightweight engine you can turn on and off instantly. You can test your glider safely without crashing, killing a potential joint venture partnership, or blowing through a lot of money.

MARKETING MISERY: NOT NECESSARY

Thousands of people go to bed every night wondering *Why? Why can't I make any sales? Why can't I earn any real money at this?*

This is not necessary, but it's a lesson that the scorched dotcoms in the late 1990s learned the hard way. They were like Langley—they focused on the engine instead of the wings. When their business didn't take off, they just poured more gas into the engine, and when that didn't work, they put it on a rocket launcher and forced it into the air. Inevitably they crashed and burned.

But you don't have the time or money to pour into product ideas and sales messages that, in hindsight, were "almost right." Your spouse won't let you blow the grocery money or college savings on a hunch.

Reality is a great teacher. The people who click on your ads will tell you what they want if you ask them, and they'll show you what they want if you watch them.

Follow the guidelines in this book, and you'll be a world-class promoter in your market, your niche, and your chosen profession. I wish you the very, very best of success.

—Perry Marshall
Chicago, Illinois

Chapter 1

Chisel Your Way In:
Frank Talk About the Google Ads of Today

Years from now, the story of you and all the other players in your market will be just like the story of Google vs. Excite, HotBot, Infoseek, AltaVista, Yahoo!, and MSN: a bunch of losers, a couple that turned out sort of OK, and one massive success story.

I want YOU to be the success story. The alpha dog.

In this chapter, I'm going to outline a few vital strategies that can determine whether you succeed or fail in online marketing and Google Ads. I'll conclude with some frank discussion of what it takes to make Google Ads work today. Stick with me a minute for a brief internet history lesson.

Remember the dotcom bubble, when half the world thought Amazon's Jeff Bezos was a genius and the other half deemed him a bloody fool? Do you remember the late '90s, when it was obvious to everybody (OK, almost everybody) that the internet was a Very Big Deal and the stakes were very, very high? That's why the dotcom bubble happened—investors and entrepreneurs alike were determined to win on this new playing field, no matter the cost.

The internet is not merely another communication medium. As my friend Tom Hoobyar said, it is a fundamental shift for humanity that's as important as the discovery of fire.

I remember sometime around 1999 or 2000, Yahoo! Auctions was trying to make a go of it. I was selling stuff on eBay at the time, so I tried Yahoo! Auctions, too. They were advertising all over the place, and their fees were lower than eBay's.

But I quickly discovered that Yahoo! Auctions didn't have as many buyers, and my stuff didn't fetch as high a price on Yahoo! as it got on eBay. I didn't want to sell an item for $17 on Yahoo! if it would fetch $20 on eBay.

As a seller, I wanted to go where the buyers were. Buyers want to go where the sellers are. This synergy between buyers and sellers is called the *network effect*. The network effect says the value of a network is equal to the number of members squared. So if in 1999 Yahoo! Auctions had one million users and eBay had two million, eBay wasn't just twice as powerful—it was four times as powerful. Yahoo! couldn't overcome the advantage of eBay's sheer numbers.

As you know, eBay went on to become the web's number-one auction site. There isn't even a close runner-up today.

The network effect is twice as big on the internet as in the brick-and-mortar world. Why? Because the internet is almost frictionless. This quality paradoxically introduces a new kind of friction: *the nearly effortless dominance of the number-one player over all competitors.* The other players are at their mercy.

This has *everything* to do with you and your quest to dominate your market. I will get to that in just a minute. First, a quick story.

Way back in April 2002, I went to my first internet marketing conference, Ken McCarthy's System Seminar. There, I heard Jon Keel speak on pay-per-click (PPC) advertising. Jon was my first true inspiration as an online marketer. He devoted most of his presentation to Overture, which was the dominant PPC service at the time. But he also spent a few minutes talking about Google Ads, which he hadn't played with much yet.

By this time, eBay was already the king of online auctions, and I knew that now they had claimed this position, it would be hard for anyone to steal it away from them. So while Jon was still talking, I raised my hand and asked:

"Jon, is it possible for a pay-per-click engine to become a search monopoly, like eBay has a monopoly on auctions?"

Jon didn't know. I had a hunch it was true, but I didn't know why.

After the seminar ended, I went home and opened my first Google Ads account. Within a few days, I knew I'd discovered the most amazing direct-response marketing tool in history and launched a beautiful magic carpet ride that has yet to end.

At that point, Google was just another player in the dogfight between MSN, Yahoo!, AltaVista, HotBot, Excite, Infoseek, and a dozen others. There was no clear winner yet—they were all just beginning to move away from the "free" model. Search engine optimization (SEO) was still easy to game.

I personally liked Google much more than the rest, but I was in the minority. Many people still didn't even know what Google was. Nobody at the time realized that Google was poised to become the 800-pound gorilla of the internet.

In those early days of Ads, I wondered:

In this frictionless world, where every search engine is only one click away from any other, and only one browser setting away from being the default, how can any one search engine dominate?

In hindsight, that was a dumb question. Here are some better ones:

If one search engine/auction site/map service/ecommerce store/butcher/baker/candlestick maker is clearly just a little better than everyone else, what is going to stop everyone from buying from them instead?

And when that fabled tipping point happens, and they get thousands or millions or billions of dollars in their coffers, what is going to stop them from reinvesting the profits and getting better and better until they are absolutely unbeatable?

A year after that conference, in 2003, Google Ads hit critical mass. It reached the point where everyone was seeing their competitors' ads on Google and wanted to know how they got there. Affiliate marketers figured out that every word in the English language (and most other languages) was up for sale. The world got sucked in by Google's irresistible gravitational pull.

Where Overture was clunky and poorly thought out, Ads was elegant and magnificently executed. Sure, Ads had its flaws, but it was fundamentally *right*. It was a marketer's dream. Over the next five years, Google exploded with breathtaking force, outpacing Overture as a PPC platform, raking in billions of dollars, and going public (in 2004).

Google, which was just a *little* better than all the other search engines, started getting a *lot* better.

Google Maps became almost otherworldly in its sophistication. Soon you could take a virtual tour of anywhere on earth with Street View. In 2006, Google bought YouTube, which became the world's number-two search engine and the default place to upload videos of your kids' ballet recitals.

Ads started adding features; eventually almost every form of targeting you could imagine became possible, no matter how granular. Local businesses started tuning into Google Maps. Consultants and agencies started pitching, "I'll get you listed on Google."

Once Google added Google News (2002), Gmail (2004), and its popular web browser Chrome (2008), it became entrenched, as unbeatable as eBay. The other search engines were and are vastly inferior. You'd have to spend a trillion dollars to unseat Google at this point, and you would *still* probably fail.

This "winner-take-all" phenomenon is what the dotcom boom was really all about. Sure, there was a lot of dumb stuff—sock puppet mascots and whatnot. People take big risks when trillions of dollars are on the line. But they knew the potential rewards were huge. The present dominance of Google, Amazon, Apple, and Facebook proves that.

So what does all this have to do with you?

The winner-take-all phenomenon is just as true at *your* level and in *your* market as it was for eBay and Google and Facebook—especially if you run a purely online business or any business with a national or international market.

In my book *80/20 Sales and Marketing*, I describe how it's a law of nature that 80 percent of the money comes from 20 percent of the customers, 80 percent of the sales come from 20 percent of the products, and 80 percent of the cars drive on 20 percent of the roads. The 80/20 rule applies to almost everything you do in business.

But here's something I don't really talk about in that book: On the internet, most things aren't 80/20. They're 90/10!

The web, the "great equalizer," the leveler of all playing fields, is in fact even more unequal than real life. Ninety percent of the customers use 10 percent of the search engines. [Ninety percent of your traffic comes from 10 percent of your ad campaigns.] Ten percent of the advertisers get 90 percent of the traffic.

Winners win big and losers lose big on the internet because it's so frictionless.

Online marketing is a blood sport. You are playing for keeps. If you think Google Ads is going to be some small task you can delegate to your part-time assistant . . . if you're planning to stick your toe in the water and dabble in it . . . or if you think you're just going to spend an hour or two buying some clicks and get rich . . .

Ditch this book right now and go find some other delusion to indulge in.

Because it's *not* going to work that way.

You're either going to do this right, dominate your competition, and return with the spoils, or you're going to go home with your tail between your legs. You'll be just another Yahoo! Auctions, and the whole thing will end up being a painful lesson and a tax write-off.

This is not some miscellaneous activity that's going to make you a little extra money. This is big—if you want it to be. If you're not serious, don't even start.

If you're in business at all, this is the game you're playing. It's a 90/10 game, and you're either among the wannabe 90 or the wealthy 10. There isn't much of an in-between. If you're not one of the top three, you're toast. This isn't just true on Google—it's true everywhere on the internet.

Some people may tell you otherwise . . . but they're lying. There's no lack of con artists on the web. So if you want to make a middling living doing mediocre work, go babysit a kiosk at the mall, where you can accost a few dozen people every hour as they walk by.

But if you're going to play on the internet, you need to pick a game you can win, and then you need to play for keeps.

It is *far* easier to be number one—and stay there—than it is to be number four or number ten and fight over the scraps with all the other losers. As the "number-one Google Ads author" for the past ten years, I can assure you it's true.

When you're number one in your market, all the traffic flows your way because people make more money sending their traffic to you than they make keeping it to themselves. You're the star—the default go-to person everyone talks about. You get treated to the best deals, approached by the best vendors, offered first right of refusal on the best joint ventures, and presented with the seat of honor at the head table. Reaching out to an adjacent niche and dominating that one, too, becomes easier and easier.

When you're number ten in your market, you just hope your spouse's salary will cover the mortgage and groceries.

With Google Ads, 2 percent of the advertisers get 50 percent of the traffic. So you need to decide to be one of the players in the top 10 percent, who share 90 percent of the spoils with Google.

Google is the gold standard. Your ability to buy Google clicks is *the* measure of your sales mojo, *the* litmus test of your ability to be number one in your market. Do you have the best sales machine? Can you be number one? Are you inching up on number one and quickly becoming a contender? Or are you fading away?

Once you know how to do Google Ads, you'll find out exactly how you measure up.

THE THREE NICHE DOMINATION STRATEGIES OF GOOGLE ADS

There are three main ways you can dominate the Google Ads game:

1. If you can afford to spend even one penny more than all your competitors to buy clicks, sooner or later you *will* be number one. This is Jonathan Mizel's famous "Unlimited Traffic Technique." When you have the best sales funnel and conversion rates, you get easy access to all the traffic, not just some of it.

2. If you can't be the big fish in a big pond, be a big fish in a little pond. This is very important, and it goes hand in hand with the third strategy:

3. If you can find a little pocket where the competition is thinner and you can dominate, you can chisel your way into an overlooked market in Google Ads. (There are millions of them right now, and there always will be!) You can grow from there—even if you're David facing off against Goliath.

Until every single person on earth who searches Google finds the thing they are looking to buy, there's room for you.

I know what you're thinking: "Yeah, Perry, that's great. But it's a Catch-22. How can I dominate a market if I can't get traffic? And how can I get traffic if I haven't yet figured out how to dominate a market?"

Every single piece of advice in the rest of this book falls under one of these three strategies. In the pages to come, Mike Rhodes, Bryan Todd, and I are going to take you by the hand and show you how to use them.

Google's job is to thin the herd. Our job is to make you fat.

Chapter 2

How to Force Prospects to Choose Your Site:
Make Them Buy from You, Not Your Competition

Google gets searched about 6.5 billion times every day. That's 75,000 searches every second.

Google can bring thousands of visitors to your website 24 hours a day, 7 days a week, 365 days a year, whether you're taking a shower, eating breakfast, driving to work, picking up your kids at school, making a phone call, sleeping, daydreaming, busting your butt to meet a deadline, chasing down a customer, typing an email message . . .

And that traffic to your site can all happen on autopilot: 100 percent predictable and completely consistent, like clockwork.

Twenty years ago, that was an impossible dream; today, it's a reality.

And of all the different traffic sources you can buy (we wrote the world's most popular book on Facebook advertising, too), Google is the steadiest, the stablest, and the most predictable. If you want traffic 24/7/365, Google is unmatched.

Think of the lengths to which we entrepreneurs, business owners, and salespeople go just to get a company off the ground or to get a sale. I could recount in agonizing detail the *years* of my life I spent working the phone, pounding the pavement, making cold calls, renting trade-show booths, going to no-show appointments, and booking meetings that were a total waste of time.

But not anymore. Now customers come to me.

They'll come to you, too.

Google Ads has been the biggest revolution in advertising in the past 50 years. Never before had it been possible to spend five bucks, open an account, and have brand-new, precisely targeted customers arrive at your website within minutes.

There are a lot of different things you might want from Google. Maybe you're adding an online component to your retail operation, looking to get steadier cash flow and deeper discounts from your suppliers. Maybe you want to make your payroll easier or position your consulting business better.

Maybe you're already getting traffic to your site, but free listings are too unreliable. Maybe you've had some success selling on eBay, and now you want to play with the big boys. Maybe you've been futzing around with social media, and you've finally decided it's time to make some serious money. Maybe you're a working parent, and you want to be able to spend more time with your family.

If you're privy to the secrets of online marketing, all those opportunities will open up to you. You'll have fresh, hot sales leads waiting in your email inbox every morning when you sit down at your desk. You'll have customers buying from you around the clock.

Instead of chasing customers, they'll come to you. Instead of trying to *guess* whether your next product launch will work, you can *know*. How is this possible? Because in the past decade, the direction of commerce has flipped.

In the old days (are you too young to remember the 1990s?), entrepreneurs and salespeople pursued customers with phone calls, letters, and newspaper ads. Now customers hunt down businesses on the web.

Back then, you had a list of prospects you would contact and try to get them to buy. Now the buyers—millions of them—are trolling the web every second of the day, looking for businesses that can scratch their itch.

Ever heard Woody Allen's saying "80 percent of success is showing up"? The phrase takes on a whole new meaning in the 21st century. If your restaurant just *shows up* on

Google and its search partners when people type in the right phrase, a starving crowd will bust your doors down. They'll fill every table and flood the kitchen with orders. If they like the daily special and the desserts, they'll come back and eat again and again. There's a feast going on—*if* you show up.

Here, you'll discover the secrets of showing up at the right places and times, and in front of the right people. And if you're already advertising on Google, you'll learn how to cut your bid prices 20 percent, 50 percent, or even 70 percent or more.

This book is for:

- Ecommerce marketers
- Local retail stores and service businesses
- Niche product marketers
- Homebased businesses
- Authors, speakers, consultants, and publishers
- B2B marketers collecting sales leads
- Nonprofits, churches, and charities
- Resellers, repair services, and parts suppliers
- Online communities and membership sites

Google Ads can help your business whether you're a little old lady selling quilts in eastern Kentucky or a multinational corporation. You don't have to be a web developer to excel at this; many of the best online marketers are nontechnical people who succeed simply because they understand their customers.

A lot of these success stories are from "invisible entrepreneurs." By invisible, I mean that their next-door neighbors have no idea what they do, but they're quietly running micro-empires from their spare bedrooms. And they're in hundreds of industries, ranging from the mundane to the ridiculous to the outrageously specialized. Some of these guys and gals are making *serious* cash: tens or even hundreds of thousands of dollars a month.

HERE'S HOW TO MAKE SURE THEY FIND *YOU* AND BUY FROM *YOU*—NOT SOMEONE ELSE

Got a watch with a second hand?

Tick. 75,000 people just searched Google and went to somebody's website.

Tick. 75,000 more.

Tick. 75,000 more.

That's 4.5 million people a minute, every minute, all day long, all night long.

Here they come: 75,000 every second.

Are they finding your website? Are they buying from you? Or are they finding someone *else's* website and buying from them instead?

They *should* be finding you. Many of them *will* come to your site, buy from you, and come back again and again, *if* you follow the simple instructions in this book.

Google Ads can be the traffic monster that feeds your autopilot marketing machine and churns out a profit for you every day and every night, hitting the entire world up for customers while you sleep. Not just bringing you tire kickers but highly qualified buyers who are actively looking for what you sell right this minute.

If the internet matters to your business, then no book you've ever bought has more potential to make or save you money than this one.

This book is written so you can blow through it fast and get going immediately on your plan to make serious money with Google insider marketing tactics. That's the fun part: quickly implementing killer tactics that will flood your business with prospects and profit.

But there's a serious side, too. I've held nothing back here. So not only will you know how to play the Google Ads game, but you'll also discover how to craft powerful marketing messages and hooks, bond with your customers, and dominate your market.

In this book, you'll discover:

- Tragic, costly mistakes that almost all Google advertisers and online entrepreneurs make—and how to easily avoid them (including techniques Google *should* teach you but doesn't).
- How to disaster-proof business startups and product launches and pound the risk out of new ventures. (Most times, you've only got one or two shots to nail it; why would you want to leave anything to chance?)
- Profiles of successful online businesses. Having coached hundreds of online entrepreneurs to success, I've accumulated a list of vital characteristics that separate the winners from the losers, many of which defy normal "business school wisdom."
- How to create ultra-persuasive Google ads and web pages that not only convert visitors to buyers but automatically improve with time as well, making it impossible for your rivals to catch up to you.
- The advanced (but simple) shortcut secrets of getting deep into your customer's head so you know exactly where their hot buttons are and how to punch them at will. The result is fanatical customer loyalty and a rabid customer base that eagerly buys almost everything you ask them to buy.

If you're already advertising on Google, you'll get 30 percent to 300 percent more visitors, for less money than you're paying right now.

While many hardcore "let's get after it" types will mark up and dog-ear this book for later reference, you can start seeing results *while* you're reading it. There are shortcuts you can use tonight and see the results before you go to bed an hour later. Your business can literally improve by tomorrow morning.

So strap on your crash helmet because you're in for a wild ride. *Onward!*

—Perry Marshall

P.S.: I've created an online supplement to this book with more than $85 worth of extended book chapters, audio interviews, information on specialized topics, and ongoing updates on Google's ever-changing rules. You can access it at www. perrymarshall.com/supplement.

P.P.S.: Here are some cool success stories I've gotten from my customers:

I'm telling everyone that your book is "required reading" if they want to market online. I actually read your "Definitive Guide" in one day, and that evening started my first Ads campaign. I now have four of them running, and the average clickthrough rate for all campaigns is above 2 percent. I also get well over a 3 percent CTR (some as high as 15 percent) on my more targeted keywords. This has increased the traffic to my sites tenfold in some cases and has made my monthly revenues much more consistent (which is always nice). Best of all, I've never had a keyword shut down by Google for low CTR, and I've only done one round of "peel and stick" with my ads. I give all the credit to my recent Ads success to you and your book.

—Ryan Deiss, Austin, TX

I first purchased Perry's Ads guide about five years ago and just recently purchased the newest version.

That's about five years of Perry Marshall information, and I've never once been offered a dream. I don't do Ads advertising because I can't afford it.

But Perry never promised me that I could get rich using Ads; i.e., he never tried to sell me a dream. I really appreciate that. Like he said, Ads is not a business. It's a tool you can use to advertise your business, and I don't know anyone that's more qualified than Perry Marshall that can teach you how to benefit from Ads.

I can promise you this. This information will save you a lot of money and possibly even an arm and a leg . . . it all depends on what kind of fish you're swimming with.

—Roger Kelley, Decatur, AL

Since your last coaching call, we made the keyword matching changes as you recommended and have the following to show you. Our overall CTR is 4.4 percent—our best ad is 12.4 percent and the worst one is a very respectable 3.1 percent!

—SIMON CHEN, THE EIGHT BLACK GROUP, MELBOURNE, AUSTRALIA

I've been a faithful Perry fan since I met him at a Dan Kennedy event about five years ago. I own most of Perry's products, I've been through the Bobsled Run twice, and I attended a four-man intensive at his house last year.

Perry always tells it like it is. He's not like most of the "gurus" out there always trying to sell you their next product or coaching program. Perry gives us rock-solid advice on how to grow our business or how to sell more products. He repeats his solid advice over and over with no sales hype. That's why we love and trust Perry. That's why I've been a longtime customer and I buy everything he offers.

Recently, I took a real job after being on my own for ten years. I'm now an online marketing/SEO analyst for a local software company. I'm managing their Ads campaigns, which are over $20,000 per month worldwide.

Using what Perry taught me, I increased their CTR from just over 1 percent to over 6 percent in just one day. They're running three times more ads on the same budget, and they're getting better-qualified leads.

Think about using your knowledge managing Ads campaigns as a consultant or for a company. There are tons of online marketing jobs out there right now, and most pay over six figures a year. I never thought I could go back to a real job, but I love getting that steady paycheck and going home at 5 o'clock every day not worrying about keeping my business going. Plus, I'm consulting on the side still, so I'm making more than I ever have."

—TED PRODROMOU, SAN ANSELMO, CA
AUTHOR, *ULTIMATE GUIDE TO LINKEDIN FOR BUSINESS*

Your Ads guide is worth hundreds of times its cost. And the free advice in your marketing emails—one story in particular about the Wright brothers and Samuel Langley—has been absolutely priceless.

—PAUL DEL PIERO, AUSTIN, TX

I was getting about 2,830 clicks per month with Google Ads at $1.06 per click. I've spent about eight hours total reading your stuff and implementing it. Based on the results of my last few days, I am on track to get 7,815 clicks in the next month and spend the same $3,000 a month . . . a savings of $23,400 per year, or

$2,925 per hour for the eight hours I have invested. This is without doubt one of the absolute best investments I've ever made, and I haven't even started! And yes, I have done most of this while sitting at home in my underwear.

—Keith Lee, TMS, Kent, WA

I had spent almost $100,000 on wasted SEO firms and websites with no real reward. I discovered Perry on another podcast I was listening to and have learned so much in only a year. I have just started employing his processes on Google Ads and am reaping the benefits already. I appreciate your delivery of information and the lack of BS in your sales tactics . . .

You bring great info to the table so we do not have to sort through to find what is useful. It's simply amazing watching my clickthrough rate go from 0.3 percent up to 48 percent in less than 30 minutes.

The most important part is I AM BEATING THE COMPETITION in cost and, better yet, finding areas of "no competition." Thanks for such awesome marketing advice. Your material is by far the most valuable I have purchased. Your concepts are working for me, and I intend on running this as a service for a lot of my web hosting clientele."

—Eddie Symonds, Upper Marlboro, MD

WOW! I got a 500 percent increase in response . . . with just a quick "Band-Aid" fix. Can't wait to see what happens when I follow all your suggestions.

—Jenny Hamby, Copywriter and Seminar Marketing Consultant, SeminarMarketingPro.com, Plainfield, IL

Chapter 3

Planning and Goals

It's a safe bet you can quickly describe to most people what your business does and how you do it. You may even be able to explain simply and clearly how you're different from your competitors. But what is the true purpose of your business?

You may have seen the Simon Sinek TED Talk "Start with Why." Customers need to believe in what you do. More important, they need to believe in *the reason you exist*.

You can and should have a larger purpose. You can marry that purpose to a specific objective. Take these as an example:

- The XYZ industry has lost its way, and my business is going to be the exception.
- People are changed for the better by what we do, and my goal is to reach twice as many next year.
- I'm doing this because I want to help promote truth in the world.
- If we grow our net profit 30 percent, we can feed three times as many children in Mozambique.
- I'm here to build a strong, reputable gathering place in the community—one I'll be proud to leave to my children and grandchildren.

It's that message—addressing why you're in business—that needs to be at the forefront of your marketing efforts. In this chapter, we'll discuss how you can incorporate your "why" into your advertising planning and goals.

YOUR WEBSITE IS NOT A BROCHURE

Measurable objectives drive everything. Specific goals, tied to your greater purpose, drive your marketing and your website.

And let's be clear: Your website is not a brochure.

Building an attractive, functional site used to take a team of graphic designers and web developers. Not anymore. With a fairly inexpensive solution, you can create a platform that gets people to take action: contact you, ask for help, make a purchase, or just fall head over heels for your brand.

A good goal is one where you identify a specific number you want to reach (either a percentage or a dollar target) and (ideally) a date before which it needs to happen.

If you're an ecommerce business, it might look like this:

Gross profit from online sales will be 20 percent more for June than it was for December.

Or, if yours is a lead-generation business, something like this:

Our volume of leads will be 40 percent higher in October than in July, while maintaining an average cost per action (CPA) of $70 or less.

Note that you can have basic goals and *stretch* goals:

- A basic goal would be: "To keep the lights on, we need to sell a minimum of 1,000 small units this month."
- A stretch goal would be: "Our aim is to grow 40 percent this month by selling a minimum of 1,400 small units."

Your website is a major part of the plan that will help you accomplish that.

Measuring Small Steps

If it's leads you're after, tracking them is simple enough. But if you're measuring something grand, like gross profit over the four-month period from early July to the end of October, how will you know at any given point—say, on a Thursday in late August—if you're headed in the right direction? What are some smaller, more immediate metrics you can use to measure your progress toward that bigger goal?

Some are obvious:

- Your number of sales
- Your number of new leads on a daily, weekly, or monthly basis
- Your various conversion rates

And some involve a little more nuance:

- For an ecommerce site, you can track return on ad spend (ROAS), or the revenue you generate for every dollar of ad spend. (A ROAS of 5.5 means you take in $5.50 for every $1 you spend on advertising.)
- For a lead-generation website, track your cost per action (CPA) or cost per lead (CPL)—that is, how much it costs you to acquire each lead.

There are other, still smaller metrics you can watch, such as impressions and clickthrough rate (CTR). But don't get too hung up on measuring impressions. Yes, it's important that people see your ads and it's important that they click, but it's an example of what we call a "vanity metric." And CTR is certainly valuable, but it doesn't measure actual sales outcomes.

HOW MUCH IS YOUR CUSTOMER WORTH?

Knowing *why* you want to bring in customers—that is, understanding the good you want to do in the world—is indispensable.

But how much does it cost you to acquire a new customer? And how much are they worth to you over time? Knowing that number will help you make this process repeatable and sustainable.

You may have heard of LTV, or lifetime value. This refers to how much, on average, each customer is worth to your business over a specific time period. For example:

- If you're a personal injury lawyer and your average client has one case with you that brings in $30,000, their lifetime value is $30,000.
- If you're an online fashion retailer and your average customer will buy three items from you each year over the next three years and spend $100 each time, their lifetime value is $900.

■ If you sell vitamins and the average person makes 12 monthly purchases from you at an average of $20 per purchase, then your customer's lifetime value is $240.

Different business models have different LTVs, along with different buying cycles and customer behavior. If you're clear on how much revenue a new customer brings you, and what your margins are on that revenue, you can calculate the maximum amount you can spend to get a lead or generate a sale.

An Example

Let's take that personal injury attorney as a lead-generation case study.

If your average client is worth $30,000 in gross revenue, and you know you need roughly 100 leads to get one client, then your break-even point is $300 per lead. (That's $30,000 divided by 100.)

That's the maximum amount you can pay to acquire the new client—or so it would seem. *But there's more you need to think about.*

Figure Your Real Costs

Namely, you have to factor in the other costs of doing business: paying your team, running the office, and keeping the lights on.

Your plan is to acquire a client, and the average client will pay you $30,000. But you're also going to spend (in this example) $20,000 servicing the client and keeping your business running.

So now it looks like you have a margin of $10,000. But be careful: this is not profit. It's *the total amount you can pay to acquire a new client* and still break even.

So the real goal revolves around that $10,000 figure. You can't spend any more than that to bring in a client. And if it takes 100 leads, then the most you can spend per lead is actually $100 ($10,000 divided by 100), not $300.

Once you know that number, every dollar you spend *less* than $100 to acquire a lead becomes actual profit—i.e., money to be reinvested in growth, money for your savings account, or money in your pocket.

Every business is different, so you'll need to calculate your own numbers. But this illustrates how vital it is to know your customer lifetime value. Having a solid back end and knowing that you can make repeat sales over time will make all the difference in the world.

BEFORE YOU SPEND A DOLLAR, WHAT'S YOUR GROWTH PLAN?

Some years ago, Mike's marketing business WebSavvy worked with a small manufacturing company in Adelaide, South Australia, that made doors and windows. One day, just three months after they started running ads on Google, the owner called Mike.

"I don't know what your team is doing," he said, "but please dial it down. The guys on my shop floor can't keep up with the demand."

What a wonderful problem to have! Mike was delighted. The WebSavvy team had optimized the account to the point that the customer was inundated with new leads.

Thankfully, Google Ads is like a tap that you can turn on or off, up or down, once you've built the machine and all its pieces are in place. In this case, WebSavvy stepped in and reduced the flow of leads while the customer quickly assembled the necessary sales and customer-service resources. With that ready, they could open the tap back up and service the flood of new leads that came in.

So think about your business. Now that you've set some goals and identified your key metrics, you need a plan to reach your target. So with a specific goal in mind and a date you've set to achieve it, consider these important questions:

- What resources do I have available that will help me achieve the goal?
- How many team members do I have who can devote time to this?
- What kind of cash can I set aside for experimentation?
- If this Google thing completely tanks, what's my next option going to be? (And is there any reason I can think of as to why it might fail?)
- If this goes supernova, can I deal with it? Can I dial it back if I have to? Can I marshal more team members and resources to meet demand?

For a copy of the *Repeatable Planning Process* that WebSavvy uses, go to http://www.perrymarshall.com/supplement.

THE THREE-PART MINDSET

We are convinced that the size and condition of your business is just an outward reflection of your inner mindset. As you grow as a person and your mindset expands, your business will do the same.

Here are three fundamental attitudes we recommend you bring to the table when working with Google Ads. They will greatly improve your odds of success.

I'm Here to Experiment—and Get Lucky

Google Ads is a game of experimentation. It's about continually testing an endless assortment of new ideas:

- New keywords
- New ad copy
- New landing pages
- New offers
- New types of ads
- New targeting methods

If you can't tolerate occasional small failures, or seeing a precious idea tank, or discovering that you were wrong, Google Ads is not for you.

Advertisers who are willing to experiment with fast and crazy ideas will reap the rewards in the long game.

Always be testing. The minute it becomes clear that an idea has failed, pause or delete it. When a new idea gets you improved results, hang onto it. Think short-term downside, long-term upside.

I'm Investing Now. Returns Will Come Later

At first it may feel like you're just spending money, with very little to show in return. But if you're testing as we described above, then what you spend with Google is a down payment toward future earnings. As Mike's old options-trading mentor used to say, "You're investing money in the market to buy data and learn fast."

I'm in It for the Long Game

If you expect Google Ads to be profitable from day one, prepare to be disappointed. It's going to take work, time, and continued investment to uncover what resonates in your market with your customers.

And remember: This is digital marketing. There's so many things you can measure and tweak. The positive feedback loops are endless. That's the power of the Google Ads marketing machine.

YOUR QUICK ACTION SUMMARY

Thinking ahead, knowing where you want your business to end up, knowing how you're going to measure it, and accepting the process—that's the key.

- Sit down by yourself, with your business partner, or maybe even with your whole team, and put down on paper why you exist. What's your larger purpose in the market and in the world?
- Answer: How do you want to grow and expand over the next month, the next quarter, and the next year?
- Identify: What numbers are you going to watch most closely as this progresses?

Chapter 4

Getting Started:
Doing Your Research

By now you've worked out why you're in business, set your goals, and built your website.

You're ready for traffic, right?

Almost. There's a little more work to do first.

It's time to kick off your advertiser shoes and step into those of your prospect.

The first thing to think about is: Where are all the places they might look for you or bump into your business? It might be through a Google search. It might be through an app or a game. They might be browsing other websites trying to find a product or service such as you offer.

Depending on where they find you, they'll encounter different kinds of ads. Let's take a closer look at the types of Google ads they might see.

THE BIG NETWORKS

Google is split into two huge networks: Search and Display.

If your prospective customer is using Google Search, they'll see one of two possible types of ads: a search ad or a Shopping ad.

The search ad is a few lines of text, typically shown at the top or bottom of the search results page on Google.

The Shopping ad is for retailers. It's a small square image that appears at the top of search results, with the name of your product, your price, and the name of your store.

Display

The Display Network consists of more than two million websites and more than a million apps. These range from huge sites like Oprah.com and ESPN.com down to the smallest blogs, forums, and niche websites.

Owners place a small piece of code on their site to tell Google where it can show ads, and Google does the rest. The system "understands" what each site is about and what its visitors are interested in.

As a visitor arrives at a website, Google takes stock of two things:

1. All the data collected about that person, including sites they've been to recently and what actions they took on those websites
2. All the information about the website itself and how previous visitors to the site have behaved

Google combines all that data and in a fraction of a second decides which ads to show the visitor. If the person clicks on one of the ads, Google will share a portion of the click price with the site owner.

The Display Network is vast. On it you'll see many different types of ads, the most common being a simple banner ad. These come in different sizes and can be static or animated.

YouTube and Gmail

No doubt you've seen ads on YouTube, the world's second-largest search engine. One type of ad is a short video that plays before your chosen video starts. Another is a banner that appears on the right side of the page as you're watching a video.

Google also owns Gmail, the world's largest email platform, with more than 1.5 billion users. You're likely to see ads there as well.

Google is constantly experimenting with new ads, formats, and placements. You'll encounter ads on your phone, on your tablet, and inside various apps.

Let's talk about Search. We'll save Display, YouTube, and Gmail for later in the book.

GETTING STARTED WITH A SEARCH CAMPAIGN

Is this your first time using Google Ads? You'll find search campaigns the easiest to set up and tweak. They're a great way to learn the fundamentals.

Pay-per-click boils down to three indispensable elements: bidding, targeting, and messaging. Let's look at all three.

Bidding

A bid is your way of telling Google how much you're willing to pay when someone clicks on your ad. You'll set it up with what's called a maximum cost per click, or max CPC. You won't always pay that full amount; Google will usually charge you a bit less, but it will never go above that limit.

How much are you willing to pay to get a new visitor to your site? If you're unsure, start with a bid of $1. You can always adjust it later.

Targeting

This is how you tell Google *who* should see your ad.

There are myriad ways to do this, but the two main ones involve keywords and audiences. When you give a keyword to Google, you're telling them to show your ad to people who are searching for similar phrases.

We'll have more on audiences in later chapters.

Messaging

What should your ad *say?*

The key is figuring out your prospect's *intent.* Why are they searching on Google right now? What do they hope to find? What itch do they want to scratch? What conversations are going on inside their head?

Then think of an ad that reflects that intent. What can you offer that your competitors can't? What can you say that demonstrates you have exactly what your prospect is looking for?

Remember, your ad's only job is to get them to click on it. It's your website's job to persuade them to take action and buy. Consider what message will trigger the click, and then think about how to continue that conversation on the landing page you send them to.

WHAT ARE YOUR COMPETITORS DOING?

The internet is transparent. You can see what other advertisers are doing and learn from them. Visit your competitors' websites often. What offers are they making? What hot buttons are they pushing? Can you do better?

Think about the keywords your prospects might use to find the products and services you sell. Go to Google and search on those. Which of your competitors are running ads on those search terms? Are they saying things or trying offers you hadn't thought of? Is their message different from yours?

KEYWORDS FOR SEARCH ADS

As business owners, we're often too close to our own services to be able to think like our prospects. So do a little asking around. Talk to people you work with. Poll your friends and family. Find out how they might go about searching for your product or service. You might even invite a friend to do a search while you look over their shoulder. You'll be surprised at what they show you. Watch and learn.

Collect keywords from your own brainstorm sessions and your conversations with others, and create a list of two- and three-word phrases. (Not single words. That way you get clearer search intent.) Later in the book, we'll tell you how to use Google's free Keyword Planner tool. But for now, start building that keyword list. It should have more than one but fewer than 100.

In the next chapter, we'll talk about how to set yourself apart from your competitors. After that, we'll walk you through setting up your first campaign.

YOUR QUICK ACTION SUMMARY

- Write down all the places your prospect might look for you or encounter your business—Google search, an app or a game, or other websites.
- Start with a Google search campaign.
- Decide what you're willing to pay to get a new visitor to your site. If you're unsure, start with a bid of $1 per click.

- Find out your prospect's intent. Why are they searching on Google, and what do they hope to find? What conversations are going on inside their head? Think of an ad that reflects that.

- Talk to people you work with. Poll your friends and family. Find out how friends and family, or people you work with, might go about searching for your product or service. Brainstorm and collect keywords, and create a list of short phrases.

Chapter 5

Vanquish the Thickest Competition with a Killer USP

Michael Strickland of Boulder, Colorado, runs Ship a Car Direct, a company that transports cars across the country. He enrolled in our 12-week, hands-on, first-click-to-first-sale marketing funnel improvement lab. Like many people who take this course, he assumed we were just going to go "ninja" to the nth degree on Google Ads.

Sure, we did that, but in the very first live small-group session, I asked him, "Michael, why should I ship my car with *your* company instead of any other company out there?"

Michael didn't have a solid, meaty answer to my question. Sure, he ran a good company, and they delivered quality and good service and all that. But it was a deer-in-the-headlights moment for him.

I told him, "Michael, you *must* create a great answer to that question." So we started building his unique selling proposition (USP) together. Two weeks later, Michael emerged with a powerful new USP and his "Damage Free Guarantee," which you can see on his website today at https://www.shipacardirect.com/index.php.

That was the tipping point of Michael's business. His sales doubled in six months. Yes, all his experimentation and optimization of Google Ads was helpful and necessary. But his ads didn't light on fire until his USP was solid. Once he had a terrific answer to "Why should I buy from you?," customers started responding, and the business went supernova.

The business ventures that fail the fastest are the ones that have no USP. The businesses that have their USP crisply and clearly defined acquire customers and grow.

So what is a USP?

It's the "thing" that makes you unique in the marketplace—it's what customers can get from you that they can't find anyplace else. You can also call it your "unique selling position" or your "value proposition."

Having a USP gives you a clear response for these questions:

- How are you unique?
- In what way are you different from your competitors?
- Why should I buy from you, rather than from someone else?
- Why should I care at all about you or anything you sell?

The term was coined by Rosser Reeves (1910–1984), a pioneer in the use of TV ads who wrote *Reality in Advertising,* one of the most respected advertising books of the 20th century.

His message on USPs was simple:

- Your ad has to have some way of clearly saying, "Buy this product, and you will get this specific benefit."
- Your promise has to be one that your competitor cannot or does not offer.
- Your promise has to win over new customers.

You see, a USP is worthless if it doesn't *actually persuade people to buy from you.* A USP is the knife edge of your chisel. A power USP enables you to "chisel your way in," anytime, anywhere. If you're not getting enough traction, sharpen your USP.

In this chapter, I'm going to give you a method for defining your USP, as well as for testing elements of your USP in your Google Ads to determine what gets you the strongest response.

SIX ESSENTIAL ELEMENTS OF A POWER USP

Any time you're communicating with a prospect, you can appeal to any one of these, a combination of them, or all of them together:

1. You're unique because of the *buyer* you serve.
2. You're unique because of *what you sell.*
3. You're unique because you have an unusual *angle.*
4. You're unique because of what your product or service *does not do.*
5. You're unique because of the *time frame* around your offer.
6. You're unique because of how you *guarantee* your product.

How many of these elements are already true of you? Or, if not, what can you change in your business so that any or all of these elements *become* true of you?

We'll explore them one at a time.

You're Unique Because of the Buyer You Serve

Your business gets traction when you zero in on a niche. Maybe you target people in a specific demographic—a certain age, gender, income level, or religious or political leaning. Or maybe you solve a very specific kind of problem—a rare health issue or a peculiar type of software malfunction. Maybe you cater to a particular hobby. If you're in B2B, you might serve a specific narrow vertical or a particular stripe of business owner. Maybe you only work with companies of ten employees or less.

In extremely rare cases, you could be unique because there's *no limit* to whom you serve. For example:

> *My hiring and recruiting system is unique because it works for virtually any position in any business, anywhere—from the ecommerce business in the UK to the information marketer in Chicago to the nursing station in the Australian outback.*
>
> —Nancy Slessenger, Vinehouse Hiring

Test the unique-buyer approach in your ads, whether you serve a unique demographic, help people with a unique struggle, or focus on a unique niche.

You're Unique Because of What You Sell

Do you offer a service where others only offer a product, or do you offer a product where everyone else is selling services?

Are *you* the thing for sale, as a skilled technician, consultant, coach, or performer? Are you the entertaining or compelling personality that makes the business what it is?

If so, beat your drum. Having a story to tell will instantly separate you from the herd. I've made a name for my business by telling my unusual story:

"How an Inexperienced 29-Year-Old Punk Ignored All the Usual 'Marketing Wisdom'—Grew a High-Tech Business 2,000 percent in Four Years, and Sold It for 18 Million Dollars!"

Test the "unique thing for sale" in your ads. For example, sell a product instead of a service, or sell your unique story.

You're Unique Because You Have an Unusual Angle

There are so many "angles" you can use to separate yourself from competitors. Here are just a few examples:

- You promise a unique and specific outcome.
- You have a noteworthy track record.
- You deliver an unusual level of quality.
- The experience of doing business with you is one of a kind.
- You offer a unique payment plan.

You can use acronyms and proprietary labels for products you sell and methods you use that get results. That approach always gets people to sit up and take notice.

You're Unique Because of What Your Product or Service Does Not Do

We call these "negative promises." They're just as powerful as positive promises—often more so.

Maybe there's some unwanted ingredient or feature your product doesn't have. Maybe there's a bad result you prevent. Maybe there's some prerequisite for effectiveness that your product lets users bypass, saving them time. Maybe your product avoids cost or waste.

You're Unique Because of the Time Frame Around Your Offer

You can promise results *within* a set amount of time or *for* a set amount of time. How specific can you actually get? The more explicit you are, the better your ads will perform.

Ads that use actual numbers generally perform better. It's practically an ironclad law. There are two reasons why: 1) the brain processes number symbols faster than written words, and 2) numbers make your message *specific*.

Prospects love promises that are specific, clear, and unmistakable. Advertising legend Claude Hopkins explains:

The weight of an argument may often be multiplied by making it specific. Say that a tungsten lamp gives more light than a carbon and you leave some doubt. Say it gives three and one-third times the light and people realize that you have made tests and comparisons.

You're Unique Because of How You Guarantee Your Product

Give your offer an "or else"—a penalty to you if you don't deliver. Refund your customer's money. Replace your product. Redo your service.

The more ballsy and specific you make it, the more your prospects will sit up and take notice:

- "Double your money back."
- "Triple your money back."
- "Your money back plus $1,000."
- "We'll refund your money and pay our competitor to come in and give you a replacement."

Combine your "or else" with a specific time promise, and your message has power.

A Killer Strategy for Generating Sales Leads

Are you trying to "chisel your way in"? Your business must have a great USP—and so should the very first offer you use to attract attention. For decades, direct marketers offered free reports and white papers to bring in sales leads. "Free report: How to cut your back pain in half in 15 minutes or less."

Those still work, and perhaps to an extent, they always will. But the amount of value you have to offer to get a prospect's email address has risen exponentially as the web has matured. That "free report" strategy is tired at best and obsolete at worst. Many times it simply does not stand out at all. Everyone has a free report or a free video. You can see that simply by scanning your competitors' ads.

A much less common strategy that still works quite well is what I call the Disqualification Approach: offer some kind of tool to help many of your visitors figure out that they are *not* your customers. Let me explain.

A Killer Strategy for Generating Sales Leads, continued

When we wrote the first *Ultimate Guide to Facebook Advertising* a few years ago, I was concerned that most people who bought the book would eventually figure out Facebook was not for them. At the time, Facebook's ad platform was still primitive, and it was not appropriate for 60 to 80 percent of businesses. (That has since changed.) I didn't want people buying my book and giving it two stars on Amazon because their ad campaigns failed.

So we created a tool, www.IsFBforMe.com. It scores people from one to ten based on ten easy-to-answer questions. After they get their score, they can enter their email address to get a customized report that explains it. If people get a score of less than six, we tell them to not even bother with advertising on Facebook.

This works extremely well. It gets lots of sales leads for us, and they're qualified sales leads because most of them are people with high scores. The fact that we actively push people away who are not good customers gives us tremendous credibility when we tell someone, "Yes, indeed, you should invest in Facebook advertising and education."

When you build a tool like this, if it doesn't disqualify a significant number of people who use it, the tool and your sales pitch are wrong. As I preach in my book *80/20 Sales and Marketing,* sales is first and foremost a *dis*qualification process. Most people are not right for you, so get rid of them at the outset.

A disqualifier lead-generation magnet helps you write better ads.

Which of these (older format) ads would you rather click on?

> Facebook Ads Are Hot
> Discover the Secrets to Mastery
> Free Online Training Video
> www.perrymarshall.com/facebook

> Or

> Is Facebook for You?
> Before (!) You Squander Time & Money
> Take This Free 60-Second Quiz
> www.IsFBforMe.com

A Killer Strategy for Generating Sales Leads, continued

Consider these two ads in terms of the offer. Which one is more appealing? Which one promises you the most immediate gratification and appeal? This is a huge aspect of marketing through Google Ads. It would be very rare for a training video to go viral, but our IsFBforME.com quiz did; in fact, many bloggers and authority sites happily recommend it.

Ultimately, the offer your ad describes is more important than the words you use to describe it. What does your customer *get* by clicking on your ad? And how fast do they get it? How soon will it make a difference in their life?

This deserves serious thought and, most of all, serious experimentation!

YOUR QUICK ACTION SUMMARY

Determining your USP is key to your Google Ads success. You can create yours by identifying what makes you unique, like:

- The buyer you serve
- What you sell
- Your unusual angle
- What your product or service does not do
- The time frame around your offer
- How you guarantee your product

Your mission: Test as many of these concepts in your Google Ads as you can find the time for. Some will completely tank—plan on it. But somewhere among these USP concepts will be a new winning ad and a new, proven way for you to approach your prospects, regardless of what media you use.

That is how you hammer out your USP in the crucible of the marketplace.

Chapter 6

How to Build Your First Campaign

When you set up a Google Ads campaign, you're actually creating a set of instructions that tell Google which ads to run, when to run them, and how much to charge you for it.

Experts say you need more than one campaign. And we agree. Why?

Here are some basic rules of thumb to help answer that question.

You want different campaigns for different types of ads. If you want to run search ads, Shopping ads, and YouTube ads, these are far easier to manage and track when they're in separate campaigns.

You want a different campaign for each country or region where you run ads. If you're spending more money in the U.S. than in Australia, having two separate campaigns will help you control the budgets for each country. It will also let you set different vocabulary and spelling in the ads themselves.

You want different campaigns to track your different products. Let's say you sell doors, windows, and shutters. You could put all these products in one campaign, but it's a safe bet that they have different price points and contribute different profit levels to your business. With separate campaigns for each product, you can see at a glance how they're working individually. Plus it lets you separate out the different budgets, which is especially helpful in seasonal markets. For example, this month you could reduce the budget on windows and increase the budget on doors to match seasonal demand, and then next month you could do the reverse. In this chapter, we'll walk you through what you need to know to build your first campaign—no matter what your goal is.

HOW TO GET STARTED THE RIGHT WAY

The first decision you'll make is what kind of ad you want to run. There are four main types: search ads, Shopping ads, display or banner ads, and video ads.

It's a safe bet you'll start with search ads, so your first campaign will be a search campaign. That's the easiest type to manage and make profitable.

Inside that campaign, you'll have a few ad groups. An ad group is just a container that holds ads and keywords—at least one of each. (Though you'll likely have more than that.)

Your campaign will also have a bid price, which is the maximum you're willing to pay each time someone clicks on one of your ads.

So when you start out, you'll have at least one campaign. In that campaign, you'll have at least one ad group containing at least one ad and one keyword, as well as a bid price. Let's look at an example.

Example: Training Dogs

Let's say you offer dog training.

You create a search campaign. Within the campaign, you create a single ad group. We'll call it "Dog training." In that ad group, you start with some keywords: dog training, Labrador training, and poodle dog training.

You write an ad.

For the campaign, you set a maximum bid price of $2 per click.

You turn it on, and it goes live.

Someone goes to Google and searches for "dog training for poodles," and Google decides to show them your ad.

If they click on your ad, you'll pay a fee to Google. The vast majority of the time it will be less than $2.

Campaign Bid Price $2		
	Name	Keywords
Ad Group#1	DogTraining	dog training
		Labrador training
		poodle dog training

HOW TO ARRANGE YOUR CAMPAIGN SETTINGS

There are a few key things you need to address when creating your first campaign. We can think about it in terms of what might go wrong:

- You could attract either the wrong people or nobody at all.
- Your ads could be irrelevant or just plain ineffective.
- You could pay too much . . . or not pay enough for your ads to show.

And to combat that, you want the right *targeting*, the right *messaging*, and the right *bidding and budget*. We're going to walk you step by step through a basic setup here in this chapter, which will adequately cover those three bases for you as you get started.

Here's how to set up your first campaign.

1. Navigate to the Campaigns tab on the left of the screen.
2. Click the big blue + button to start the process.
3. Click New Campaign.
4. You'll have the option to choose a "goal." This can help you get started easily, but it can also limit the features available to you. For the most flexibility, choose Create a Campaign Without a Goal. If you're already overwhelmed, choose Leads if your site is designed to get leads or Sales if you're selling products.
5. Next choose your campaign type. We recommend starting with Search.
6. Then choose the result you want (website visits, phone calls, or app downloads). We'll cover call tracking later in the book, so pick Website Visits for now.
7. Click Continue to get to the General Settings page.
8. Choose a name for your campaign.
9. Choose the networks you want to show ads on (uncheck Google Search Partners and Display Network for now).

10. Choose the location where your ads will show. Start with the smallest, most local option, e.g., your local town or state, rather than the whole country.

11. Ignore Audiences for now; we'll start with just keywords.

12. Set your daily budget. Pick a small amount of money that you're prepared to lose.

13. Bidding: You'll have to dig a bit here to find Manual Bidding, which is what we recommend when starting out. Choose Select a Bid Strategy (as seen in Figure 6–1 below) and then Manual CPC (Figure 6–2 below) from the drop-down menu.

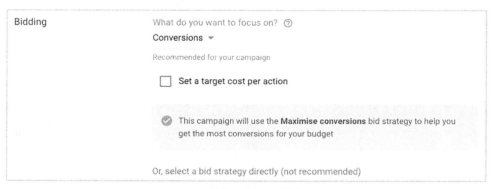

FIGURE 6–1. Select Your Bid Strategy

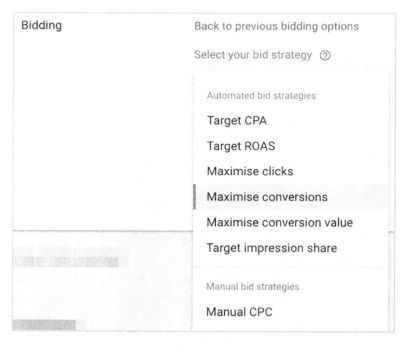

FIGURE 6–2. Choose Manual CPC

14. You'll be prompted to use Enhanced CPC, which is fine. This allows the system to make a few decisions for you without ignoring your direction completely.
15. You can ignore the other settings for now.

Other Options

You'll be prompted as part of your campaign setup to add in some ad extensions. Ignore those for now.

You can set start and end dates for your campaign. In most cases, you wouldn't use this option unless you were setting up a campaign for a specific promotion or holiday period and you wanted your ads to shut off after a certain date.

You'll be given a few URL options to help with tracking and measurement. Ignore these for now.

Unless you're targeting a specific minority language group, set your campaign to the single dominant language in your geographic area.

You'll see sections on audiences, ad scheduling, and ad rotation. Again, you can skip these for now. We'll cover them in more detail later in the book.

WHAT DOES AN AD GROUP DO, EXACTLY?

We mentioned above that you'll have a few ad groups within your campaign. But why do you need more than one?

For starters, consider this:

- If I'm searching for "Labrador dog training," I'm much more likely to click on an ad that talks specifically about training Labradors than about dog training in general.
- If I'm searching for "puppy training," I'm far more likely to click on a dog training ad that specifically mentions puppies.

So imagine that you offer dog training. You create an ad group with a couple of ads and 50 keywords. Those keywords are about dogs, dog training, puppies, Labradors, poodles, and more.

But your ads only talk generically about "dog training." They don't mention Labradors, puppies, or poodles. That's a problem. If I'm searching for training for my Labrador, I'm more likely to ignore your ads.

That's where separate ad groups come in. You can move your Labrador keywords into a new ad group with one or two new ads written specifically about Labradors. Then move your puppy keywords into a different ad group where your ads talk specifically about working with puppies.

This way, you know people typing in those keywords will see relevant, targeted ads.

Even better, you can direct those Labrador ads to a landing page specifically about Labrador training and the puppy ads to a page about puppy training.

Again: Targeted and relevant. With this method, we know exactly what your prospect searched for, which keyword has been triggered in our account, and which ad they saw. Now our job is to send them to a page that matches all that, maintaining the chain of relevance to ensure the best experience. They've searched, they've seen an ad, and now they land on a page with consistent messaging.

A Google ad works best when you can take a visitor to the page most relevant to them.

You can take this concept quite far. Maybe too far. Many advertisers create what we call single keyword ad groups (SKAGs). That's an ad group containing only one keyword, and an ad written exclusively for that search term.

SKAGs can perform very well, but there are a couple of issues with them. One is the drain on your time and resources. If you've collected 5,000 keywords, building separate ad groups for each of those search terms is completely unrealistic.

The second concern is something we'll cover in more detail in Chapter 26, when we talk about automation. With such narrowly targeted ad groups, each individual group will accumulate very little performance data over time. That becomes an issue, as Google's machine learning requires lots of data to perform well. You don't want to hamstring Google.

So which approach do you take?

Start with a small number of ad groups. That means five to ten, if you have around 50 keywords. Group those keywords together in small clusters around tight themes, and make sure in each ad group that every ad reflects its accompanying keywords as closely and literally as possible.

Campaign #2		
	Name	Keywords
Ad Group #1	Puppy Training	puppy training
		puppy school
		puppy obedience
Ad Group #2	Labrador Training	Labrador training
		Labrador school
		Labrador obedience

To review, each ad group contains three things: at least one ad, at least one keyword, and a bid.

We suggest that you bid only at the ad-group level at this point. Ignore the option to set separate bids for individual keywords.

HOW MUCH SHOULD I SPEND?

Understand that Google Ads is a competitive auction. The more advertisers that are bidding on a particular keyword, the higher your bid price will need to be. It's not unlike the auction on a house: The more people who want to buy the house, the higher you'll have to bid if you want to win the auction.

There's one key difference, though: In Google Ads, the spoils don't all go to the highest bidder. You can't buy and own a keyword the way you can own a house, in other words. (There are people who believe that if they bid enough money, they own access to a keyword, and no other advertiser can use or benefit from it. That's simply not true.)

The higher you bid, the more likely it is your ad will appear when somebody searches for your keyword and the higher on the page your ad will show. But the ad at the top of the page does not necessarily belong to the advertiser who's willing to spend the most money. It's more nuanced than that.

We'll go into it in more detail later in the book. For now, we suggest you bid an amount you're comfortable with *and that you can tolerate losing* in the short term. Bid too high, and you'll waste money. Bid too low, and your ads won't show. The trick is to find the amount that's just right.

In the beginning, err on the side of caution and pick a relatively small amount. If your ads don't show often enough, you can always increase your bid.

Recall that you also have the fail-safe of your campaign's daily budget, to ensure that you never overspend on any given day. As a simple rule of thumb, set your budget to at least five to ten times the amount of your bid. So if your bid price is $1 per click, set your daily budget to $5 or $10 per day. Likewise, a bid of $10 per click means a daily budget of $50 to $100.

YOUR QUICK ACTION SUMMARY

What separates profitable Google advertisers from unprofitable ones? The profitable advertisers are prepared to put in the work and optimize their campaigns over time.

To recap, let's take a look at the most important steps you need to take when building your first campaign:

- Create the campaign.

- Set a small budget for the campaign—an amount you can afford to lose.
- Inside that campaign, start with one ad group.
- Research and gather your keywords.
- Add the keywords to the ad group.
- Write at least one ad.
- Set a bid for the ad group.
- If you have additional sets of keywords around other themes, create a new ad group for each separate theme.
- Turn them live.
- Keep what works; tweak or delete what doesn't.
- Rinse and repeat.

The next thing you'll need to put in place is tracking, which we'll cover in the next chapter.

Chapter 7

Conversion Tracking:
How to Know Where Every Penny You Spend Is Going

A few years ago, before Google's conversion tracking was as sophisticated as it is today, my team and I had determined that a certain keyword was a great target keyword for us. We fed $15,000 a month into that ad campaign for years.

Then I brought on a new marketing manager, Jack Born. Jack did some more conversion tracking, and one day he called me.

"Hey, Perry, you know that one ad campaign?" he said. "I don't think it's bringing you any paying customers. I think you're only getting tire kickers from that keyword."

This seemed totally counterintuitive to me. We were getting lots of email signups and, in fact, lots of customers from that campaign.

Jack said, "I carefully connected the dots, and I don't think this is the thing that's paying your bills. Let's pause that campaign and see what happens to our sales."

So, with much fear and trepidation, we paused $15,000 per month of traffic.

Sales did not change one iota.

Dang. We had spent $300,000 on traffic that wasn't converting at all.

Ugh! Ever wish you could get $300,000 back?

Well . . . if you're not tracking conversions from that initial click to sales lead to sale, then the odds are 80 percent of your traffic is *not* converting to sales—you just don't know it.

If that's the case, you might as well find out right now!

What's the difference between a novice airplane pilot and a veteran? Ask any flight instructor and they'll tell you a beginner relies on sight and gut feeling, while an experienced professional relies on their instruments.

This sounds counterintuitive. You might think experienced pilots with thousands of hours of flight time would reach the point where they could ignore their instruments and fly on instinct alone. But it's quite the opposite. Novice pilots are unfamiliar with the complex range of cockpit instrumentation and are naturally inclined to rely on their basic senses. Veteran pilots, on the other hand, know your senses can deceive you, and so can your instincts. Instruments, being machines, are far less likely to give you faulty information.

Marketers can be vulnerable to the same errors. We sit down to write a new ad or create a new offer, and we think we know instinctively what will get clicks, what will sell, and what won't.

But forecasting markets and predicting buyer behavior is nearly impossible. Worse still, determining which keywords, ad groups, and campaigns bring in the best customers can be a completely opaque black box.

Truly experienced marketers understand that *nobody* knows what works until the target audience has cast their vote. And nobody knows which advertising dollars create the best return until we've looked at the hard data.

Fortunately, Google gets this. Their conversion-tracking tools are engineered so you don't have to guess what's working and what isn't. The "instruments" in the Google Ads interface let you measure every last bit of prospective and current buyer activity in precise detail. With these tools in place, even the smallest business can go head-to-head against large competitors knowing exactly where their advertising dollars are having the greatest impact.

Google's conversion tracking can break down your numbers and tell you where each conversion came from. It can even show you the path your visitors took to find you. Most important, it shows you where the waste is.

Relying solely on gut instinct can kill your PPC results. Do you want to learn how to see exactly where your dollars are going? This chapter will teach you. We'll show you how to make solid decisions based on hard data by setting up your conversion tracking right the first time. We'll also show you how to use a thank-you page to welcome new customers and create upsells. We'll start by looking over the options available to you, and then we'll walk you through a specific example of how it works.

THE FOUR TYPES OF CONVERSIONS YOU'LL WANT TO TRACK

For every business owner, a "conversion" can refer to a number of different actions that a prospect or customer might take. Some are more valuable than others:

- To a blogger, it might be a visitor reading at least three posts.
- To a service provider, it might be a visitor picking up the phone or completing a registration form.
- To an ecommerce site owner, it might be a visitor making an online purchase.

Google makes it easy to track all these and more. There are four essential types of conversions you'll want to consider. See Figure 7–1 below.

Type 1. Track When Someone Lands on a Specific Page

This includes the person who sees your thank-you page after completing your newsletter signup form or the buyer who arrives at your download page after purchasing your software. It is the most common type of conversion tracking and the most basic, so it's worth knowing how to set it up even if you plan to largely

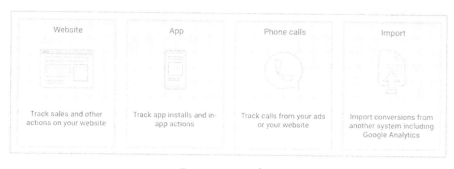

FIGURE 7–1. Four Types of Conversions

focus on other types. We'll give you an example later in this chapter on how to do just that.

Type 2. Track When Someone Calls You After Seeing Your Ad or Visiting Your Site

According to one survey, 70 percent of mobile users at some time or another have seen an advertiser's phone number on a Google results page and called it.

Putting your phone number in a Google ad is an effective strategy, but you'll need to do it the right way: by using a call extension or a "click-to-call" ad. Best of all, it's easy for Google to track.

We'll talk more about ad extensions in Chapter 10, and we'll discuss how to set up phone call tracking in Chapter 19. That said, there are a couple of tracking options we'll share with you here.

One is to use code to swap your regular phone number for a Google forwarding number for visitors arriving from Google Ads. That way, any time someone calls the forwarding number, your ads get credited with a conversion, whether they saw the number in your ad or on your website.

This is available only in certain countries (check the Google website to see if it is available in yours), but if you can take advantage of it, you get access to better reporting. You can even specify to Google that only calls of a certain length will count as a conversion.

The two main benefits are that 1) it's free (Google will create as many numbers as you need, and they don't charge you for the calls), and 2) it integrates perfectly with the Google Ads system.

There are also a few third-party tracking options you can try. One is CallRail.com, which is particularly popular in the U.S., but there are other good call-tracking services you can find by searching online. The main benefits of using these are that they track multiple sources other than Google Ads—i.e., you will have separate numbers for your Facebook, email, and organic traffic. In each case, the system is more robust, but you will pay for each phone number and each call.

You're not allowed to include your actual phone number in the text of your ad. Instead, Google gives you three options:

1. *Call extensions or call-only ads let you display a phone number in your ad.* This can be on desktop, tablet, or mobile. We'll discuss these in more detail in Chapter 10 on ad extensions. We also cover call-only ads in Chapter 12 in the section on special campaign types.

2. *You can display a Google tracking number on your website.* If someone clicks through to your website from a Google ad, you can track phone calls you receive as a result

of that visit. You need to do this tracking to understand the full value of Google Ads; you're only getting half the picture if you are just tracking website form fills, for example. So many businesses get the majority of their leads or sales via telephone, so it's important to connect the dots from incoming calls back to your Google Ads campaigns.

3. *You can track phone number clicks on your mobile site.* With this feature, a mobile user who clicks on your phone number on your mobile site to call you will be counted as a conversion. You keep your current phone number, and Google tracks both your clicks and your calls. (This method requires you to add a piece of code to your website.)

Type 3. Track When a Person Downloads Your Mobile App

If you have an app on Google Play or Apple's App Store, Google can track downloads and count them as conversions. One method is to find the URL for the App Store download page you want to use and make that the destination URL of your ad.

If you have an Android app, it's easy to track app downloads and actions, as this functionality is built into Google's system and can be set up automatically to track in-app activity and billing.

If you have an iOS app, there are other options, where you'll need to add some code inside the app itself. We recommend Google Analytics App + Web, which is a great tool built specifically for tracking app behaviors. (It's the future of analytics for apps, especially if you are doing any marketing for apps or app creation; however, it is beyond the scope of this book.)

Type 4. Track Conversions That Happen Off-Line

What if your primary business model involves calling leads and closing the sale over the phone? Google has off-line conversion tracking, which lets you connect off-line sales back to your Google Ads accounts.

Let's say you discovered that 80 percent of the leads who arrived from Google Ads ad groups A, B, and C converted to a sale, but only 5 percent of the leads who came through ad groups D, E, and F ended up buying. This might frustrate you initially, but just think how useful that information would be to you in the end.

With this kind of conversion tracking, you can know in advance which leads are most likely to become customers. That could save you huge amounts of money on your Google ad spend, and it could save your sales team tremendous amounts of time and effort.

Off-line conversion tracking can be a bit involved, but it's worth it, and it's likely to become more important as the use of cookies becomes difficult or even impossible due to ever more robust privacy laws. Read more about offline conversion tracking here: https://support.google.com/google-ads/answer/2998031.

HOW TO SET UP CONVERSION TRACKING THE RIGHT WAY

Let's say you run a lead-generation site where a visitor can fill out a form in exchange for a free consultation with you and a free brochure. We'll walk you through how to set up your Google account to track it.

Step One: Select Conversion Type

First, tell Google what kind of conversion you want to track. Click on the Tools & Settings icon at the very top of your Google Ads page and select Conversions. On the resulting page, click the big blue + Conversion button.

Next select the Website option, since you're tracking something that happens on your site.

Step Two: Set Your Conversion Category

You'll be asked to choose one of the following categories for your conversion type (see Figure 7–2, below).

- Sales (with various subcategories)
- Leads (also with subcategories)
- Other

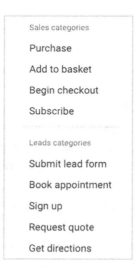

FIGURE 7–2. Conversion Categories

In this example, Submit lead form is probably the best choice.

Step Three: Name Your Conversion Action

Choose a name that tells you what the conversion is (e.g., "Opt in for brochure").

Step Four: Set a Conversion Value

If you're not running an ecommerce site, you may be tempted to skip this step. Google will let you do so. But please don't. Setting a conversion value right from the beginning, for every conversion-tracking program you set up, will make your data far more valuable in the long run.

Don't think of the conversion value in terms of dollars. Instead, think of it as a points system that rates the relative value of the different types of conversions in your business. For example, a conversion that involves a visitor completing your quiz might be worth 5 points, but if they complete a "please call me" lead-capture form, it would be worth 100 points. If your site is very basic and offers only one conversion action, then you can simply set the conversion value as 1.

When it comes to reporting and sifting through your data, setting a conversion value is vitally important. You'll thank us later. More on this in Chapters 8 and 19.

Note: If your site is far less basic, that is, you're an ecommerce site owner, you can set conversion values to adjust automatically based on the revenue of each product sold. Talk with your web developer about implementing this. For example, you might sell a range of products that run from $5 to $5,000; you can use the dollar value of the sale as the value of your conversion goal.

Step Five: Set a Conversion Count

There are two options: you can choose All Conversions—Every (the default) or Unique Conversions—One.

Every, as the name would suggest, measures every individual sale or lead. If you pick One, then if your visitor takes the same action multiple times, it would count as just one conversion.

Do you want Google to count all conversions in total or only unique conversions? In other words, if someone clicks on your ad and then makes a purchase from you every day for the next three days, do you want that to be recorded as one conversion or three?

Your choice often depends on the type of online business you operate. An ecommerce site owner, for instance, usually wants to keep track of every product purchased, so they would select All Conversions—Every. On the other hand, an information marketer who provides PDFs for download might be more interested in knowing the total number of individuals who download one or more items, rather than the total number of downloads. So they would choose Unique Conversions—One.

If you're not sure, go with the default All Conversions—Every. That way you still get data for both types. (If you select Unique Conversions—One, you get less data, and you can't change your mind later on without deleting and re-creating the conversion from scratch.)

Step Six: Set Your Conversion Window

This indicates how many days or weeks you want Google to keep tracking the user after they click on your ads the first time. The default is 30 days. That's more than adequate for this exercise. If a person clicked on your ad but didn't opt in for your brochure within 30 days, they're probably not worth following anymore. Unless you have a very good reason for a different conversion window, leave this on the default setting.

That said, you have eight options available: 1, 2, 3, or 4 weeks, or 30, 45, 60, or 90 days. You can also set a window for view-through conversions—people who saw your ad and didn't click on it, but who came back to your site and converted from another channel, such as an organic search. If you have this setting activated, then, for example,

---

A Word of Warning

Measuring conversion events accurately and assigning correct values to them is absolutely critical. If you do conversion tracking right, you can make fast, accurate decisions about very complex issues with absolute confidence.

But if you measure conversion events wrong (like accidentally counting one conversion event twice because someone stuck an extra conversion pixel where it didn't belong) or assign wrong values (like counting a $10 sale as a $25 one), it's like trying to fly an airplane with a malfunctioning altimeter. You think you're cruising along at 20,000 feet, and then suddenly you smash into the side of a mountain.

Your flying is only as accurate as your instruments. And please remember that even the best tracking software can only give you an approximate, relative answer. The only numbers that are *real* are the deposits in your bank account, so take extra time at the beginning to verify that the conversions in your ad-tracking system match up to the sales in your shopping cart.

---

by purchasing within that 30-day default window, a visitor would be counted as a view-through conversion.

Step Seven: Decide What to Include in Conversions

You now get to choose which conversion types should be included in the total conversions count. For example, if your site is an ecommerce store, you might want to have two conversion actions. One would be for every time somebody adds a product to their shopping cart, and another one would be for when they buy a product. If you're using Smart Bidding (see Chapter 8), or if you simply want to optimize your bidding for actual sales, then you would not include the first action in your conversions column. It would omit those people adding products to their carts but not buying them from the total number of conversions and include only buyers under "all conversions."

When in doubt, stick with the default setting (which is Yes to include).

Step Eight: Choose Your Attribution Type

A visitor may have clicked through to your site multiple times and from multiple places. This setting is where you tell Google which of those clicks gets credit for the sale. Google defaults to the setting called Last Click. We recommend you stick with it for now. We'll discuss the other attribution models briefly in Chapter 27.

Your Thank-You Page: A Great Tool for Upsells

Thank-you pages are important—and not just for conversion tracking. They also keep your visitors happy. Nobody likes opting in and then being shunted off to some unrelated offer without first being acknowledged and thanked for taking the action—or, worse, being dumped unceremoniously back onto the homepage.

Only a small percentage of your visitors actually put up their hand, so to speak, to indicate that they might be interested in doing business with you—perhaps between 5 and 10 percent. So treat them with care and respect. A well-designed page that thanks your prospect for their interest is a great way to get your relationship started on the right track.

You might provide your visitor with relevant information about what steps to take next. You could give them your contact information, ask for that Facebook like, or post a short thank-you video for them to watch.

Step Nine: Install Code

You're ready to ensure that your site has the necessary code to allow Google to track your conversions. You have two options: 1) install it manually, in which case Google will give you a snippet of code to place on your key pages, or 2) enter the email address of your web developer, and Google will send the code there, along with instructions.

In Chapter 27, we'll talk about how Google Tag Manager can help with this process. But for now, if you're not comfortable handling this part of the process and you don't have a web developer, you can hire a freelancer or ask one of the many talented PPC practitioners in Planet Perry to handle it for you, such as in our private New Renaissance Club, www.perrymarshall.com/new-renaissance or www.Marketers247.com.

Important: The most reliable way to keep your conversion tracking running smoothly is to ensure that your conversion action always directs your visitor to a separate landing page with a unique, static web address.

What do we mean by this? If you want visitors to complete a lead-capture form, don't let your web developer talk you into using some fancy Ajax-style onsite messaging that keeps the user on the same page or generates a dynamic URL.

In our current example, once your visitor completes the lead-capture form, redirect them to a unique thank-you page with an ordinary static URL. If you create multiple landing pages, each with a lead-capture form, you can have one thank-you page for all of them, or you can have a different thank-you page for each one.

Either way, simpler is better. This is the only way to ensure that your conversion tracking doesn't break farther down the line and you don't end up making decisions based on bad data.

Who Is the Real Winner?

Before you become obsessed with dramatically driving down your cost per action, remember this golden rule of thumb from marketing guru Dan Kennedy: *The winner is not the business that gets the cheapest leads. The winner is the business that can afford to pay the most per lead.*

There's nothing wrong with paying less for your conversions. Profit is a worthy goal. But if you want to grow your market share, or even your market, then by decreasing your cost per conversion by a few dollars, your lead volume or quality may suffer. The best strategy to lock in market share and secure profit for your business over the long term may be to pay more, not less.

Just be sure you have the resources to handle the increase in customers!

TAKE ADVANTAGE OF ANALYTICS

One final note: If you're also a Google Analytics (GA) user, you can connect your Google Ads conversion tracking to your GA account. This saves you from having to install additional code on your site, and it gives you some measuring options that aren't available through conversion tracking alone.

For example, if you own a blog and your goal is for a visitor to read three pages on their visit, this is simple to set up in Analytics.

There are some caveats, though. Analytics uses different methods for counting conversions, so your GA numbers may not perfectly match those in your Google Ads account. Analytics can also have a bit of a delay sending data to Google Ads (usually less than 24 hours). We'll cover Analytics in more detail later in the book.

YOUR QUICK ACTION SUMMARY

Google Ads is the apex of direct-marketing automation, but you cannot use it effectively if you don't first enable conversion tracking. Don't forget to:

- Create your conversion action.
- Choose a category.
- Name it and set a value.
- Choose the conversion count and whether to include all conversion types in the total count.
- Install the conversion tracking code on your website, or delegate this to your web developer.
- At first, check to make sure your tracking reports match up to physical reality. Compare these numbers to your shopping cart, email signups, etc.
- Review your data closely to make necessary adjustments and improve your Google Ads results.

Chapter 8

Bidding Strategies:
Tools to Keep Your Spending Smart

How much do I put on the table to start the game?

That's a vital question you must answer. Fortunately, Google's tools make it far less of a crapshoot than it used to be when you first launch a new campaign or ad group. Mastering bidding is absolutely essential to your success as a Google advertiser. The good news is that the better you get at it, the less it will cost you.

Every single time someone does a search on Google, an auction runs in the background to decide which advertisers are eligible to show ads. As with any auction, it's a competitive game. The more you bid, the more likely you are to have a chance to show your ad. However, the "quality" of your ad also matters a great deal. In Chapter 24, we'll dig into the details of how Google uses its Quality Score algorithm to determine ad placement.

For now, you just need to know that the more relevant your ad is to search results, and the more clicks your ad gets compared to your competitors, the greater your chances of success.

In this chapter, we'll spell out all the strategies and tools you need to ensure that you spend only what you can reasonably afford and get feedback on your ads as quickly as possible.

START WITH MANUAL BIDS

Manual bids are the best way to understand firsthand how your dollars and cents are working (or not) for you. We don't advise starting out with Google's automatic bid settings. Start with numbers that you can personally see, respond to, and adjust.

Frankly, Google's system is not good at figuring out what your bids should be until it has a significant amount of data to work with. You'll need to be getting at least 50 conversions a month (at the campaign level) before you can start using automated bidding.

WHERE DO YOU SET BIDS?

Google display, video, and shopping campaigns work a little differently. We'll discuss those in later chapters. For now, let's focus on search campaigns.

Search gives you two options. The first (and easier) option is to set bids at the ad group level. This is the option we recommend if you're just starting out. The second is to set them at the keyword level. Like a manual vs. an automatic transmission, keyword bidding gives you more control, but you'll be left with far more bids to carefully watch and manage. That can be overwhelming if you're new.

What to Use as a Starting Bid

To get started on keyword bidding, we suggest you use Google's Keyword Planner tool (https://Ads.google.com/home/tools/keyword-planner). Enter your keywords, and it will suggest a reasonable starting bid. If you're not comfortable with Google's recommendations, start with $1 or $2 per click. (This will of course depend on your budget and appetite for risk.) Whatever you use, it's only a starting point. You'll be changing it often.

There are three extra columns of data that you'll want to add next to each of your keywords to use as a guide for getting your ads seen affordably. You'll find these under the Keywords tab: Click on the Column Chooser and then, under the Attributes section, add the three columns labeled Estimated First Page Bid, Estimated Top Page Bid, and Estimated First Position Bid.

Different advertisers have different goals and numbers they're optimizing for. For our purposes, we're not aiming for more impressions, clicks, or even video views. We're interested in conversions and your conversion data. Hopefully, by now you have your tracking set up, conversions are happening, and you're starting to accumulate conversion data.

Remember, This Is a Maximum Bid

The amount that you bid is a maximum cost per click, or max CPC. This is the most that you are willing to pay, if and when somebody clicks on your ad. However, your cost is usually less, and typically you'll find you pay between 50 and 90 percent of your max CPC.

BID STRATEGIES

Under the Shared Library in your account, you'll find a section called Bid Strategies, where you'll find the option to create various strategies for bidding:

- *Enhanced Cost per Click (ECPC).* This is the next step up from manual bidding and is a good place to start. You select your default bid as usual, and Google increases or decreases your bid based on their calculations as to whether a particular click will lead to a conversion. The downside of this option is that sometimes you can pay a lot of money for a single click. But it generally works well and is a good way to dip your toe into using Google's machine learning. It may well become the default option for Google Ads in the future.

- *Target Cost per Acquisition (tCPA).* If you're using conversion tracking (which you should be), you can select this bid strategy, which used to be known as Google Conversion Optimizer. With it, Google works to maximize your number of conversions while still hitting your desired CPA. You set your tCPA dollar amount at the campaign or ad group level; Google then decides when to show your ads, who to show them to, and how much to charge for each click so you can reach your goal. For example, if you set your tCPA at $80, you're telling Google that you are willing to pay $80 for each lead, and it will choose how much to charge you for each click to try to meet that target.

  Pro tip: Use your target CPA to adjust the total spend for your campaign. If you want to reduce your incoming traffic, don't decrease your budget; instead, decrease your tCPA. This forces Google to work harder to find cheaper leads or sales. Google's machine learning is improving all the time and it is very good at meeting these targets most of the time, but proceed with caution. With tCPA, when it gets things wrong, Google tends to get them very wrong. The machine also needs data, so the more data it has, the better it can meet your targets. If you're not getting more than 100 conversions per month, per campaign, you should probably stick with manual bidding for the time being.

- *Target Return on Ad Spend (ROAS).* This is another option if you're using conversion tracking. In this case, the strategy is to hit a target return (just revenue/cost). This means you're going after a *conversion value* rather than a total number of conversions. This is typically used by ecommerce businesses that sell a products with a wide range of prices. For example, you might sell everything from a $20 lamp to a $6,000 dining room table. Having an average CPA of $200 doesn't help you much if all your sales were $20 lamps. But if all your sales were $6,000 tables, you'd be very profitable. In reality, you're probably getting a mix of both, and individual sale costs will be less of a concern as long as the return is there.

- *Max Conversions.* This model aims to maximize the number of conversions that you get for your budget. It's less concerned with the CPA number than with trying to maximize the number of leads or the number of sales. Use caution, however—while the average CPA may be on target, Google will often massively overpay for individual leads or sales using this model.

- *Max Conversion Value.* This is similar to Target ROAS and is a useful model for campaigns with low budgets. The machine will try to spend your entire budget. This is good for less sophisticated advertisers who just want a decent return without having to actively manage a campaign. But if you need to hit a particular ROAS goal, it's best to avoid this model and stick with Target ROAS.

BID STRATEGIES TO AVOID

Some bid strategies are more useful than others. Some are just about vanity (for example, always seeing your ad at the top of the page or wanting to beat a particular competitor). But vanity is a bad business model. Here are three bidding models you can largely ignore for now.

1. *Maximized Clicks.* With this method, Google automatically adjusts your bids to maximize the number of clicks you receive. You can set a maximum budget, but Google has free rein to adjust your bids in whatever fashion its system believes will deliver the most clicks. We frankly don't advise using this. If sheer traffic

volume is more important to you than conversions, you may find this worth testing. Otherwise, steer clear.

2. *Target Impression Share.* Google adjusts your bid based on whether you indicate you're merely looking to get onto the first page of search results or to the *very top* of results. Be cautious with this one. Getting to the top of the page can be expensive, so be aware that you're giving Google permission to spend your money.

3. *Target Outranking Share.* You specify a website domain name, most likely one of your main competitors, and tell Google to show your ads above that specific competitor's. You can also specify the percentage of time you would like to outrank them on the page. Note that Google doesn't guarantee you'll always rank above your competitor; that depends on how much your competitor is willing to bid. This is a risky strategy for beginners. If your competitors are bidding high, you may end up spending far more than you intended.

WHAT IS SMART BIDDING?

Google is all about artificial intelligence, and they're constantly searching for ways to have the machines do more of the work.

Smart Bidding is the technology used in four of the bid strategies we listed—Enhanced CPC, Target CPA, Max Conversions, and Target ROAS. It's you handing over the reins and letting Google decide how much to charge every time your ad enters an auction. It does this using a huge range of contextual signals. The full list of these is vast (and not publicly available), but the most important include the device being used, the location, the time of day, whether the user is on a remarketing list, the type of ad, the search query, and even the browser and operating system.

So why use Smart Bidding? We are fast approaching the point where there is simply too much data for any one human to process. Even if you could spend all day tweaking your Ads campaigns, there are just too many signals to account for. Google has more data than God (OK, maybe not that much). They have access to every account and every party in the auction, and they know an enormous amount about each person searching. We will soon reach the point where there is simply no beating the machine. You'll want to test out Smart Bidding if you're not already using it.

UPPING YOUR GAME WITH BID ADJUSTMENTS

If you choose to use manual bidding, there are many other adjustments you can make to various properties inside your account.

Based on what you know about a particular prospect, you can choose to increase or decrease a bid. Sophisticated advertisers love this additional control. However, Google seems to be phasing this out over time in favor of having all advertisers use the machine learning. Until that day comes, we recommend that you at least understand how to use this feature, even if you choose to use Smart Bidding instead.

Each keyword in your account has a base bid. Let's say you choose $1 as yours. Once that's determined, you can adjust it based on various criteria, which we'll explain below.

You can instruct Google to decrease your base bid as much as 90 percent in one circumstance or increase it 900 percent in another. In this example, if you add a bid adjustment of +100 percent, you are effectively telling the machine to double your bid up to $2. A bid adjustment of 0 percent makes no change to the base bid, and a bid adjustment of –20 percent would reduce the bid from $1 down to 80 cents. This can be very confusing, especially to new advertisers. It is not necessarily intuitive that a bid adjustment of +200 percent will actually triple your base bid.

Here are a few methods of adjusting your bids based on device, geography, time of day, and more.

Device

This is the most common bid adjustment you can make. It can be done at the campaign or ad group level (most other adjustments are campaign-only). It allows you to change the bids for three device categories: desktop, mobile, and tablet.

You may find that people who come to you via their desktop behave very differently from people who find you via mobile or tablet. They may convert better; they may convert worse. You'll want to watch and see over time. And these bid adjustments allow you to reach the various devices differently if needed.

For example, you can leave the desktop bid as is (0 percent adjustment = $1), you can decrease the mobile bid by 60 percent (= 40 cents), and you can increase your bid on tablets by 20 percent (= $1.20).

If you like, you can set a particular device type at –100 percent, which tells Google to stop showing ads on that device entirely. So if you set your tablet bid at –100 percent, your ads will only show on desktops and cell phones going forward.

Location

Expect some regions or cities to perform better than others. Skilled Ads practitioners sculpt the geography of their campaigns to target hot customers in prime areas and reduce or eliminate the places that underperform. If in Chicago you're getting a CPA of $50, but in Florida every conversion is costing you $150, try decreasing just your Florida bids. Previously you would have needed two separate campaigns for Chicago and Florida, but now you can add a bid adjustment to match the performance level of different locations in the same campaign.

Time

Don't confuse this with ad scheduling, which allows you to turn ads *off* on specific days or during specific time periods. The time bid feature lets you move your bid *up* or *down*, depending on the time of day or day of the week. Let's say you discover that clicks in the evening are more profitable for you. You can tell Google to increase your bid by 25 percent from 7 to 11:30 P.M. Or if weekends are quiet, you can have Google decrease your bids by 40 percent on Saturday and Sunday. There's no need for you to manually adjust these in real time; bid adjustments will do it for you automatically.

Advanced Bid Adjustments

We don't recommend these if you're brand-new to Google Ads, but they are worth exploring once you have a bit of experience under your belt.

- *Audiences.* You can bid differently based on whether a person belongs to a particular audience, such as a remarketing list or one of Google's predefined audiences. (We'll discuss these more in Chapter 14.) If you have an ecommerce site, you might increase bids by 10 percent for everyone who is on your remarketing list and has been to your site. You could bid 50 percent more for someone who made it all the way to checkout without buying.
- *Demographics.* You can consider age, household income, and gender and then, for instance, bid 50 percent less on men. (Note that this feature is not yet available for Shopping or YouTube.)
- *Top Content.* This is a little-known and rarely used setting for Display Network campaigns. You can bid higher and have your ads shown on what Google considers "top content"—sites or pages that are trending or hot right now. You might bid up to 500 percent more to be seen on a news page that's going viral or next to a popular YouTube video. It's a strategy worth testing—that's where all the people are!

RISKY! BEWARE OF BID STACKING

This is a bit technical, but it's important to be aware of this effect. *Bid stacking* is what happens when you activate more than one bid adjustment at a time. If you don't know the risks before playing around with bid adjustments, you can end up paying considerably more than you intended for clicks.

When calculating bid adjustments, understand how Google does their arithmetic. Not changing a bid (a 0 percent adjustment) does *not* mean "multiply by 0." If you want to keep a bid the same, you multiply by 1. (Multiplying a number by 1 equals that same number; multiplying a number by 0 equals 0.) If you want to boost a $5 bid to $7.50 (a 50 percent adjustment), you multiply by 1.5, *not* by 0.5.

> 0 percent = multiply by 1
>
> +50 percent = multiply by 1.5
>
> +200 percent = multiply by 3 (multiplying by 2 means doubling; 200 percent means tripling)
>
> −20 percent = multiply by 0.8
>
> −90 percent = multiply by 0.1

You must also understand how multiple bids impact one another. Let's say you increase your bid by 10 percent for people living in London, and *also* increase your bid by 10 percent on Wednesdays. When someone from London clicks on your ad on a Wednesday, Google will apply *both increases* to your spend. Here's what that looks like:
Your regular bid is $5.

- A user from London (+10 percent) clicks on your ad on a Tuesday (no adjustment), which increases your maximum bid to $5.50 ($5 x 1.1).
- A user from London (+10 percent) clicks on your ad on a Wednesday (+10 percent), which increases your maximum bid to $6.05 ($5 x 1.1 x 1.1).

Got it?

This applies to decreasing bid adjustments as well. Let's say your regular bid is $5. You bid −30 percent for Chicago dwellers and −20 percent for mobile users at the same time:

- A user from Chicago (−30 percent) clicks on your ad via a desktop device, which decreases your maximum bid to $3.50 ($5 x 0.7).
- A user from Chicago (−30 percent) clicks on your ad via a mobile device (−20 percent), which decreases your maximum bid to $2.80 ($5 x 0.7 x 0.8).

Let's try one more. Grab a calculator and see if you can work out the answer yourself.

Your regular bid is $10. You set bid adjustments to be −25 percent for mobile users, +200 percent for users from Florida, and +20 percent on Tuesdays and Thursdays.

What would be the bid for a mobile user from Florida, clicking on a Tuesday? (*Answer at the end of this chapter.)

Note: If there are multiple bids that need to be stacked together, you might worry that your final bid could be many times larger than your original. Don't worry—even if your $5 bid looks like it could turn into a $1,000 bid with all the adjustments, Google won't let that happen. The maximum bid adjustment is capped at +900 percent. In this case, $5 may become $50, but at least you won't spend hundreds or thousands per click.

EVERY CAMPAIGN NEEDS A BUDGET

Your budget is a campaign setting. But the size of that budget is determined by your business goals and the plan you set for yourself earlier. That said, a rule of thumb is that your budget should be at least ten times your typical CPC. For example, if you're spending $1 per click, your campaign budget should be at least $10. If your typical CPC is $10, then your budget needs to be more than $100.

If your average CPC is $10 but you set a very low budget—say, $5 or $10—it will just confuse the machine and you'll get hardly any traffic. That also means you won't get the data you need to help improve your results. Let's consider some best practices for setting a budget so this doesn't happen.

Start with a Budget You Can Afford

There are many ways to set a budget. Some retailers will look at their predicted revenue for the month ahead and set a budget as a percentage of that. Some businesses will have a monthly spending target, or an amount they need to spend to justify future budgets. Our preference is to base the budget on maximizing your profit.

As we said earlier, having a large budget just for its own sake is a vanity metric. It is far more important to invest your money profitably so that you can afford to continue showing ads month after month.

So start with an amount you can afford to lose, but one high enough to get data flowing through your account. The only way you can improve your account is by investing in clicks and collecting data. You can then use that information to refine your ads, making them more profitable for you over time.

Set Either a Daily or a Monthly Budget

If you choose to set a daily budget, Google won't exceed 30.4 times that daily amount in any one month. For example, if a campaign has a budget of $10 per day, the most you can spend on it for that month will be $304.

Do note that if you set a monthly budget, there's no corresponding daily limit. Which means you'll want to be careful not to spend all of your budget in the first few days of the month.

Shared Budgets

There's a setting in Google where you can set one budget across multiple campaigns. For example, you can have five campaigns that share a single total budget of $100 per day. This is designed for lazy advertisers who don't want to spend much time managing their accounts. The risk is that your budget may get used up on a single expensive campaign, because that's where the traffic is. It's far better to set five separate budgets so that you can control your spending in each campaign.

Google Ads requires a mindset of *investment*. It is not realistic to expect any campaign to be profitable in the first week, or even the first month. Your plan should be to invest some money, learn from the market, make changes to your account, and over time increase the profitability of your campaigns.

If you're a beginner, we recommend starting at the bottom of the funnel with high commercial-intent keywords, as well as your own brand keywords. You probably shouldn't bid on informational or research terms just yet.

YOUR QUICK ACTION SUMMARY

Google's range of flexible bid strategies and bid adjustments offers a whole new level of control that's worth exploring. The ability to zero in on locations and device types and modify bids makes sculpting your campaigns much easier than it used to be.

- Review your bid adjustments and consider changing device and geographical settings based on your CPA data.
- Test various bid strategies; start with Enhanced CPC, and move on to Target CPA once you have enough conversion data.
- The answer to the question on page 64 is: Your maximum bid would go from $10 to $27.

Chapter 9

Keywords:
Ads Success Starts Here

My friend, colleague, and client Matt Gillogly was running Google Ads in real estate. As you might expect, real estate keywords are ferociously competitive, especially nationwide. He was looking for an edge.

One night he was watching a real estate TV show, and it occurred to him: "Hey, I bet a lot of people who watch this show are my perfect target customers because they're amateur real estate investors."

He started bidding on the name of that TV show as a keyword. To his delight, he discovered that 1) yes, there are a fair number of searches for that show, and 2) yes, those customers buy!

It pays to be a little more resourceful than everybody else when you do keyword research!

Keywords are the heart and soul of Google Ads. There are certainly other elements you need to learn, but fail to understand keywords, and your business will tank—guaranteed.

Many online marketers think of extra keywords like finding a few bucks under the car seat and slap a few of them onto an existing marketing campaign, in hopes of generating a little extra profit.

Not so! You need to be deliberate. Different kinds of keywords demand different strategies. Keywords are the foundation of your ad campaign. Get the right keywords in place from the beginning, and everything that follows becomes much easier.

Think about how many times in an average day that you do a search on Google, whether you're researching a project for work, browsing for a cool new gadget, checking football scores, looking for that one how-to video, or settling an argument over whether it's possible to sneeze with your eyes open.

Nearly everything we do online begins with a search. And that involves thinking up the best phrase that represents the problem we're trying to solve, the question we're trying to answer, or the itch we want to scratch. This is why keyword research is a step you cannot skip in your Google strategy.

Let's say you run a website that sells the latest tablet computers. Put yourself in the shoes of someone who is about to search for tablets and places to buy them. What keywords would they type in?

This exercise isn't new. Marketers and salespeople throughout the ages have formulated winning pitches by figuring out what's going through the heads of the people they want to sell to. Decades ago, master copywriter Robert Collier famously said, "Always enter the conversation that is already taking place in the customer's mind."

Think about that. Too many business owners are trying to *create* a conversation in the mind of their customers when what they should really be doing is figuring out the conversation that is *already there.*

None of us wants to be told what to think. But we love people who can echo exactly what we're already thinking and feeling. Stepping in to help customers get where they *already want to go* and do what they *already want to do* is where true PPC magic happens.

The amazing part is that before the internet, the conversation in a customer's mind was private, a mystery you could only guess at. But in the Google age, your customer literally types it into the search bar! In fact, the way we search has itself changed dramatically over the past ten years and will continue to evolve as more of us search by speaking to a device rather than typing on a keyboard. Some have speculated that by the end of 2020 somewhere between 30 and 50 percent of all searches wouldn't involve a screen at all.

Google's research shows that around 15 percent of the searches made every day have never been done before. We may not be able to predict the exact keywords an individual is going to use, but 99 percent of the guesswork has been removed from the process, and as we'll see later, absolute precision isn't necessary anyway. The keywords you choose as your campaign begins are just the starting point. They will change over time, so don't overanalyze it. Just get going.

So here's where we start: Imagine your ideal customer, and picture what they're likely to type into Google. By doing that, you're a giant step closer to constructing a highly effective PPC campaign. That's what this chapter is all about.

HOW TO FIND THE MOST PROFITABLE KEYWORDS

By now, you've likely figured out that once you start trying to predict the keywords your customers are using, you're going to end up with a very, very long list.

Not to worry. The longer your list of keywords, the wider the array of customers you'll reach. That said, don't spend months trying to create an exhaustive list. Start by narrowing things down a little. You can find the people who are most interested in your product or service by understanding the three major groups of online searchers:

1. *Informational searchers* are people looking for general information on a topic. It's usually hard to tell exactly what each person is looking for. One might be doing research for a term paper, while someone else might be killing time waiting for a bus. The vast majority of this group are not ready to buy and probably never will be.

2. *Comparison searchers* are definitely interested in your product, but they're still at the research stage, checking out reviews and comparing prices. Some folks from this group will be ready to buy in a matter of days or even hours, but for others it may be weeks, months, or possibly never.

3. *Buyers* are typing with one hand and holding their credit card in the other. They know exactly what they want, and the only barrier to making a purchase is finding the right place and the right deal.

So how do you tell which of these three groups a person is in? By studying the keywords they enter into the search bar. As a general rule of thumb, the more specific the search, the closer they are to the "Buyer" group.

If someone types in the word "microphones," does it mean they're looking to buy a microphone in the near future? Not necessarily. If they type in "Rode podcaster alternatives," they've done enough research to know about Rode's products, but they're still looking at other options.

Then there is the person searching for "Rode PodMic near me." They know exactly what they want, and they're as ready to buy as anyone you'll come across.

Recently we had to move away from our old favorite analogy of "top, middle, and bottom of the marketing funnel." The customer journey in the 2020s is far more complicated and involves dozens or even hundreds of touch points across a range of devices.

Every time somebody searches, Google uses its machine learning to predict who is most likely to buy. But the phrase they type in is just one factor. Google considers all the other terms that person has searched on in the past, how they typically shop, which device they're on right now, what the time of day is, what the weather is like—even the apps they have on their phone. A search term that looks like a simple informational query may actually be from someone who is ready to buy.

If you're just getting started with your Google Ads campaigns and budget is your biggest concern, it makes sense to target only the buyer group. These folks are the easiest to convert to customers. As your experience grows, you can extend your reach to the comparison searchers and, to some degree, even the informational searchers as well.

So let's start with a group of buyers and put together a first draft of our keyword list.

Step 1: Scour Your Website

Browse through your site and your entire product range and make a list of everything you sell. You probably know your product line pretty well, but try to step into your customer's shoes and assume they're unfamiliar with what you sell. Think of synonyms they might use. Then combine those with some of the common buyer and comparison keywords.

Sticking with our microphone example, if one of your products is a Rode PodMic, you might come up with these keyword combinations:

- Rode PodMic
- Buy Rode PodMic
- Best Rode PodMic
- Compare Rode PodMic

Step 2: Sniff Out Your Competition

Take a look at your top competitors' websites. You'll almost certainly find a few phrases and expressions you hadn't thought of. Add these to your list as well.

Step 3: Ask Your Customers

Do a survey. Have a casual phone chat with a few of your most recent buyers. Ask them specifically how they found your site and, if they can remember, the keywords they searched on in the process. Also quiz them about the kind of keywords they use in their searches in general. At this stage, you won't hear much that surprises you, but you'll definitely pick up a handful of new keywords or modifiers to add to your list.

Step 4: Ask Your Staff, Family, and Friends

This is an extension of Step 3. At this stage, you may feel like you're scraping the bottom of the barrel. But that's the point—it's all about quickly compiling as exhaustive a list as you can.

Step 5: Dive into the Keyword Tools

For the most part, Google's Keyword Planner is good enough. As you gain experience, however, third-party tools will allow you to dig even deeper. This is especially true if you're managing PPC campaigns for clients.

There are plenty of software applications, like SEMrush, to choose from; these can be helpful but aren't essential when just starting out. Most keyword tools of this type work by figuring out what your competitors are bidding on and feeding the data back to you. There are limits to how accurate this supply of information can be. But they will give you keyword ideas you would otherwise have missed.

HOW TO GET THE MOST FROM GOOGLE'S KEYWORD PLANNER

If you've been diligent with the previous steps, you should now have a long list of keywords. We'll use Google's free Keyword Planner to add a few more and then begin the refining process.

You don't need to be running PPC ads to use Google's tool, but you do need a Google Ads account. If you haven't opened one yet, now's the time.

The advantage of the Keyword Planner comes from Google's massive storehouse of data that it uses to find you new keywords and to predict their cost and value.

You'll find the Keyword Planner under the Tools section. Use the Discover New Keywords option and type one or two fairly broad keywords into the tool—e.g., *microphone* or *podcast mic*. Click on the Get Results button.

You will then be provided with a list of hundreds, maybe thousands, of keyword suggestions, sorted by relevance. Don't copy all these keywords into your account. For now, just use the tool to give you an idea of the keywords that *could* most likely convert either into leads or sales.

How Many Keywords Do You Need?

Once you've finished refining your list, you can either download the keywords to add to your existing list or import Google's list directly into a campaign. The choice is yours. Either way, you may still want to do some additional trimming.

PPC beginners frequently fall into the trap of assuming that keywords are all about volume and trying to hit every possible angle. In practice, having too many keywords is worse than not having enough. You want to find that "Goldilocks zone" where you have enough keywords to give you results but not so many that you dilute your efforts and end up with overload.

If you're just starting out, go for a minimum of 20 keywords and an absolute maximum of 250. (You can certainly have more than that, but let's keep things simple at first.)

So what do you cut, and what do you keep?

Imagine that you're an archer looking at your target. The bull's-eye represents the keywords that are right on the money and a near-perfect match for what you're offering. The ring just outside the bull's-eye represents keywords that are still closely matched but not quite as exact. The next ring out contains keywords that are still good but are bringing you more shoppers and comparison searchers than buyers. Every other keyword that does not fit this description of the bull's-eye and those two rings, pause for now or delete.

STEP UP YOUR GAME USING KEYWORD MATCHING OPTIONS

When you're ready to import your keyword list into Google, there's a final step to consider. And beware: Skip this step, and you'll burn through your budget in a matter of days, or even hours. Plus, your conversion rates will be pitiful.

Remember, we're first and foremost targeting buyers. You've likely spent considerable time crafting your keyword list to focus on this group. But if you simply import those keywords into your ad groups as they are, you may unintentionally waste all your hard work.

Google provides keyword matching options as a means to pair your keywords with genuine, real-world searches. This process is entirely in your hands, so let me explain your options.

1. Broad Match

If you don't tell Google how and when to show your keywords, it will default to this setting and show your ads for any search it considers relevant. This could include searches that use your keywords in any order, or don't contain your keywords at all.

So if you have "formal shoes" with no punctuation or brackets on your keyword list, then Google could show your ads for any of these searches:

- What are formal shoes?
- Will formal shoes get me a better job?
- Buy shoes online
- Good work shoes
- Smart shoes for prom

Can you see the problem here? The first two are informational searchers who are a long way from spending money. The next three searches are vague and will pull in people looking for products you may not even stock.

As a result, you will waste money on tire kickers or get a very low clickthrough rate. If that happens, Google's Quality Score rules kick in (more on this in Chapter 24), which could make your campaigns far more expensive.

This is one of the biggest pitfalls facing new operators. It's Google's "stupidity tax." Broad match searches generally get lots of impressions—which makes it look as if your campaign is working—but their clickthrough rates and conversions are usually abysmal.

The solution is simple. Google lets you input your keywords with some simple punctuation that more specifically indicates what kinds of searches you want your ads to show for. We'll look at those options below.

2. Exact Match

This option gives you the most control. You'll get fewer impressions and fewer clicks overall, but you won't have to worry as much about wasting clicks on useless searches. Just enter your keyword with square brackets around it, like this:

[buy formal shoes]

Ads connected to this keyword will now show when people type in this exact keyword phrase. It used to be that if someone searched for a keyword phrase other than your exact keyword, your ad wouldn't show. But over the past few years, Google has continually expanded the meaning of these match types. They call these *close variants*.

So now *exact match* will also match close variations of the intended search query, where Google believes those terms have the same meaning as your keyword.

In the above instance, your ad will show for this search:

buy formal shoes

But it might also show for any of these:

- buy formal shoes online
- formal shoes buy
- buy shoes for formal
- purchase formal shoes

The Google machine is not perfect—it can misinterpret the intent behind a search query. And that's why exact match is a two-edged sword! You avoid wasted impressions at the expense of missed opportunities. That brings us to . . .

3. Phrase Match

Enter your keyword in double quotation marks. People will see your ad when they type in the keyword in that exact order, just as with exact matches, but your ad will also display if they type in additional words before or after the keyword:

"formal shoes"

With this keyword, your ad will show for all of the following searches:

- formal shoes
- buy formal shoes
- formal shoes buy
- purchase formal shoes
- buy formal shoes online

However, it won't show for searches that insert anything between the keywords or use them in a different order. For example:

- shoes formal
- formal black shoes
- buy formal work shoes
- formal men's shoes

Phrase match is useful because you get more impressions than with exact match but you still retain a level of accuracy—at least that's the promise. As Google continues to broaden the definition of close variants, this may change and they may match your keywords to a wider selection of search queries.

You may *still* miss out on some opportunities, however. So let's move on and look at the fourth option.

4. Modified Broad Match

This option behaves like broad match, but you can specify that one or more of the words in your keyword must always be present (or at least close variants of those words). Add a plus sign immediately before the non-negotiable word, like this:

+formal shoes

This keyword will show for any search that Google considers relevant if the person searching included the word "formal." This way your ads will show for all of the following searches:

- buy formal shoes
- buy formal footwear
- affordable formal black shoes
- what are formal shoes?
- formal shoe shop

But your ad will not (typically) show for:

- buy work shoes
- best smart shoes
- buy black evening footwear
- smart cheap black shoes

These days, because of the changes to close variants, you may find that your keyword is being matched to search queries where Google believes the intent is the same.

It always comes back to intent. What is the conversation taking place in your ideal customer's head? Most people who use the word "buy" in a search are looking for websites that sell the product in question and are ready to spend money.

Modified broad match offers a superb balance between flexibility and accuracy and is an important tool you should learn to use well. However, when you first start out, it offers many opportunities for mistakes. The problems we identified with broad match can easily manifest themselves here as well if you put the "+" in the wrong place!

Google suggests using what it calls a "broad to narrow" approach. In other words, start with very broad terms and, as you gather data, narrow down your keyword selection to the ones that get you the best results.

But we suggest the opposite. If you're putting together your very first campaign, and especially if your budget is tight, start with just exact or phrase match and pin down the most targeted searches for your product or service. Only expand once you're profitable!

NEGATIVE KEYWORDS

What are *negative keywords*? They're a way to stop your ads from showing when certain words or phrases appear in a search query. This is a dynamite method for improving your CTR—one tiny change can literally *double* your results—but it's definitely not for total beginners. One wrong negative keyword can flatline your account. If you decide to give negative keywords a try, roll them out carefully into your campaigns or ad groups, a couple of keywords at a time, and allow a few days between attempts so you can measure the results of your changes. Look for the Negative Keywords section in the tree view on the left of your Ads screen. (See Figure 9-1 below.)

Imagine you sell microphones, but not microphone stands. One of your keywords could be the phrase match "Rode podcaster microphone," which might match the search query "Rode podcaster microphone stand." But since you don't sell stands, you won't want your ad to show for that search.

FIGURE 9-1. Select Negative Keywords

That's where negative keywords come in. Open the Keywords tab, go to the Negative Keyword section, and enter the words you want to exclude (negative keywords are indicated with the minus sign):

> –stand
>
> –stands

Note that negative keywords do not use close variants, so you would need to include both the singular and the plural version to block all irrelevant search queries.

You can apply a set of negative keywords to one specific ad group or to an entire campaign. We recommend using the Campaign option for now.

You can also use a feature called *negative keyword lists*, which you'll find in the Tools section of your account. Lists are a great way to apply the same group of negatives to multiple campaigns.

Negative keywords are powerful because they eliminate irrelevant impressions. If you have 1,000 impressions and 50 clicks, your CTR is 5 percent. If you use negative keywords to cut out half of those impressions and show your ad to just 500 people, but you still get the 50 clicks, then your CTR just went from 5 percent to 10 percent.

Fewer irrelevant impressions mean a better CTR and a better Quality Score. That's the power of negative keywords.

How to Build a List of Negative Keywords

The easiest way to find negative keywords is to go back through your keyword research and pick out words that you rejected because they referenced product lines or services that you don't provide.

Once you start running ads, the best place to find negative keywords is in your search terms report. This should be reviewed regularly to look for terms that are irrelevant to your business (such as those people searching for microphone stands). To find your search terms report, go to the Reports icon at the top of your Ads screen, then Predefined Reports > Basic > Search Terms. See Figure 9–2 on page 78.

Whenever you find a good negative keyword, think about what other words someone might use for it. For example, a microphone stand might also be called a boom arm. So if you're going to add "stand" and "stands" as negative keywords, you'll also need to include "boom arm" and "boom arms."

Google will show you all the search queries they chose to display your ads for, along with data on how you're performing for each one. Finding underperforming terms and turning them into negatives is a great way to improve the performance of your keywords and ads. That said, be sure to apply negative keywords slowly and monitor your numbers carefully.

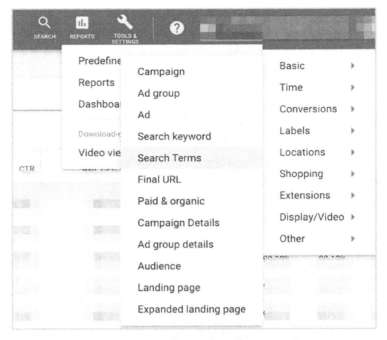

FIGURE 9–2. Generating a Search Terms Report

YOUR QUICK ACTION SUMMARY

Keywords are the foundation of a strong Ads strategy, but they're only the starting point. Don't obsess over building the perfect keyword list for your first campaigns. Good enough is good enough, and to be frank, the keyword list you have 12 months from now will probably look nothing like the one you have today. After you've spent a few months eliminating ineffective or costly keywords, finding variations of the winners, and reviewing your search terms reports to see how searches are changing, your keyword list will have grown and evolved into something far more interesting, finely targeted, and profitable.

But all journeys begin with a single step. Here's a quick review of what you need to do to get started:

- Set up your Ads account.
- Brainstorm keyword ideas.
- Use Google's Keyword Planner to expand your keyword list.
- Start with exact or phrase matches to identify the most targeted searches.
- Use Google's search terms report to find irrelevant and underperforming terms and add them as negative keywords.
- Refine your keyword list with options and filters.

Chapter 10

Supercharge Your Clickthrough Rates:
How to Write Google Ads That Pass the Test

Your ad is the most important part of your entire Google account. It's the one piece your prospect sees. They don't care how many keywords you have, how often you change your bids, or whether you're using Google's latest beta. All they care about is if your product or service can solve their problem.

That means what you say in a Google ad should be nearly identical to what you would say on the phone or when sitting across from your prospect, persuading them to buy. It's the language of the living room, the bar, or the street—not the ivory tower.

Speak to your customers in the same language they use in everyday conversation, and you'll click. Be clear, straightforward, interesting, customer-centered, and (most important) relevant.

Remember: It's not your ad's job to make the sale. That's your website's responsibility. Your ad just has to get your prospect to click on it.

In this chapter, we'll explore the various ad types available to you. We'll share copywriting tips and tricks to ensure that your ads don't break any of Google's rules. And we'll show you how to make use of ad extensions to gain an edge over your competitors.

You'll access these ad types from the page menu on the left. (See Figure 10–1 below.) Click on Ads & Extensions and choose Ads. Then click the blue + button and Google will give you a list of possible ad types to choose from.

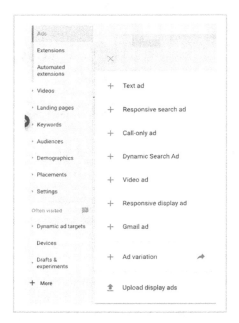

FIGURE 10–1. The Many Different Ad Types Available

REGULAR VS. RESPONSIVE ADS

We mentioned earlier that Google gathers 70 million combinations of signals in real time as users perform their searches. That's more data than any Google Ads manager could possibly analyze. This is why we're seeing a departure from old-school A/B split testing in the 2020s. It makes more sense to allow Google's machine to work out what the best ad is for any one person at any particular moment in time.

Rather than forcing the machine to choose from one or two ads, you can offer a range of ad "assets" to let it mix and match. These are called responsive ads.

The machine is far from perfect, but it's getting better all the time. We suspect that someday responsive ads will be the only option available to advertisers. However, at the time of this writing, you can still use regular ads, known as expanded text ads.

Let's take a deeper look.

Expanded Text Ads

Expanded text ads are so named because they're very similar to the old legacy text ads, but with room for more characters. You can now have up to three 30-character headlines and one or two 90-character descriptions in your ad.

Your job is to write two or three ads like this for each ad group and see which one gets the best results.

Responsive Search Ads (RSAs)

With responsive search ads, you write up to 15 headlines and up to four descriptions. These are the ad assets, or elements, that the machine will use to craft the best ad in real time. And if (for example) you want the first headline to be just your brand name, you can "pin" it so that it always appears as the first of the two or three headlines to be displayed.

But be careful. If you choose to "pin" certain ad elements in place, it will greatly limit the amount of testing the machine can do, hampering your results.

Reporting for RSAs still leaves a lot to be desired. You'll see very little transparency as to which of your ad assets are performing well and which ones need replacing. But the Google machine appears to favor RSAs. They get better clickthrough rates (CTRs), even if those clicks lead to fewer conversions.

COMPONENTS OF AN AD

The main challenge with those tiny Google Ads is the limited space. You'll need at least two headlines—and as many as 15 if you want to test responsive ads. Each headline can be up to 30 characters in length.

You'll need at least one description per ad, up to 90 characters in length. For responsive ads you'll need up to four of these.

Note that Google gives you a bit more creative freedom with responsive ads, but you can never use emojis or ASCII art.

Your landing page URL, which Google calls your "final URL," can be up to 1024 characters long. This is the page a user is taken to when they click on your ad.

Paths

Related to this, there's a feature called a *path* that lets you add some text to the URL displayed to the searcher (known as your display URL). This isn't the actual text of your final URL, but Google is fine with that.

Let's say you sell microphones, and you know there's high demand for particular models that you can use to do high-quality podcasts. You can create one path that says "podcasting" and another that says "microphones."

And now your display URL would show up in your ad as:

example.com/podcasting/microphones

This is another way for you to squeeze in more information and make your ads more relevant.

OUR TOP TEN FAVORITE AD COPY TESTS

Most of us make the mistake early on of thinking we already know the single best and most compelling way to describe our product or service to our prospects. But different people resonate with different kinds of ad copy. Expand and test a range of ideas for your ads, and you'll reach more people.

Whether you're using regular expanded text ads or you want to try responsive ads, here are ten things you can test.

1. *Price.* Add your price. Or omit it. Then measure the impact on both your CTR and your conversion rate.

2. *Call to action.* Include a clear and compelling call to action to get more people to click and to encourage a specific action once a visitor arrives at your website. Do this with strong verbs:
   - Maximize
   - Complete
   - Grab
   - Claim
   - Download

   There's one phrase you *cannot* use in an ad: "Click here." Google considers that a waste of space.

3. *Features and benefits.* Features describe your product itself. What it includes, or how big or small or robust or thorough it is. Benefits are the personal and emotional payoffs your customer will get from using it. You can certainly list the features of your product or service. But providing a list of benefits will tell your customer how they will actually be helped by it.

Let's say you're selling a coaching course. Instead of saying that your course teaches "12 timeless principles"—which is a feature—try saying, "Apply any one of these 12 techniques immediately and see instant results."

4. *Point-of-difference benefits.* If possible, have your ad clearly answer the question "Why you?" Explain what makes you different from your competition, and what your buyer can only experience by coming to you. (For more on this, go back and read about USPs in Chapter 5.)

5. *Empathy.* Express a pain or a frustration your customer is feeling or verbalize something good or positive they want to experience.

6. *Special offers.* Mention a deal or a special offer, particularly if it's available only for a limited time.

7. *Simplicity.* Choose words any fifth grader can understand. Keep your headlines and descriptions sweet and succinct. Use strong verbs and short sentences.

8. *Scarcity and urgency.* Consumers respond to scarcity—just be sure it's genuine. If you only have 50 units available, say so. If there are only two days left to act, announce it in your ads. An advanced option might be to add a countdown timer to your ads that changes the number of days or hours leading up to a buying deadline.

9. *Logic and emotions.* We make decisions emotionally and then justify those decisions rationally, after the fact. Use your ad copy to highlight the emotional

---

You Don't Have to Be a Poet or a Master Copywriter

We can't teach you in this short space how to be a great copywriter, but we can point you toward some timeless books on the subject and recommend you read at least one:

- *Advertising Secrets of the Written Word* by Joseph Sugarman

- *Scientific Advertising* by Claude Hopkins

- *Tested Advertising Methods* by John Caples

- *Breakthrough Advertising* by Eugene Schwartz

- *The Advertising Solution* by Craig Simpson with Brian Kurtz

Recall that your ad is the only part of your account visible to the public. As the Google machine becomes more proficient with the data, the advertiser with the most persuasive copy will come out on top.

---

payoffs of using your product or service. Far too many ads are too dry in their wording. Add some spice.

Alternatively, if all your competitors are using strictly emotional appeals, aim instead for something logical. Offer some form of incontrovertible proof of your claims, for example.

10. *Specificity*. The more specific you are, the more believable your message is. For example, explain how your software "has helped 31,493 people," instead of "thousands of people." But be sure your claims are factually correct.

SEE IN ADVANCE HOW YOUR ADS WILL LOOK

If you want to write great ads, don't try to reinvent the wheel. The simplest, clearest, and most truthful ads are almost always the ones that end up winning in split tests.

For inspiration, try Google's Ad Preview and Diagnosis tool, which lets you see how your ads will appear on search pages. It will also show the ads your competitors are running. Click on the Tools & Settings icon at the top of your Ads account, and under Planning select Ad Preview and Diagnosis. From there, simply enter your chosen keywords to see other ads that are appearing for those keywords.

Sure, you could just search for those keywords on Google, but the Ad Preview and Diagnosis tool gives you much finer control. You can select different versions of Google, different languages, different locations, and even different devices to see which ads are targeting which profiles.

And while we don't recommend that you copy anybody else's ad, you can certainly look to other businesses' ads for ideas. If you really want to dig deep, you can use paid spy tools to see all the ads in a competitor's account, and even how those ads have changed over time. Tools like SEMrush or Adbeat are highly recommended for the more advanced advertiser.

Also don't forget to get inspiration from ads in other channels, such as magazine, radio, or billboard ads. Always be on the lookout for a great hook or call to action that you can modify and use in your own advertising.

FOLLOW EDITORIAL GUIDELINES AND KEEP GOOGLE HAPPY

Over the years, Google has refined its policy on what is and isn't acceptable in an ad. Although most of its rules are common sense, this has still resulted in a lengthy list of dos and don'ts, which can be found on Google's Advertising Policies Center page.

Here's a quick summary of some of the most important rules:

- *Capitalization.* You can't write in all caps in your ads. If your ad says "FREE," for example, it will be disapproved.
- *Punctuation and symbols.* You can't use emojis or ASCII art in your ad copy, nor can you use excessive punctuation or symbols. Putting a greater-than symbol (>) at the end of your ad to trick people into clicking on it will get the ad disapproved.
- *Adult content.* While some adult content is allowed in the Google system, it will often limit the serving of your ad, sometimes greatly—which will also limit the amount of traffic it generates.
- *Style and spelling.* Perfect Queen's English isn't required, but you do need to use commonly accepted grammar and spelling.
- *Unacceptable spacing.* Just as you can't use excessive punctuation and symbols, you can't insert extra spaces (or run words together).
- *Repetition.* Needlessly repeating words, such as "Sale! Sale! Sale!" will get your ad disapproved.
- *Phone numbers.* You can't put a phone number in the text of an ad. You can use call extensions, however. More on that in the next section.
- *Trademarks.* If you're a reseller of a product, you can use a registered trademark in your ad copy. Note that Google will sometimes incorrectly disapprove an ad for trademark reasons. If this happens to you, search the Google Help Center for *Help for trademark owners* to find out how to correct it.

SUPERCHARGE YOUR CLICKTHROUGH RATES WITH AD EXTENSIONS

It's simple: Ad extensions boost clickthrough rates.

Some folks dismiss ad extensions as unnecessarily complicated and fussy. But those extra links and lines of copy make your ads more visible and more relevant. And when you improve your visibility and relevance, you increase your CTR and Ad Rank. (More on Ad Rank under "How to Improve Your Impression Share" in Chapter 24.)

Ad extensions let you expand your ads and introduce more specific information, which makes your ads stand out on the page and entice more clicks. This gives you an automatic advantage over other advertisers.

Google wants you to use ad extensions. Users get more value and Google makes more money. For many years now, they have included the use of extensions in their secretive Quality Score algorithm: "If two competing ads have the same bid and quality, the ad with greater expected impact from extensions will generally appear in a higher ad position than the other."

Let's look at the different types of extensions that are available and how to make the best use of them.

Ad Extension #1: Sitelinks

If your ad is showing in one of the top four premium spots, you can show sitelink extensions. These appear as additional links underneath your main ad. As shown in Figure 10–2 below, you'll typically see two, three, or four (or maybe even six) links that point the user to different pages on your site.

These can work wonders for you. They don't cost you any extra money, they offer more specific and relevant options for your prospects to click on, and they let you take visitors directly to the most relevant page. Best of all, they take up more space on the Google results page, pushing your competitors and the organic search listings farther down and out of the way.

Let's say your website sells a particular brand of men's shirts. You bid on the brand name as a keyword and write an ad that specifically offers a deal on long-sleeve crewnecks. With sitelinks, you can also add three or four other links in your ad that take visitors to special offers for turtlenecks, short-sleeve shirts, or even hoodies, all from the same brand. Or you can highlight other information that may be of interest to the searcher, such as your About Us page or your Shipping and Returns Policy page.

These extensions are easy to add and update. You can even create sitelinks that are specific to mobile devices and schedule them to show at specific times, which is especially valuable if your offers are seasonal or expire after a certain date.

FIGURE 10–2. Examples of Sitelinks

Google has greatly improved their reporting for sitelinks, making it far easier for you to see which ones are getting the most clicks and activity.

A word of caution: Google allows you to set up different sitelinks for different ad groups, which sounds like a great idea in theory. However, it adds a level of complexity that only the most experienced Google users should be grappling with. If you're just getting started, stick to activating sitelinks at the campaign level.

Ad Extension #2: Callout Extensions

As with sitelinks, callout extensions offer additional text in your ad—making your ad bigger and pushing your competitors' ads and organic listings down the page. Typically, you can add three or four useful snippets of copy to your ad with callouts, but unlike sitelinks, they are not clickable. Google recommends that you limit yourself to 12 to 15 characters per callout; the hard limit is 25.

Ad Extension #3: Structured Snippet Extensions

Despite being easy to create, structured snippet extensions are overlooked by most advertisers. Yet they're another great opportunity to add more (nonclickable) text to your ads. Whereas callout extensions allow you to type in whatever you like (up to 25 characters), structured snippets—as the name suggests—are more restrictive.

First you choose from a range of attributes based on what you sell. Options include types, styles, brands, amenities, courses, and models, plus a few more.

Most of the time you will just use "types" or "brands." Services is a good place to start if you sell a range of products or services. See Figure 10–3 below.

You then enter a range of values for that attribute. For example, if you sell training courses, you might enter "personal development," "business training," "leadership," "time management," and "public speaking." These will show as an additional line underneath your ad.

But remember: Google gets to choose when to show each extension.

[Ad] melbourne.goldlaw.com.au/Family_Law ▾ (03) 9322 2777

Family Lawyers Melbourne | Goldsmiths Lawyers - Melbourne

Family Law Solutions - Call Us! Specialist Family Law Practitioners. Proven Expertise. Qualified Lawyers. Established 1961 Types: Property Settlements, Protection of Assets.

FIGURE 10–3. An Example of Structured Snippets

Ad Extension #4: Call Extensions

Google no longer allows you to type your phone number directly into the text of your ad; you now have to use call extensions instead. If you're in a country that allows you to use a Google forwarding number, you can get access to additional reporting features this way.

Call extensions are most useful because they allow you to count a phone call as a conversion. You can even specify the minimum length of a converting phone call. For example, a call might only count as a conversion if it's longer than 45 seconds.

The cost to have a mobile user click on your telephone number is the same as a regular click, making this an extremely cost-effective method of driving calls to your business. This is also a good feature to combine with ad scheduling if, for instance, you only want your call extensions activated during business hours.

How Much Does Google Charge You for Calls?

Charges for phone calls and clicks on your ads can get tricky. If someone clicks on your call extension to ring your phone number directly, you'll be charged the cost of a regular click. If that same user also clicks on your ad's URL to visit your landing page, you'll be charged a second time. You won't, however, be charged a third time for any subsequent clicks on the same ad by the same user.

Ad Extension #5: Location

Location extensions allow you to show your business address next to your ad. This is relevant if you're showing ads to people just in your area, as it's a signal to them that you are in fact local.

Note that Google decides whether showing your address next to your ad will be useful for the person searching. They may display a link for driving directions as well.

If you want to show location extensions in your ads, you need to link your Google My Business (GMB) and Google Ads accounts. You can find more information about this process at https://support.google.com/google-ads/answer/7189290.

Ad Extension #6: Price

A price extension allows you to list your products below your ad. Once again, this allows your ad to take up more onscreen real estate—especially on mobile devices—and push your competitors down the page.

When you create your extension, you'll choose your language, the type (as we mentioned earlier with structured snippets), your currency, and a price qualifier. The qualifier adds either "From" or "Up to" before your prices, or you can choose to display no qualifiers at all. For each product item, you'll enter a header and a description (with a maximum of 25 characters each), a price, and a final URL. (All your price extensions can use the same URL, e.g., your homepage.)

We recommend you enter at least five items. Google will test these and typically show the three that perform best.

YOUR QUICK ACTION SUMMARY

Not only do ad extensions increase your visibility and CTR but they also expand your ads to considerably greater sizes, giving you a bigger piece of Google real estate at no extra cost.

- Try your hand at Responsive Search Ads.
- Start with number one and go through the list of the top ten things to test in your ads. Always be running tests of these different kinds of elements.
- Pick the two or three ad groups you feel have the most potential early on and add sitelink, callout, and structured snippet extensions, and use the reporting interface to see how they're helping your results.
- If your primary goal is to generate phone calls to your business, activate call extensions.
- If you're a local brick-and-mortar business, link your Google My Business page to your Google Ads account to enable location extensions to show.

Chapter 11

Landing Pages:
Making Powerful First Impressions That Convert

Imagine you're walking past a sporting goods store and you see an amazing pair of sneakers in the window. But when you walk into the shop, the sneakers are nowhere to be found. Or, worse, a security guard stops you at the door and demands to know your address and phone number.

Not a great first impression.

Your landing page is the same way. When you make a promise in your ad, your visitors expect you to deliver on it when they arrive at your page. They won't stick around otherwise.

If, for example, you promised an answer to a puzzling question, your page has to supply the answer or your visitors will bail. If you offered a report or a free software trial, then that's what you must deliver.

Always match your landing page to your ad, and give your visitors enough information that they can decide whether your offer is truly for them.

WHAT IS A LANDING PAGE?

A landing page is a stand-alone page on your site, separate from your homepage, designed for visitors to "land on" as soon as they click on your ad. You craft it with a single outcome in mind—the specific action you want your visitor to take, whether that's opting in to your newsletter, registering for a webinar, downloading an ebook or white paper, or calling you on the phone.

Why Don't I Just Send People to My Homepage?

A well-designed landing page with a crystal-clear call to action will seem far more relevant to your visitor, and will convert at a far higher rate, than your homepage. If your prospect arrives on your site and has to search for information, or even *think* about what they're doing, they'll hit the back button and leave.

Most web developers just want a site that looks pretty. Your goal, however, is to get your prospect to take immediate action. You don't *have* to use the same headline on your page as you did in your ad. And in the case of display ads, you don't *have* to use the same image on your page that your prospect saw in your ad. But the page should clearly continue the story without confusing your visitor.

Pick one goal for each landing page you create. If you want one slice of your traffic to opt in to your webinar and another slice to try your free software, then create separate landing pages for each one. If you have multiple offers in mind and you're not sure which one will convert best, create a split test.

Whatever you do, don't overwhelm visitors with multiple offers on a page. A confused mind always says "No." Stick with one offer and one call to action for each page.

MAINTAIN THE "SCENT"

Your landing page will perform best when it looks and feels like a natural continuation of your ad. What key words or phrases made your ad sing? What colors or images got people's attention? What ballsy promise did you make? Don't lose your prospect! Match those same elements on your landing page.

Google's editors look for this same pattern. They want to see an uninterrupted chain of relevance—a "scent"—starting from the initial search query, to the keyword, to the ad, right through to the landing page.

The landing page keeps the visitor in a familiar environment. The original offer is clearly visible. There's no confusion. The page has eliminated all need to think; the visitor can complete the required action quickly and easily.

THE TWO PEOPLE YOU NEED TO KEEP HAPPY

Your landing page needs to make two people happy—not just one.

First, there's the Google editor who will review it. If they decide your landing page is unacceptable, your ad will be disapproved. In some cases, Google will suspend or even ban a Google Ads account based on the content of a landing page. Keeping the editor happy is critical to your mission.

Google currently lists five main items they believe make for a good landing page experience:

1. *Have relevant, useful, and original content.* The copy and images on your page must maintain the scent and clearly relate to your ad text and keyword.
2. *Promote transparency and foster trustworthiness on your site.* Be open and transparent about your business and its product and services. Be clear with visitors (on your page or via a link) what you plan to do with the personal information they share with you.
3. *Make mobile and computer navigation easy.* The simpler the better. When your visitor can easily find on the page what you promised in the ad, they'll stick around and take action.
4. *Decrease your landing page load time.* Pages that load slowly fare poorly with your visitors and with Google. We suggest using the PageSpeed Insights tool (https://developers.google.com/speed/pagespeed/insights) you can use to check your pages' load times. Just enter your URL and click on the blue Analyze button to receive suggestions on how to optimize and improve your page loading speed.
5. *Make your site fast.* The fact that Google has two points in this list about speed should tell you something about how important speed is to Google. This is especially true of your mobile site.

The second person you need to please is your customer or prospect. Maintain the scent. Give them what they came for. Craft a landing page that perfectly matches what they saw in the ad. If you make it easy for them to take the required action, they'll do it.

THE ESSENTIAL LANDING PAGE CHECKLIST

There are many things you can do with a landing page, but it's important to get the fundamentals right before you start experimenting. Provide these key elements on your page, and you'll keep Google on your side:

- *A clear business model.* If a Google editor manually reviews your site, they should be able to tell in less than 20 seconds what you actually do. How do you make your money? Are you selling a course, a product, or a service? The editor wants assurance that you're not harvesting emails in order to spam. Your page should describe what will happen once your visitors opt in and what value they'll receive in exchange for their personal information.

- *Friendly design.* You never get a second chance to make that first impression, as they say. Invest the time and a little money on a professional, well-designed page that's easy to navigate—the simpler the better. Your content might be fantastic, but if the design is outdated or user-hostile, it will cost you. In the first second or two after your prospect lands on your page, they need to think, "Yes, this is relevant to what I was looking for; yes, there's obvious value here; and yes, it's clear what action I'm going to take." Think about where you're drawing your visitor's eye. Use imagery that adds value. Avoid obvious stock photos. Show people using your product or service and the end result they can expect: the contented sleeping baby, the perfectly mowed lawn, the happy podcaster, and so on.

- *A clear call to action.* Be sure you have one clear and obvious call to action per page. If you ask a prospect to do more than one thing, they'll usually choose to do nothing.

- *A compelling offer.* One of the fastest ways to boost your results is to improve the offer. Have you done enough to show your prospect why your product or service is different from and better than your competitors? If not, revisit Chapter 5 on unique selling propositions.

- *Persuasive copy.* We talked a little about persuasive copy in Chapter 10. Your landing page also needs to sell the benefits of the product or service, not the features. Remember, it's always about them, not you. So try to use words like *you* or *your*, not *I* or *we*. And here's a tip: Don't always used the word "submit" on buttons on your website. Match your call to action in the header of the form on your site with the form's call to action button, as this can often increase results.

  If you're trying to decide whether to use long- or short-form copy on your page, test which works better for you. Long-form copy will convert well as long as it's persuasive and not just there to make the page longer.

- *Fast page speed.* Sites like Amazon have trained people to expect very fast-loading websites. Amazon's site loads in around one second. Google's latest research suggests that if your site takes more than three seconds to load, people will get bored and leave. Faster pages will also convert better and, for ecommerce sites, typically lead to a higher average order value (AOV). You may also want to consider using AMP pages to help your mobile site load faster.

- *Social proof.* You're free to use case studies, reviews, or testimonials from past customers who have gained value from your products and services. (Use customer ratings where possible.) If you have a great track record and can support the claims you make, use them. Just be careful of which claims you make if you're in the health space. You can also use company logos, pictures of the people who have left reviews, or even screenshots of reviews they've written on Facebook.

- *Contact details.* It's not a hard requirement, but Google prefers you make your physical address—not just a P.O. box—available on your site. This helps build trust, as it demonstrates that you're a real business with an actual front door. At the very least, you'll need a working phone number or a functional email address.

- *Clear policy.* Ensure you meet the policy requirements. As a minimum, have a link to your privacy policy available on every landing page. You might also want to link to terms and conditions, shipping and return policies, or any appropriate disclaimers. These are particularly important in the health space. Also make sure that your website is crawlable by Google, so your Ads account doesn't get suspended.

ENSURE YOUR LANDING PAGES ARE COMPLIANT

As with the editorial guidelines we mentioned in Chapter 10, Google has dozens of pages dedicated to its landing page policies. We highly recommend that you read these pages, but we'll give a very high-level summary here to help you get started quickly.

Have a link to your privacy policy on every page. You can copy a competitor's privacy policy as a starting point and edit it to match your business. Depending on where you're based, and where your customers are, you may also have to comply with legislation such as Europe's General Data Protection Regulation (GDPR) and the California Consumer Privacy Act (CCPA). We recommend talking to a lawyer to ensure your policies are legally correct.

Not all industries are equal in Google's eyes, so depending on your industry, you may need to add other disclaimers, particularly about your customer reviews or claims you're making. Often the phrase "results are not typical" is a wise phrase to add to your site.

Search for the Google Ads Destination Requirements policy, which details what to avoid in your landing pages—such as interfering pop-ups.

GIVE YOUR WEB DEVELOPER THE DAY OFF: CREATE YOUR OWN LANDING PAGE

There are scores of great tools available these days to help you create an inexpensive landing page. You won't need a web designer, and you don't have to hassle with complicated coding. The best tools offer a range of fully customized templates where you can change colors and text, add images, and quickly build a working page yourself. Here are a few you can check out:

- Unbounce (https://unbounce.com)
- Webflow (https://webflow.com)
- Leadpages (https://www.leadpages.com/)

You can also use WordPress or whatever platform your website is built on. The platform isn't important; what matters is that you end up with a page that converts.

Always Be Testing

Sending paid traffic to a page that isn't being tested is a crime against humanity.
–Avinash Kaushik

It may sound harsh, but Kaushik, a data analytics expert at Google, has a point. He's a huge fan of A/B split testing, and so are we. How do you know if your current offer is the one that will convert best? How do you know if your chosen headline and landing page copy will convert better than something else? Without split testing, you don't. You put time, work, and money into your page, and you want to be sure you're getting maximum results.

In an ideal world, you would split-test every page you're actively sending traffic to. Start with the elements on the page that have the biggest impact on results: the headline, any images at the top of the page, and the layout and placement of your opt-in form. (Other elements you could test include the order or wording of bullet points, your color scheme, and your call-to-action buttons.)

Of these, the headline will always make the biggest difference, so start there. And always test just one major page element at a time. For further help, check out Google Optimize, Optimizely (https://www.optimizely.com/) and VWO, or Visual Website Optimizer (https://vwo.com/testing).

The wonderful thing about the web is how transparent it is. You don't have to be concerned about staring at a blank page when designing your landing page. There are plenty of places to get inspired. We suggest keeping a swipe file of pages that you notice when reading other websites.

If a page stands out to you or persuades you to buy something, keep a note of it and revisit that for ideas when you're designing your own landing pages.

Blogs on websites like Unbounce.com and Leadpages.com frequently showcase great landing pages and explain why they work well. These can be a great source of inspiration. Of course, you can also look at what your competitors are doing. However, don't copy them; use them only as a launching pad for your own ideas.

YOUR QUICK ACTION SUMMARY

You want your paid traffic to generate the highest ROI possible. When you improve your landing pages, your conversion rates go up, you end up with more leads, and you can afford to buy more traffic in greater volume.

- Know what the single purpose for your landing page is. Create it with that one conversion goal in mind.
- Maintain the scent! Be sure your page is the natural extension of your ad. Use the same design and content with the original promise or offer clearly visible.
- Keep Google happy by following their five guidelines on what your page should include and how it should function. Read the full list here: https://support. google.com/google-ads/answer/2404197.
- Be sure that your visitor's first impression is of an established, trustworthy business. Include your contact details and a privacy policy, and provide access to enough valuable information that they can opt in or purchase from you with confidence.
- Split-test the major elements on your landing page. Start with your headline, and then test images. Constantly work to improve your conversion rates.

Chapter 12

Choosing and Mastering Search Campaigns

Thanks to Google's two main networks, Search and Display, there are a number of different types of ads your prospect might see as they browse and search the web.

When a user goes straight to google.com, or the Google homepage in their country, and performs a search, they are on the Search Network. Among the search results, they might see a text ad (roughly 300 characters in length) or a shopping ad.

(They might also see those ads on Google's search partner sites. These are typically either second-tier search engines that syndicate their results and ads from Google, or else large sites that have done a special deal with Google and show ads from the Search Network.)

The Display Network contains more than two million websites and a million apps—everything from Oprah.com to small blogs you've probably never heard of. There are also two large Google properties that are part of the Display Network: Gmail and YouTube. The ads on those two sites have their own unique characteristics, so we'll cover each of them separately (YouTube in Chapter 16 and Gmail in Chapter 17). We'll also cover remarketing ads in Chapter 14.

In this chapter, we'll look at the different search campaigns that can produce top results for you and show you how to master them. We'll also briefly cover a new type of search campaign launched by Google in 2019: a discovery campaign. App campaigns are used by less than 1 percent of Google advertisers, and therefore won't be addressed in this book.

DECIDING WHEN A SEARCH CAMPAIGN IS RIGHT FOR YOU

Not all campaign types will suit your business. It will depend on what you're selling, who you're trying to sell to, and where your target audience might be looking for you.

The following questions will help guide you through which campaign types you should consider for your own advertising:

- *Are people searching for you or your company by name?* If they are, or if it's likely that they will be soon, you'll want to create a search campaign using keywords relating to your name or your business name.
- *Are people searching for the product or service you sell?* Again, you'll want to create a search campaign. This time, however, the keywords you choose will relate directly to the product or service you sell. These are known as non-brand keywords. Examples might include "Italian restaurant" or "digital marketing agency."
- *Do you sell a physical product?* If you sell physical products, such as microphones, maternity wear, or riding lawn mowers, you'll want to experiment with a shopping campaign.
- *Does your product or service benefit from being advertised visually?* If so, consider the Display Network or even a YouTube campaign.
- *Are you more concerned with reach than cost?* If your advertising objective is to show as many ads as possible to get people interested in a new product or service, you should consider display or video ads.
- *Do you have an app?* You'll want to consider an app campaign to get your app in front of and downloaded by more users. Those are beyond the scope of this book but you can contact WebSavvy if you'd like more details.

This chapter will focus on search campaigns; we'll cover the other types in subsequent chapters.

SETTING YOUR CAMPAIGN GOALS

When you create a new campaign in the Google Ads interface, you'll first be asked what your goals are. There are seven to choose from:

1. Sales
2. Leads
3. Website traffic
4. Product and brand consideration
5. Brand awareness and reach
6. App promotion
7. A campaign without the guidance of a single goal

The last option sounds scary but is the one most often used by search professionals, as it gives the advertiser more choices. If you choose one of the first six goals, Google will limit the features available to you. This makes things easier when you're just starting out, but as you become more proficient, you'll likely choose to have "no goal" for later campaigns.

Figure 12–1 gives you a quick-glance view of which types of campaigns allow you to achieve which types of goals.

There are additional campaign types such as smart, local, and hotel campaigns, but those are beyond the scope of this book. For now, let's dive into search campaigns.

Goal Type	Sales	Leads	Website Traffic	Product & Brand Consideration	Brand Awareness & Reach	App Promotion	No Goal
Search	√	√	√				√
Display	√	√	√	√	√		
Shopping	√	√	√				
YouTube	√	√	√	√	√		
Discovery	√	√	√				
App						√	

FIGURE 12–1. The Seven Campaign Goal Options

MASTERING SEARCH CAMPAIGNS

If you're just getting started, you'll want to do so with a search campaign. Search is the most common campaign type and the easiest to learn. Search campaigns typically have a higher conversion rate than display or video, and they give you a far greater chance of starting off profitably and with less hassle.

Search ads show up on the results page at google.com (google.co.uk, google.com.au, etc., depending on your country), on Google Maps, and on Google's search partner network.

BACK TO BASICS, BRIEFLY

We'll show you some examples of search campaigns soon. But first, let's recap some basics.

We've explained how a single Google Ads account can have multiple campaigns within it. As a rule of thumb, each campaign should feature a different type of ad. For example, you should have one campaign exclusively for search ads, one for YouTube ads, and one for shopping ads. Avoid mixing the different ad types together into one campaign.

But do you need more than one search campaign?

Maybe. To dig more deeply into that question, let's return to the idea of *intent* (which you read about in Chapter 9). There are three main levels of intent, or what people are looking for when they search: people looking for *information,* people searching in order to do *comparison,* and people searching with intent to *buy.*

If you're bidding on keyword groups that clearly have different levels of intent, you'll want to split them up into separate search campaigns. Your *buying* keywords are likely to have the lowest CPA, or cost per action. Your *informational* keywords will have a much higher CPA. You'll want to manage these keyword sets quite differently.

Another reason for separate search campaigns is when you're selling products and services in multiple locations. For example, if you sell your products in Australia, the U.S., and the UK, there are at least three good reasons to separate these countries into different campaigns:

- The CPA is likely to be different in each location.
- The amount you spend in each country will be different.
- For each country, you may need to use different spellings or local words and phrases.

You might also use separate campaigns for separate products. If you sell doors, windows, and shower screens, as one of our WebSavvy clients does, then having these three types of products divided among three separate campaigns makes it much faster and easier to see the relative performance of each one at a glance.

Here are some additional principles for launching your campaigns the right way.

Campaigns Contain Multiple Ad Groups

Just as your account can contain multiple campaigns, each campaign can contain multiple ad groups—up to 20,000 apiece (if you ever need that many).

You don't want all your keywords in one gigantic ad group, because different keywords express different intent. And different intent means you want to show different ads and take visitors to different pages of your site.

At the other extreme, you could have a separate ad group for every single keyword in your campaign. (We call these SKAGs, or single keyword ad groups.) This method has worked well for many search professionals over the years, but there's a downside: each ad group contains very little data. As we increasingly become a world of machine learning, this method is falling out of favor, since it doesn't give Google's system enough information to optimize results.

So just as with Goldilocks, you'll want to settle somewhere in between the two extremes. Aim for a sweet spot where you're using multiple ad groups, but not too many, to keep the right keywords grouped together and your ads relevant to those keyword searches. See Figure 12–2 below.

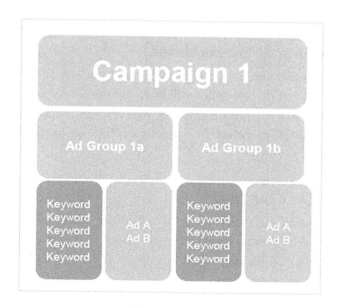

FIGURE 12–2. A Basic Campaign Structure

Build Your Message Around a Single Page on Your Site

Now that you've placed your keywords into multiple ad groups, pick one ad group and decide which page on your site is the most relevant for people searching for those specific keywords. Write two or three ads you think would entice someone to click through to that web page.

When you're just starting out, choose Text Ad, not Responsive Search Ad (see Figure 12–3 below). You'll get set up faster this way.

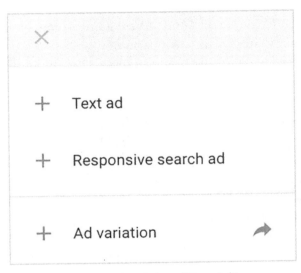

FIGURE 12–3. Select "Text Ad"

Start with Keywords as Your Targeting Method

While Google has made many changes to search targeting over the years, keywords are still the core method, and they probably will be for a long time yet.

Don't spend weeks or months on your keyword research. Whatever list of keywords you choose to start with is just that: a beginning point. Your list will grow and change over time.

Set Your Bids at the Ad Group Level

You could set bids at the individual keyword level if you wanted. But when you're new to Google Ads, it's easier to set bids at the ad group level, so that a single bid applies to all the keywords in that ad group.

As we mentioned in Chapter 8 on bidding, you'll want to start with manual bidding. It's the best way to learn the fundamentals. As you build data and gain more proficiency in search, you can test one of Google's Smart Bidding models, such as Target CPA.

THREE TYPES OF KEYWORD SEARCH CAMPAIGNS

There are three main types of search campaigns: brand, non-brand, and competitor. Let's look at each one in more detail.

Brand Campaigns

The keywords in a brand campaign center on the name of your business or your products. That can include your own name if that's something your prospects search for.

There has always been debate over whether brand campaigns are necessary, particularly if you already hold the top position in organic results. If prospects already find a free link to you at the top of the page, why would you pay money to get people to click on an ad?

Google has published a good deal of research on this, and WebSavvy's own tests have shown that running a brand campaign, even when you're number one in the organic results, does in fact give you an advantage. Here's why.

It Makes It Harder on Your Competitors

Bid on your own brand name with a matching ad, and Google will recognize it as highly relevant, so they'll give you the traffic very cheaply. Meanwhile, if competitors bid on your brand name—which they are allowed to do—they will have to pay more than you, because Google sees their ad and website as less relevant to the search than yours.

If you choose not to show brand ads, you'll often find three or four of your competitors showing ads on searches for your brand, and those ads will appear *above your organic search results*. This is a big disadvantage for you, particularly on mobile devices, where the screen is much smaller. However, if you run brand ads, your competitors' ads will almost always fall to the bottom of the page, if they show at all.

Prospects Perceive You as the Leader

If you show an ad and appear in the top organic position, your prospects will see you as the relevant business. You'll also find that users often scroll past your ad to click your organic listing, which saves you money.

It Gives You More Control

It's far easier to tweak and split-test the copy in paid ads than to change the snippet in your organic listing. Plus, in your paid ads you can determine the exact page you send your prospects to. That's very difficult with organic traffic.

Virtually every one of our WebSavvy clients runs a brand campaign. We recently had one who insisted on turning off the brand campaign to save $3,000 a week. Within a few weeks they realized they were on track to lose $150,000 a month in sales revenue and quickly agreed to turn the campaign back on.

Think of a brand campaign as cheap insurance. Brand terms should generally take up just 5 percent of your total budget—a small price to pay for the rewards you reap.

Non-Brand Campaigns

Keywords in a non-brand campaign center on the products and services you sell, not the name of your company, for example, "marketing consulting" rather than "Perry S. Marshall and Associates."

Again, if you expect different keywords in your collection to have different CPAs, or you wish to measure different outcomes (such as different types of conversion actions), you'll want to use more than one non-brand campaign.

Also remember that if you're running ads in multiple locations, consider using a separate campaign for each one. This is not required, but it can make things easier.

Start by using keywords that express the strongest buying intent, get those campaigns running, and then test additional keywords. Think about what keywords a person might use when they're poised and ready to make a purchase.

Competitor Campaigns

You are allowed to bid on your competitors' brand names. Pay special attention if you have competitors who have chosen not to run brand ads. It may be worth your time to bid on their brand terms. Typically you'll find that this traffic converts at a level somewhere between your brand and non-brand campaigns.

DYNAMIC SEARCH AD CAMPAIGNS

In this campaign type, Google helps out by supplying keywords you might have missed.

The search queries your prospects use change all the time. It's impossible to predict in advance what all the possible search queries might be. Google doesn't want you to miss out on those potential prospects. (They also don't want to miss out on the revenue from those extra clicks.) So they developed a type of campaign called Dynamic Search Ads (DSAs).

When Google spots someone they believe is a good prospect for you using a search term that doesn't match any of your keywords, they fill the gap with a DSA, showing them your ad even though you don't have that exact keyword in your account.

How to Set Up a DSA Campaign

As with other campaign types, the best method is to create a new campaign just for DSAs. Launch a new search campaign as you would any other, but in the campaign settings toward the bottom of the page, click Show More Settings. You'll also need to choose a targeting source, which tells Google which pages on your site to mine keywords from. Here you can select by categories of pages, by specific pages, or choose every page on your site. (We don't recommend the last option, though, as it's quite cumbersome.) See Figure 12–4 below.

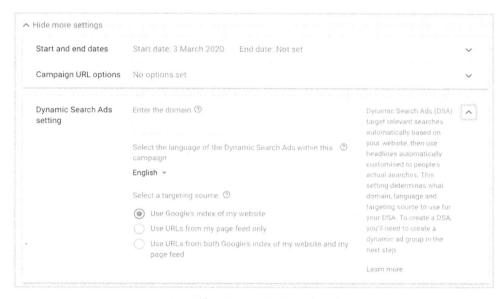

FIGURE 12–4. The Dynamic Search Ads Setting

For your ads, you'll write just two lines of description. Google will create the headline for you.

With a DSA campaign, you control your maximum bid, the description lines in your ad, the copy in your ad extensions, and which pages you allow Google to direct traffic to. You can also add negative keywords (we highly recommend this!) and specifically exclude certain pages from Google traffic. For example, you don't want to send paid traffic to your privacy policy, returns policy, contact information, or blog. You can create rules that tell Google to ignore pages under certain conditions, such as when a page contains the phrase "out of stock," for example.

Google controls the headline and decides dynamically which landing page to send your prospect to. They also decide what to charge for the click, though they'll never go above your maximum bid.

Optimizing DSA Campaigns

Having a good site structure will make your job far easier when it comes to DSA campaigns. If Google is confused by your website, and their machine can't clearly discern which pages are category pages and which are product pages, your ad campaigns will suffer.

Compare the performance of your DSA campaign with your regular ad campaigns and adjust your bidding accordingly. Keep an eye on your search terms report to ensure that Google understands what your website is about and is showing your DSA ads to the right audience.

You can also mine this report for useful keywords to add to your regular search campaigns and identify new negative keywords, which you can then include in your DSA and regular search campaigns.

Be sure to check your landing page performance as well and exclude any pages you need to.

DSA campaigns are particularly useful for large ecommerce sites where the product mix changes regularly, or for advertisers who feel they've maxed out their regular search campaigns but still want a higher traffic volume.

CALL CAMPAIGNS

Call campaigns are designed solely to generate phone calls to you.

Note that there's a difference between call campaigns and call extensions, which may not be immediately obvious at first glance. Call extensions add a phone number to your regular search ad, while call-only ads (see Figure 12–5 below) replace the headline of your ad with your phone number (or sometimes your business name). With a call-only ad, which appears on mobile platforms, there's one action the ad is aimed at getting the prospect to take: call the advertiser.

FIGURE 12–5. A Call-Only Ad

When a user clicks your call-only ad, a message pops up on their phone to ask if they want to call or cancel. At that point, you've already been charged for the click. Most users will go on to confirm and call you.

Setting Up Call Campaigns

To use call campaigns, you first need to set up a new conversion action. Figure 12-6 below shows how to select the source of phone calls you'd like to track.

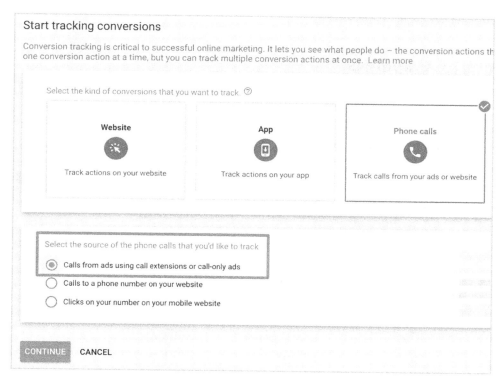

FIGURE 12–6. Setting Up a New Conversion for Call-Only Ads

By default, Google won't count a conversion if the call doesn't last at least 60 seconds. (You can change that value if you like.) Once you've established the conversion action, you'll create a new campaign designated for call-only ads.

Be sure to include your proper business name. Don't add any promotional text (such as "Free coaching at WebSavvy"). The ad will show a display URL, but remember that people cannot click through to your website. Google uses the URL to verify that your website contains the same phone number you've entered for the ad. They also require you to state your business name when answering calls from call-only campaigns. (How rigidly they enforce this is debatable, however.)

You can also add scheduling to your call campaigns so that your ads only show during business hours.

Many advertisers choose to raise their bids for these calls, as they can be more valuable to a business than leads generated through a web form.

We recommend you review the Google Help Center for country-specific information about call-only ads, as it tends to change often.

TIP

Google's call reporting is basic at best. You might want to consider using a third-party call tracker such as CallRail.

SMART CAMPAIGNS

Google Ads can feel complicated and even overwhelming for small-business owners. Google understands this, so they created Smart campaigns, a simpler, more stripped-down, automated version of Google Ads. The downside is that you have less control and you're given sparser data showing what's working and what your prospects are searching on.

Smart campaigns are for business owners with little time or desire to learn how to do Google Ads properly. If you're reading this book, it's safe to assume they're not for you.

DISCOVERY CAMPAIGNS

At the time of this writing, Discovery campaigns are still fairly new.

They aren't available for all Google Ads accounts yet. So why are we telling you about them? Because we suspect this campaign type will grow significantly in coming years and you should be aware of it. In this section, we'll fill you in on what makes these campaigns worth watching.

As with a display campaign, a Discovery campaign is designed to show visually engaging ads using the standard audience targeting you're used to. The difference is in 1) where the ads show and 2) the formats available to you.

Discovery ads may show on a user's YouTube home feed and in Gmail. But more than likely they'll show in the Google Discover feed. This is like the Facebook news feed, but it's found on Android, the Google app, and Google.com on your mobile device. Google claims that Discover reaches more than 800 million people, so it's worth testing it out.

The big difference with Google Discover is that an individual's feed is algorithmically generated based on the content they've read in the past and the content Google predicts they'll be interested in next. It's worth exploring if you want to get your product or service in front of a lot of new people in a visually engaging way.

Setting Up Your Discovery Campaigns

There's not much you can control with a Discovery campaign. The audience targeting is very similar to regular display campaigns (see Chapter 13) and the ads themselves are very similar to responsive display ads.

You'll need to enter:

- Up to five headlines (up to 40 characters in length)
- Up to five descriptions (up to 90 characters in length)
- Up to 15 marketing images
- Up to five logos

You'll also need your business name, the call-to-action text from a list that Google supplies to you, and your final URL.

Just remember that Google's standard editorial guidelines apply here as well, which means your ad can't have anything resembling a clickable button, a clickbait headline, or a low-quality image. A full list of these guidelines can be found in the Google Ads Help Center.

What to Expect from Your Discovery Campaigns

We're still in the early days of this new campaign type. Mike and the team at WebSavvy have run some initial tests and found that the CTR for these tends to be quite good. However, the profitability and performance tend to be below that of a standard display campaign. This is to be expected, as Google is targeting people earlier in the buying process, before they've started searching for specific products or services. This is likely to be a campaign type that Google wants to use more and more, so it's definitely worth running some tests.

YOUR QUICK ACTION SUMMARY

- Decide if a search campaign is right for you.
- Determine the goal you want to reach for your new campaign.
- Create more than one ad group, with keywords grouped tightly together in each one and ads written to match those specific keyword searches.
- Build your message in each campaign around a single page on your site.

Chapter 13

How to Get Your Ads on Millions of Websites with Google's Display Network

f you wanted to see your ads on Oprah's website, how would you do that?

You could try going the traditional route and see if your budget has room for the tens of thousands of dollars you'd expect to spend. Make endless phone calls, engage in dozens of email conversions, and battle through the layers of gatekeepers and decision-makers until you reach someone with the authority to discuss the advertising opportunity with you. Finally, assuming you managed to agree on terms and have your content approved, line up behind all the other businesses that also want their products and services featured on Oprah's high-traffic website.

Fortunately, you don't need to do any of that, thanks to the Google Display Network (GDN). The GDN is perfect for mass-appeal consumer offers, and it can deliver *tremendous* volumes of traffic to the tune of millions of clicks per day. GDN can be potent for B2B and small niches as well.

Just log in to your Google Ads account and create a display campaign that targets Oprah.com. You can even choose a specific page on their site if you like (see Figure 13-1 below). Then decide how much per click you're willing to bid for the privilege.

That's the power of GDN. Extend your Google Ads campaign beyond mere search pages, and you instantly have access to *more than two million websites* that have agreed to place Google ads, plus a million apps.

In the years since introducing the program that website publishers know as AdSense, Google has become one of the largest advertising networks in history, connecting publishers and advertisers from all corners of the globe.

At its simplest level, it's a beautiful system:

■ A website owner (the "publisher") produces some content and is eager to start monetizing the traffic that their site commands.

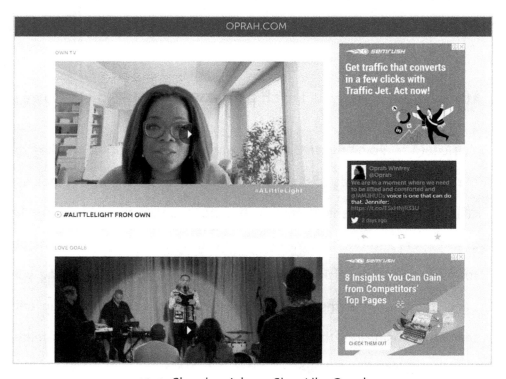

FIGURE 13-1. Showing Ads on Sites Like Oprah.com

- They place code on their website, essentially an invisible box, which Google can use as they see fit.
- People (the "advertisers") pay Google to place their ads on the site in the invisible boxes.
- Google then shares a portion of that income with the publisher.

The publisher doesn't know exactly what ads will appear on their site, but they trust Google to properly screen and manage the advertisers. As a result, they don't have to spend huge amounts of time looking for advertisers and managing clients themselves.

As a Google Ads user, you have access to the entire GDN, and you can add it to your campaigns with just a few clicks. However, just like the rest of your Google ad campaigns, the difference between a stunning ROI and complete failure lies in how well you understand the options available to you and how well you prepare and implement your strategy. In this chapter, we're going to show you how to reach more than 90 percent of internet users through a single network, how to get your ads in front of YouTube and mobile app users, and how to tap into Google's inside knowledge of pretty much everyone on the internet!

DISPLAY VS. SEARCH

Let's start with a quick comparison. The most obvious difference between GDN and Google's Search Network is the range of locations on which you can advertise. The Search Network gives you access only to Google's sites and only to people who are actively looking for information. In contrast, GDN gives you access to every kind of site imaginable, reaching people who are engaging in all manner of different interests.

Just how huge is GDN? Those two million sites we mentioned earlier mean the number of individual web pages you can target reaches into the billions. From small blogs and forums that receive only a few hundred visits per day to internet titans like CNN, Tripadvisor, and ESPN, the audience spread across GDN is mind-boggling.

And that's *before* you factor in YouTube videos, Gmail, and mobile apps!

There's also a less obvious but more important difference—namely, the mindset of the people who see GDN ads. People go onto Google's Search Network looking for information, so they see your ads as a potential solution.

But the people who see GDN ads are *not* searching for your information—they're just browsing a website that interests them. They may see your ad as an interruption, in much the same way that people see commercials on TV and radio as an intrusion into what they really want.

That doesn't make the GDN useless; it just requires a different approach—what some people refer to as *interruption marketing*. You must present an offer that is so

ULTIMATE GUIDE TO GOOGLE ADS

engaging that viewers will feel compelled to stop what they're doing and give your ad a healthy moment of their attention.

If the Google Search Network is like playing checkers, GDN is chess. They both involve strategic thinking. But while the latter requires more thought before each move, it offers vastly more options to win!

On GDN, you can do far more than just text ads. You can craft image ads, which are great for branding and make for eye-catching campaigns.

You can also get away with more creative approaches than with search, since your ads will show in so many different contexts.

BIDDING FOR GDN

Display ads are like search ads in that you set your bids at the ad group level. The biggest difference comes when you adjust your bids.

When you bid more on a search campaign, you can expect to get more of the same type of traffic. Bid less, and your ad will show lower on the page and get fewer clicks.

Display is less "linear." The amount you bid will determine which *websites* (also known as "placements") your ads get shown on. That means if you change your bid—say, from 50 cents to $1 per click—you're not just going to get more of the same type of traffic. Your ads might show on completely different placements in the network, giving you different traffic, possibly without improving your results.

We're not suggesting that you never change your bids. We just want you to understand what a change in bids will mean here compared with search.

Display campaigns require far more nuance and a lot more testing than search campaigns. That's why many advertisers give up on them. But that means there's an opportunity for you here if you're willing to put in the work.

So if bidding more doesn't guarantee better results, how *do* you improve a display campaign and make it profitable? The answer lies in targeting and messaging.

TARGETING

Google gives you a range of options when it comes to targeting. Let's walk through them here.

Managed Placements

With this option, you enter the web addresses of the sites where you want to advertise. If those sites have space available, Google will show your ads there. You can even target a specific area on a site. For example, you can select www.nytimes.com, which will give you access to the entire *New York Times* website, or you can or you can use the URL www.nytimes.com/section/technology, which will limit your ads to the Technology section.

This is a good option if you want a lot of control over your placements, but it greatly limits your reach. Google doesn't publish its entire list of partners, so you'll need to research what's available, and you'll inevitably miss some prime opportunities. Even if you spend days or (more likely) weeks handpicking a hundred sites, you'll only be reaching a fraction of the sites Google has access to.

This form of targeting was popular a decade or more ago. With advances in Google's machine learning, it's a less attractive option now.

Contextual Targeting

Google categorizes all the pages in all the sites in their network into various topics. Using this option, you can choose broad or narrow categories of sites on which to show your ads.

The more specific your choice is, the better your targeting will be. For example, "Arts & Entertainment" is extremely broad, but you can drill down to "Arts & Entertainment > Entertainment Industry > Recording Industry > Record Labels" for terrific precision. Keep in mind that by using this method, *you aren't targeting people who work in those industries, but rather people who are visiting pages and sites on these subjects.* Many of those people could become your customers.

Topic targeting is an easy place to begin, but it's still quite broad. For even better results, target by keywords.

Every page on each of the two-million-plus sites in GDN has been assigned one or more "themes." Google looks at the text on the page, links, page structure, and various other "signals" to determine those themes.

You then use keywords in your display campaigns to tell Google which themes to look for, and they find pages to match your chosen keyword themes.

Big Google Is Watching

It probably comes as no surprise that Google is watching most of what you do while you're online. Between the Chrome browser, the Android operating system, Google Analytics, YouTube, Gmail, and more, Google has a very good idea which products and services you might be in need of in the near future.

As an advertiser, you get to leverage this data when trying to determine who to show your ads to.

While this form of targeting can still work well, it can be far more effective nowadays to target your audience based on their past behavior rather than on the page they happen to be reading right now.

Affinity Targeting

With this method, you target people based on their long-term behavior over the course of many months, taking into account the types of websites they've been to and the searches they've done. (This is akin to how TV advertising is bought and sold.) Google has broken down the available market into roughly 140 segments, or populations of people with a particular interest or affinity. Examples include beauty mavens, fast-food cravers, theater aficionados, and thrill seekers.

In-Market Targeting

Unlike affinity targeting, in-market targeting selects for people based on their online behavior over the past one to two weeks. It includes searches they've performed and sites they've visited. This is how Google knows what you're looking to buy in the very near future. So if you've been searching lately for new wheels for your car, payroll services, or animation software, Google will categorize you as being in the market for those particular products.

Custom and Combined Audiences

Google has around 750 predefined audiences that you can layer on and target, allowing you to take advantage of their vast trove of user data. But if the existing audiences don't suit your needs, you can always build your own or create combinations of them.

Life Events

This allows you to target people in the middle of a major life change, such as finding a new job, getting married, buying a home, or starting a business.

Behavioral Targeting

So far we've looked at targeting various behaviors people engage in online when they're not on your site. Now we'll turn to targeting people based on their behavior on *your* site. Here are three methods you can use:

1. *Remarketing.* This is where you show an ad to a repeat visitor based on the actions they previously took on your website—which pages they looked at, the amount

of time they spent on your site, which traffic source they came from—and how recently they visited. This is like sending out a gentle reminder to past visitors to nudge them back to your website.

2. *YouTube remarketing.* If you're running videos as ads, you can retarget every person who views, comments on, or likes any of your videos. You can build entire lists of those people and target them further with advertising. (See Chapter 16 for more on leveraging the power of YouTube video ads.)

3. *Your email list.* With this feature, you can upload a CSV file of email addresses, and the ones Google recognizes will be targeted with ads. (Note: You cannot upload a purchased email list; you can only use email addresses you've collected directly from your users.)

Demographics

Google has quite a bit of information on the demographics of its individual users. You can target a person by their age, gender, household income, parental status, education level, and homeownership status. And the list is growing.

Layering Targeting

You're never limited to just one targeting option. You can mix and match several of these to create sophisticated and complex display campaigns. A word of caution, though: Keep your targeting experiments conservative until your display campaigns have proved profitable. Layering too many targeting options at once can confuse Google's machine to the point that your ads will barely show.

The Display Grid

Google's targeting methods allow you to create a huge range of different ad campaigns. Mike has developed a free visual guide for this, available at www.TheDisplayGrid.com. There are videos there that can walk you through the targeting methods and campaign options. The Display Grid makes it easy to visualize all the available GDN strategies in one place. You can also use it to decide which combinations of ad targeting and ad types you want to test first. And you can use it to keep track of the results you get from testing all these combinations.

MESSAGING

With GDN, you're not limited to just text ads. Here are three additional main ad types you can experiment with.

Responsive Display Ads (RDAs)

This is the most common type of display ad. As with the responsive search ads we discussed earlier, your job is to provide various ad assets such as images, headlines, and descriptions. Google will then mix and match these elements in real time in an attempt to show the best ad to each person as they're browsing.

To create your RDA, visit https://support.google.com/google-ads/answer/7005917 for a detailed list of the assets you'll need along with text and image specifications.

HTML5 Ads

These are great for animation and more advanced techniques. They come with certain prerequisites, however, such as a minimum spend threshold and length of account history.

Uploading Your Own Ad

Uploading your own static ads means you, not Google, get to decide what they will look like. That's good if you prefer having creative control. The downside is you probably won't get as many ad impressions.

The list of allowable ad sizes changes regularly, so please check the Google Help Center for these and other technical specifications.

As we said in Chapter 11, maintaining the scent from your ad to your landing page is vital—especially with display ads. The imagery you use in an ad sets an expectation in your prospect's mind as to what they'll see on the landing page. Make sure you meet that expectation.

BUILDING YOUR GDN CAMPAIGN

We strongly recommend running your display ads in separate campaigns from your search ads. But how many campaigns you need is ultimately up to you. It depends on how granular you want to go and how much time you want to invest.

The simplest option is to create one display campaign with a separate ad group for each type of targeting. This is where we suggest you start.

First, decide which types of targeting you would like to test and determine what your testing budget is. From there, decide how much you're willing to pay per click. This will give you a rough idea how much traffic to expect.

Your campaign settings will be very similar for both search and display. The biggest difference is that for display, you need to set a frequency cap, which is a measure of how many times you want your ads to be seen by any one person. This keeps your prospects from seeing your ads again and again when they're clearly not going to click on them. You can set it per day, per week, or per month. (See Figure 13–2 below.) We suggest a maximum of five to ten impressions per day.

FIGURE 13–2. Setting a Limit on Your Impressions

MEASURING YOUR GDN CAMPAIGN

We mentioned in Chapter 7 that there are two sets of conversions you can show in your Google report: *conversions* and *all conversions*.

Conversions covers the most important actions you can track. It's also the conversion type that's compatible with Google's Smart Bidding algorithms.

There are a number of actions people can take on your site that won't necessarily affect your bids but that you want to track anyway. That's where the concept of *all conversions* comes in. People who see your display ad are typically much earlier in their buying process. They're not likely to opt in, complete a form, or buy your product on their very first visit. You want to measure smaller, less important actions than that.

And this is the difference between a *micro* and a *macro* conversion. A *macro conversion* is when a prospect fills out a form, calls you on the phone, or makes a purchase. A *micro conversion* would be a prospect downloading a PDF, watching a video, viewing one or more key pages, or spending a significant amount of time on your site. You can even measure how far down a particular page a visitor has scrolled.

So how do you measure these actions? You can use Google Ads' native tracking. In more advanced cases, you can use Google Analytics. (More on tracking conversions in Chapter 19.)

MANAGING YOUR DISPLAY CAMPAIGNS

Most of your effort on improving your display campaigns will be spent on two things: identifying and eliminating targeting methods that aren't working and honing your message.

The exclusions for GDN campaigns roughly mirror the various targeting options listed earlier in the chapter, and using these will help you set aside what isn't working so you can perfect your message.

If there are certain sites (or placements) you know you don't want traffic from, you can exclude them. Add a list of these under the Placements tab, and Google won't show your ads there. WebSavvy employs a more advanced method: using various Google Ads scripts to exclude sites by the hundreds of thousands.

Keywords and Topics

Google uses keywords and topics to classify web pages by theme. You can exclude a particular keyword, but this may or may not block the actual sites you want if Google's interpretation differs from yours. So proceed with caution. Using keyword exclusions on the GDN is not as straightforward as using negative keywords on the Search Network.

Audiences

Google defines an "audience" as a group of people selected based on their interests and habits, what they're actively researching, or how they've interacted with your business.

You can exclude audiences as easily as you can target them. The most common groups to exclude are people who have already bought from you or signed up for your offer.

To do this, choose Audiences from the page menu on the left and then the Exclusions tab at the top, as shown in Figure 13–3 below.

Choose the display campaign you want to work with and click on the Browse option. From here, you can exclude people based on their demographics, their habits and interests, things they're researching or planning, or ways they've interacted with you already.

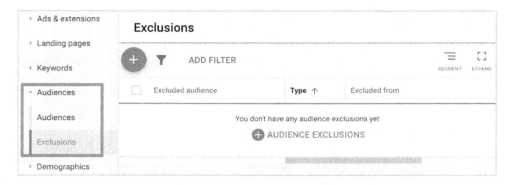

FIGURE 13–3. Setting Up Audience Exclusions

Mobile Apps

You may not want your ads to show on mobile apps, but preventing this is harder than it used to be, since Google believes their machine can best decide where to show your ads. Be warned: This can involve Google spending hundreds or even thousands of your dollars before their machine determines that mobile apps don't work that well for you after all.

That's why we recommend you block mobile apps from the outset. But this can get complicated, and it's constantly changing. Your best option is to search Google for "how to exclude mobile app categories from GDN campaigns" and follow the recommendations there.

We've saved the best for last: The first and most profitable GDN campaign you should set up is a remarketing campaign, and the following chapter is a deep dive into how to do that.

YOUR QUICK ACTION SUMMARY

Make sure you've carried out all these steps carefully:

- Think of a simple free offer or quiz that can form the foundation of your GDN campaign.
- Go to Mike's www.TheDisplayGrid.com and research the topics, interests, keywords, and audiences you could target.
- Decide whether now is the best time to try a display campaign: If you're a beginner, you may wish to skip it for now and come back to display later once you've gained some valuable experience on the Search Network.
- Check that your website is configured to record conversions. You cannot carry out effective GDN advertising, or any Google Ads advertising, without good tracking mechanisms in place.

Chapter 14

Remarketing:
The Single Most Profitable Online Advertising Strategy

Have you ever gone on *The Huffington Post* (or another news site) and suddenly noticed an ad for the espresso maker you were looking at on Amazon a few days ago?

That was no coincidence. You had a bull's-eye painted on your head. You were targeted by a remarketing campaign.

Remarketing, also called behavioral retargeting, is a way to advertise to people who have previously visited your website.

One member of my roundtable (my highest-level peer advisory group) sold an SaaS (software as a service) solution that employers could use to monitor their workers' performance. This was a product that people probably would not go looking for but intrigued them when they saw it. That made it a great candidate for GDN. However, a quick look and a 30-day free trial offer were usually not enough to persuade visitors to buy.

He discovered that people would download the free trial, forget about it, and move on. However, retargeting ads were effective at coaxing prospects into installing the software on their employees' computers. Once they had experienced its full value, they bought it.

That's an interesting use of retargeting ads, don't you think?

Imagine you ran a hardware store, and every visitor who came through your door willingly handed you their mailing address, whether or not they made a purchase. What could you do with that?

That's the power of remarketing.

Set up a remarketing campaign in your Google Ads account, and you have the freedom to reach out to every person who visits your website, long after they've left.

Consider all the visitors to your site who showed interest in your product in the past month. They may have added items to their shopping cart, but for some reason they left without completing the checkout process. Maybe they got distracted. Maybe they weren't going to get paid until Tuesday. Maybe the price was just beyond their budget.

Whatever the reason, they came very close to adding to your bottom line. This is where remarketing gives you a second chance—actually, as many chances as you like—to regain the attention of your previous visitors and give them a reason to come back for another look.

In pay-per-click terms, you'll never have a group of people to advertise to with more potential for profit than the folks who have visited your site. They know your brand, they've already demonstrated that they have at least some measure of interest in what you have to offer, and many will only need a slight nudge to go from warm lead to new buyer.

Remarketing is most popular among ecommerce site owners, but it's just as effective if you're a content or affiliate marketer whose primary goal is to add subscribers to an email list. Even if your website is so efficient that a full 20 percent of your visitors complete your lead capture form, that still means 80 percent of your audience is leaving without taking action. Ecommerce fares even worse, where 95 to 99 percent of visitors leave without making a purchase. These people are ripe for targeting with a remarketing campaign.

Much of the setup process is fairly self-explanatory, but in this chapter, we're going to highlight some of the areas that people sometimes forget to address and answer some questions that our students ask most frequently.

FIRST, UPDATE YOUR PRIVACY POLICY

You should already have a privacy policy that addresses your use of cookies and data. In fact, the wording in your fine print may already be broad enough to cover your use of remarketing campaigns. Even so, make sure you don't skip this part. Google is very strict about its remarketing campaign users having a properly worded privacy policy. Make those changes before you set up your first campaign.

Visit https://support.google.com/google-ads/answer/2549063?hl=en, and follow the directions carefully. Be sure your privacy policy is updated to include:

- A description of how you're using remarketing
- Notification that the ads you display will show on third-party websites, including Google itself
- Notification that these third-party websites will use cookies to select appropriate ads
- Guidance on how to opt out of Google's cookies (which users can do by clicking through to http://www.google.com/settings/ads)

CREATE AND INSTALL YOUR CODE

You'll need to create a small snippet of code that will be added to every page on your website. Depending on the size of your site, this may be a bit of work, but it's a one-time job. Once the code is in place, every visitor who comes by will have a cookie installed on their computer that will automatically track which pages they visit during their stay and how much time they spend on each page.

Click on the Tools & Settings drop-down menu at the top of your Google Ads account page. Under Shared Library, select Audience Manager (see Figure 14–1 on page 128).

Once you're on the new page, select Audience Sources on the left, as in Figure 14–2 on page 128.

Start with the most basic option on the upper left: the Google Ads tag. Click Details. On the resulting page, scroll down to Tag Setup and follow the instructions to install it. There are three ways to do this:

1. Email the code to your web developer. (This is your best option if you don't know how to code.)
2. Use Google Tag Manager to install it.
3. Install it yourself. (This assumes you're familiar with the back end of your website.)

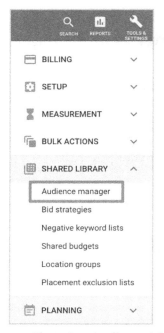

FIGURE 14-1. Choosing Audience Manager

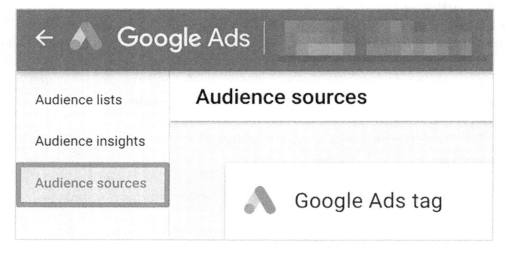

FIGURE 14-2. Choosing Audience Sources

HOW TO BUILD AN AUDIENCE TO REMARKET TO

Your next and most important job is to create and define your remarketing audiences, sometimes also referred to as lists. Simply put, an audience is a list of people who meet certain criteria. You can see at any time how many people are on each list you build, but beyond the criteria you select, you won't know who they are or anything else specific about them. Google keeps this information confidential for obvious privacy reasons.

And because these audiences are created using cookies, the process is invisible to your visitors.

Your lists grow automatically, but it may take time to build up a sizable audience that you can remarket to—days or even weeks, depending on the volume of traffic your site receives. The sooner you complete the audience-building step, the better.

There are hundreds of different types of audiences you can create, based on hundreds of actions and behaviors. We suggest you start by creating three basic lists, as follows:

1. *Everyone.* Every individual who visits your site, regardless of which pages they looked at or the actions they took.
2. *Buyers.* Everyone who took the desired action, whether it was making a purchase, completing a lead-capture form, or something else. Simply give Google the URL of your thank-you page, and anyone who completes an action and lands on that page will get added to this list. (Note that every visitor on this list will also be on the Everyone list.)
3. *Interested.* These people arrived at your site and visited certain key pages during their stay, such as a particular product page or a sales letter. Again, you can provide Google with the required page URLs that a person must visit to qualify for this list.

To create an audience, go to the Tools & Settings drop-down menu at the top of your Google Ads page. Under Shared Library, select Audience Manager. On the resulting page, be sure the menu on the left says you're in Audience Lists, as in Figure 14–3.

Let's focus on the most common type: a website visitor list. To create a new list, click the big blue + button on the upper left and choose Website Visitors.

1. *Audience Name.* Give your list a name that will make it easy to identify its purpose.
2. *List Members.* Stick with the default option, Visitors of a Page.
3. *Visited Page.* Google will populate your list by using some basic rules. Let's say you want to create a list of everyone who's been to your Joe Smith website. Here, under

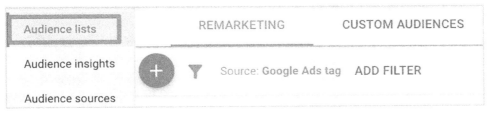

FIGURE 14–3. Choosing Audience Lists

Visited Page, go with the default choice URL and Contains. In the empty field, you can enter your domain, e.g., "joesmith.com." Going forward, everyone who visits the site will be added to this remarketing audience.

4. *Pre-fill Options*. You can start with an empty list or have one pre-filled for you. If you want a pre-filled list, go with the default setting, Pre-fill List with People Who Matched the Rules Within the Past 30 Days.

5. *Membership Duration*. You can choose how many days someone stays in this audience. The default is 30 days, but you can set this number to anything between 1 and 540 days.

HOW LONG DO I KEEP PEOPLE ON MY LIST?

Membership duration—or the length of time individuals remain on an audience list before Google removes them—is key. For example, if you set this at 60 days, anyone who visits your site will drop off your audience list after two months.

Note that if they visit your site *again* during that period, their membership duration is reset, and they'll remain on your audience list for 60 days after their most recent visit.

Keep in mind that the longer it's been since the prospect has visited your site, the lower the relevance of your remarketing ads.

As your remarketing techniques get more advanced, you will probably create multiple audiences with multiple durations. But early on, aim for shorter-duration lists. Thirty days or fewer. The more recently a person was on your website, the more likely they are to convert.

OTHER AUDIENCE LIST EXAMPLES

Once you're familiar with creating basic audience lists, you can branch out to other criteria in order to expand (or refine) who sees your ads.

Above, we showed you a sample "website visitors" list, made up of people who visited certain pages on your site. You can also create a list of people who visited between certain dates. (That could be all the people who looked at your discount offer on Black Friday, for example.) When you click on the blue + button from the Audience Lists page, you'll see that you have a number of other list options:

- A "YouTube users" list can bring you people who may not have been to your website but have interacted with your videos or channel on YouTube.
- You can upload your email list, or a portion of it (Google calls this a Customer Match audience), and show ads to people who, say, signed up for your newsletter but haven't bought from you yet.

- Under Custom Combination, you can build similar audiences to YouTube, remarketing, and Customer Match lists. In custom combination lists, Google uses machine learning to build a larger audience of people with attributes similar to the list you originally targeted, much like Facebook's Lookalike Audiences.

HOW TO CREATE A REMARKETING CAMPAIGN

Now that you've created one or more audiences, head back to the Campaigns screen and click the blue + Campaign drop-down button. Figure 14–4 below shows how you choose Display and then Standard Display Campaign.

FIGURE 14–4. Selecting a Standard Display Campaign

Now you can choose the name, bidding strategy, and daily budget for this campaign.

Your audience lists may start out empty, but over the coming days and weeks you'll watch their numbers grow. While you're waiting for this to happen, make good use of your time by crafting your first campaign with ads aimed specifically at your remarketing audiences.

A word about these settings: Pay special attention to the following three areas.

Bid Strategy

All the major bidding options are available for remarketing campaigns—cost per click (CPC), cost per thousand impressions (CPM), and cost per action (CPA)—but we suggest starting out with CPC. You can change to CPA later on if you're getting especially good results from your remarketing campaigns.

You should also consider bidding at least double your usual amount. These people are warm leads, so you can expect a higher conversion rate, which will justify the expense.

Geography

Google doesn't recommend adjusting this for remarketing campaigns. If your product is digital, you may be fine showing your ads all over the world. But if you supply physical products or services and can only reach certain geographic areas, then it's essential to modify this setting to reflect your target locations.

Frequency Capping

You don't want to annoy people by showing too many ads. You can set your number of impressions per day, week, or month, and apply it per campaign, ad group, or ad.

This setting is unique to display campaigns and allows you to specify how often any one person sees your ads. If you unintentionally show your ad hundreds of times a day to the same people, it'll kill your CTR, and it won't endear your brand to anyone. We recommend a maximum of three impressions per day for image ads.

HOW TO WRITE REMARKETING ADS THAT GET CLICKS AND CONVERSIONS

One of the most attractive elements of remarketing is the way you can write ads specifically to people who have already seen your products and your brand.

However, you never want to forget the golden rule of remarketing ads: *Don't be creepy!*

Remember the first time you became aware that you were being targeted by a remarketing campaign? How did it feel? *"How does Cracked.com know I've been thinking about buying a heated toilet seat? Who else knows about this?"*

Remarketing has been around long enough that most people are now accustomed to it. But some people are uncomfortable seeing their web browsing habits follow them around from site to site.

The solution is to never draw attention to the fact that you're remarketing to people!

A giant image of your logo with the message, "Hey, we miss you—when are you coming back?" is not smart.

We try to observe two simple methods for getting people's attention without highlighting the fact that they're a recent visitor:

1. Invite them to take the next step with you *without mentioning* any previous actions they've taken. Let's say you have a three-step conversion process: A person can watch your video, take your quiz, and then purchase your training course. And let's say you want to target visitors who watched your video without taking either of the subsequent steps. For them, you can write an ad that's simply an invitation to take your quiz. For visitors who have already watched the video *and* completed the quiz, your ad can be an invitation to purchase the course.

2. Follow the "FBI approach." You can spot a real-life stalker fairly quickly once you notice the same guy hanging around your street every day. The FBI is smarter than that. They employ a number of different people and rotate them frequently. If the FBI were following you, odds are you'd have no clue. You can accomplish the same level of stealth with your ads. Simply create a wide array of visual ad campaigns and use frequency capping to strictly limit how often each ad is shown on any given day.

SHOULD YOU TRY CUSTOMIZED LANDING PAGES?

In short, yes. But that comes with caveats.

Creating a whole new set of landing pages just for your remarketing campaigns could be a substantial amount of work. We'd rather you set up a remarketing campaign that sends people to your existing landing pages than overwhelm yourself with work and give up on the whole project.

However, if you're willing to put in the extra effort of creating landing pages with customized offers, your conversion rates will likely be substantially higher.

The key is to identify why your visitor wasn't initially willing to go through with the purchase and then create an offer that overcomes their objection. If your most common barrier is price, create an ad that offers a 10 percent discount. This is where that customized landing page becomes essential. If an ad promises a 10 percent discount, the landing page needs to back it up.

Experiment with different ads and offers to see which generates the best results. If a 10 percent discount doesn't do the trick, follow up with another campaign that offers a deeper discount or an exclusive bonus offer.

> ### How to Rescue a Failing Remarketing Campaign
>
> Want an example of how to save a bad remarketing campaign?
>
> Let's say you write an ad that mentions a promotional code for use during checkout, but you don't bother repeating the code on the landing page. If the customer can't remember the promo code from the ad, they'll give up trying to find it again, and you'll lose the sale. Bad remarketing!
>
> But there's an easy way to fix this.
>
> Have your web developer program the promotional code into the URL so the discount is automatically applied to the shopping cart when your customer clicks on the ad. That's less work than creating new custom landing pages. And it's less "friction," too. The easier you make it for your visitors to get what they came for, the higher your conversion rate will be.

As with all PPC work, watch your metrics carefully to ensure that your campaigns are profitable.

SOME ADVANCED REMARKETING TIPS

If your first remarketing campaigns are a success and you want to dig a little deeper, give these advanced techniques a try.

Analytics Remarketing

This is an incredibly powerful option that pulls data from your Google Analytics account to create audiences. Inside Google Analytics are more than a hundred metrics, and once your remarketing campaigns have been running for a few weeks, you'll have access to a virtually unlimited array of audiences based on almost any metric or combination of metrics you can think of.

Want to target people who spent at least five minutes browsing your site? Done. Want to create an ad offer that is only shown to people who read at least six of your blog posts? No problem. Want to reach out to people who arrived on your site via Facebook? Easy.

This is why remarketing is one of the most underutilized areas of marketing. You can easily turn it into an art form. And it's one of your best hedges against rising click prices and competition.

If you're not currently using Google Analytics, it's worth installing it simply to give you access to these features.

Dynamic Remarketing

This advanced use of remarketing is only available for ecommerce sites that use the Google Merchant Center. In this scenario, Google already has your product feed and can create ads that feature the products your visitors have been looking at. If you have a large number of products, it can create hundreds or even thousands of precisely targeted ads on the fly. This is incredibly effective and doesn't require a huge investment of time or manual labor.

Facebook Remarketing

We recommend also running Facebook remarketing ads. (See our *Ultimate Guide to Facebook Advertising*, 4th edition.) It lets you remarket to the people who are most likely to convert on your site.

Remarketing Grid

Mike Rhodes' Remarketing Grid tool lets you fine-tune your audience selection process and make it easier to set up the campaigns and ad groups you will need by helping you visualize and institute your remarketing strategy. Read Mike's full article at https://www.digitalmarketer.com/blog/remarketing-grid/.

YOUR QUICK ACTION SUMMARY

Unless your website is achieving unheard-of conversion rates, the vast majority of your visitors are leaving without taking your desired action, and, unfortunately, most will never return, unless they're prompted to do so. For years, internet marketers have tried to overcome this problem by using pop-unders and exit ads. These had limited success and were extremely annoying.

Remarketing is the ultimate solution to this problem of "bouncing" visitors. Not only does it allow you to maintain contact with almost 100 percent of the people who have been to your site, it does so in a way that's completely invisible and carries minimal risk of irritating people.

Yes, remarketing is a bit more involved than most PPC strategies. But if you don't make use of it, your competitors will. For whatever setup effort you put into it, remarketing will return you benefits and profits tenfold.

Here's a quick reminder of the basics and the steps you need to take to get started:

- Update your privacy policy with four key adjustments discussed in this chapter (https://support.google.com/google-ads/answer/2549063).
- Install the code on your website (or send it to your web developer to handle).
- Build three basic audiences ("Everyone," "Interested," and "Buyers").
- Create a new remarketing campaign containing one ad group for each audience you wish to target.
- Set frequency capping for the campaign.
- Create at least one ad for each ad group.
- Activate your campaign.

Chapter 15

Google Shopping Campaigns:
A Huge ROI Boost for Ecommerce

Are you an ecommerce site owner? Google Shopping campaigns can give you a better clickthrough rate *and* a higher return on your advertising investment than regular text ads.

Shopping ads have exploded in the past few years, becoming one of Google's largest profit centers. Around 70 percent of non-brand search clicks are now on Shopping ads, especially during the holiday season of November and December.

Google Shopping ads are the small, square image ads that appear at the top of Google's search results pages, sometimes under the premium ads on the left, or sometimes in the upper-right-hand corner. You can see examples in Figure 15–1. Google will show between four and nine of these, each one featuring an image of the product, the name of the store, the price, about 30 characters of the product's title, and some optional promotional text.

FIGURE 15–1. Examples of Shopping Ads

These typically have higher conversion rates than non-brand search ads. One reason is that a user doesn't need to click through to five different sites to compare pricing; they can do it right there on the Google site. When you're the consumer, this is great—you can see the product and the price before you click.

If you're selling physical products, you owe it to your business to give Google Shopping a try.

In this chapter, we'll show you three simple steps to set up your own Google Shopping campaign, with a little help from your webmaster.

HOW TO SET UP A GOOGLE SHOPPING CAMPAIGN

Unfortunately, there's no way (yet) to just click a button and connect your ecommerce site directly to your Google Ads account; you'll have to use a Google Merchant Center (GMC) account. But there's a step you must take even before that. Here's how to set this up.

Step One: Create a Data Feed

How easy is it to plug your product inventory into Google Ads? That depends on the technical makeup of your site and shopping cart. Assuming you're not a technical wizard with the ability to code your site entirely by hand, you'll probably want to speak with your webmaster about exporting your product list as a *data feed,* a specially formatted file containing a list of all your products and all associated relevant information, such as price, brand, image, and availability.

The vast majority of modern ecommerce platforms make this easy to do with plug-ins and extensions, so you should expect this step to be quick and straightforward for any competent webmaster.

Step Two: Open a Google Merchant Center Account

Visit http://google.com/merchants to read about this. It's free. The main purpose is to plug in the data feed from your site. Again, you may prefer to arrange for your webmaster to handle the process by giving them the login information for your new GMC account.

This should be a one-time job. If you set up and install the data feed correctly, it will update automatically as your inventory changes. For best results, set this to update your feed daily. (Google likes fresh data!)

Step Three: Link Your Google Merchant Center Account to Your Google Ads Account

GMC acts as a kind of middleman, assessing your feed, keeping an eye on the data, and making sure the format is correct.

Linking your Merchant Center to your Google Ads account is a two-step process. You'll need to send an approval request from the Merchant Center to your Google Ads account. See the Merchant Center help site for more information.

HOW TO GET YOUR GOOGLE SHOPPING CAMPAIGN UP AND RUNNING

You can now create a new Shopping campaign. Go back to the Campaigns tab, click the blue + Campaign button, and choose the Sales option. Then, for the campaign type, choose Shopping. Be sure your Merchant Center ID is displayed correctly and choose the country where your products are sold.

You can then choose between a Smart Shopping Campaign (which you can ignore for now) and a Standard Shopping Campaign, as you'll see in Figure 15–2 on page 140. We highly recommend you master the fundamentals of a manual campaign before relying on Google's automation. While Smart Shopping sometimes gets exceptional results, there are also many examples of costs going through the roof and sales drying up.

Mastering the fundamentals first will ensure you have the skills to diagnose any problems with smart campaigns later, should you wish to experiment with them.

Once the setup process is complete, your products will automatically be placed into one ad group called "All Products."

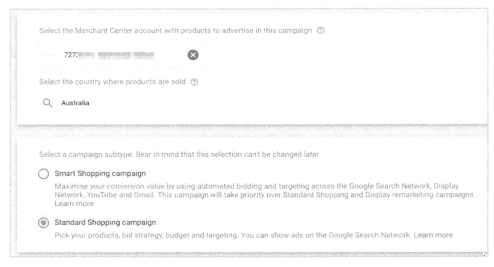

FIGURE 15–2. Smart vs. Standard Shopping Campaigns

You could, if you were so inclined, immediately activate your campaign and set your ads running at this point. For most ecommerce site owners, however, this would be a bad idea. Why?

Because all the items in a group will have the same cost per click. You wouldn't want to bid the same price per click for a 50-inch flat-screen TV as you would for a cheap pair of wireless headphones.

So start by dividing the All Products group into a set of subgroups so you can have separate bid prices for each. You can create subgroups of products based on any number of attributes those products might share, such as:

- Category
- Brand
- Product type
- Condition
- Item ID

In this example from a WebSavvy client in Figure 15–3 on page 141, the ad groups reflect the various categories of clothing available on the website.

Let's consider another example. You might choose to divide up the groups by brand. You could create a subgroup for every individual brand you sell, and, based on the attributes recorded in your data feed, Google will find and automatically transfer the appropriate products into each of these new subgroups.

You can then divide each subgroup into a further set of subgroups, based on either the same attribute you just used or a completely different one.

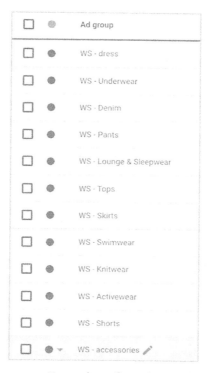

FIGURE 15–3. Examples of Product Subgroups

And you can continue to subdivide and subdivide and subdivide, down to seven levels of subgroups.

Again, why subdivide them? So that you can bid separate amounts for the items in each subgroup.

Using our electronics store example, here's how you might subdivide a group:

1. You create the All Products group, which contains your entire inventory: 500 individual items that are available to purchase from your store.

    All Products (500 items)

2. You subdivide this group by category. Your store features five different categories of products, each of which (for this example) contains 100 different items. This gives you one main group called All Products with five subgroups, each containing 100 products.

    All Products (500 items)
    > TVs (100 items)
    > Set-Top Boxes (100 items)
    > Videogame Consoles (100 items)

> Sound Systems (100 items)
> Smartphones (100 items)

3. You subdivide TVs by the brand attribute. Your store features TVs by five different manufacturers, each of which has 2o different items in your inventory. So you now have one main group called All Products, five subgroups containing 100 products each, and one of these subgroups, TVs, divided into its own set of five subgroups, each containing 20 items:

All Products (500 items)
> TVs (100 items)
>> Samsung (20 items)
>> Philips (20 items)
>> Sony (20 items)
>> Toshiba (20 items)
>> Finlux (20 items)
> Set-Top Boxes (100 items)
> Videogame Consoles (100 items)
> Sound Systems (100 items)
> Smartphones (100 items)

4. Keep on subdividing as you see fit. Maybe you subdivide your Sony TV subgroup by another category, this time screen size. Next you subdivide sound systems by category as well.

Once you've finished subdividing, you can customize each subgroup, adjusting the maximum CPC for each one or even excluding particular groups from being advertised entirely. There is no ideal one-size-fits-all system for dividing up your products.

A Smart Shopping campaign works with just one ad group and one product group. That includes all your products, even if you have tens of thousands of them. Google pulls together an enormous amount of data to determine how much you pay for each click.

Regardless of which type of Shopping campaign you use, you won't need to create any ads. Those are automatically built for you based on the information in your data feed.

BIDDING

Set up your conversion tracking to specify the actual revenue of each sale as the value of each conversion. This allows you to set bids for your Shopping ads based on the return on your ad spend, rather than just the number of items sold.

To see this in your Google Ads account, add the column called Conversion Value/ Cost. This is the equivalent of return on ad spend (ROAS), a valuable metric.

As with most things in Google Ads, you're looking for outliers. Increase what's performing well; decrease or eliminate what's performing badly. For your Shopping campaign, this means finding individual products that have sold consistently and profitably. You'll want to increase the bids for these products to encourage Google to show them more often. However, don't be tempted to make huge bid increases at once. A "little and often" approach is better. You shouldn't typically increase the bid for any item by more than 10 percent at a time.

Remarketing audiences (see Chapter 14) can be a powerful addition to your Google Shopping campaigns. You can identify previous visitors to your website—people who made it as far as your cart, or even buyers—and increase your bids on the Shopping ads you show them.

NEGATIVE KEYWORDS

Since it's not possible to target individual keywords with Shopping campaigns, you may be tempted to ignore the keyword section altogether. That would be a mistake. You can add negative keywords to keep your Shopping ads from showing when people search for particular terms. Regularly review your search terms report to identify and add new negative keywords. (Note that with Smart Shopping campaigns, you won't have access to search terms reports.)

You can start with terms like "used," "vintage," or variations on "secondhand." This is of course assuming you don't sell secondhand goods!

SOME ADVANCED SHOPPING CAMPAIGN TIPS

All these steps are vital to creating an effective Google Shopping campaign. But you can do even more to amp up your results. Here are some advanced tips for getting the most out of Google Shopping.

Multiple Campaigns

As you get more proficient at using Google Shopping, it's possible—and advisable—to have more than one Shopping campaign in your Google Ads account. This allows you to "sculpt" various search queries into specific campaigns. For example, you might wish to split your Shopping ads between search queries that contain your brand and queries that don't. You would need two separate campaigns to do this.

Multiple Countries

If you're showing Shopping ads in multiple countries, be sure your feeds are accurate in terms of prices, currency, available inventory, and such.

Troubleshooting

Having trouble? Try these advanced tips for troubleshooting:

1. *Disapproved ads.* If your Shopping ads get disapproved, check its attributes for compliance with Google's standards and make the necessary changes. (See https://support.google.com/google-ads/answer/6275312.) The following is not an extensive checklist, but it should get you started.

   - In most countries, your feed must include at least two of these three attributes: brand, MPN, and GTIN.
   - The currency of your feed needs to match the currency displayed on your website.
   - Check that your shipping details are accurate.
   - The price of every product in the feed needs to match the price shown on the website.

2. *Diagnosing problems.* Make use of the Diagnostics section in your Merchant Center to see how many products are disapproved and the possible reasons why.

ONGOING MANAGEMENT OF YOUR SHOPPING CAMPAIGNS

Once you're up and running, you should start thinking about how to optimize your campaigns going forward. Here are a few of the most important elements you can work with that will get you the best results.

Search Queries

Regularly take a look at your search terms report. You'll find new keywords as well as potential negative keywords to add to your search campaigns.

For more advanced tweaks, consider using a Google Ads script to create an n-gram report of the Shopping queries.

Predefined Reports

Longtime Google Ads users will fondly remember the Dimensions tab and the plethora of useful reports it provided. You can see from Figure 15–4 on page 145 that these are now housed in the Predefined section of your reports, which you'll find at the top of the page.

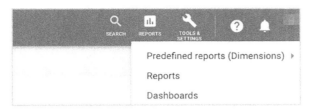

FIGURE 15–4. Where to Find Predefined Reports

You'll also find a section on Shopping reports, but these aren't especially useful in managing your account. You'll spend most of your time on the product groups page, which shows you all the main performance metrics for your various product groups.

Shopping campaigns also give you a few additional columns to add to your interface. One of the most useful is "Benchmark CPC." This lets you see how much you're paying per click compared with your competitors. On the same screen, you can also see the number of products in your feed that are approved, active, and ready to serve.

On the Ad Groups tab, you can see your Auction Insights report. If you've accumulated enough data, this will show how you're performing compared to similar retailers.

Depending on your traffic volume and bidding model, you may also see bid simulator data. This shows you what the effects would be of making significant bid price changes.

Local Inventory Ads

In 2019, Google introduced a new ad type called local inventory ads (LIAs). They combine your local product feed and local product inventory feed, allowing you to promote items that you only sell in your store, not online. We expect this to become more popular.

Dynamic Remarketing

So far, we've talked about how to create a standard remarketing campaign, which shows a set of image ads to various audiences, typically people who have previously visited your site, exhibited certain behaviors, and taken certain actions. *Dynamic* remarketing lets you combine this with your Shopping feed, so if a visitor came to your site and looked at certain products, you can show them those same products in your remarketing display ads as they browse.

We recommend dynamic remarketing for any ecommerce store, but to set it up you will need to get your web developer involved—it can be a bit tricky. (There are 53 individual steps involved!)

We've created a two-hour training set specifically about dynamic remarketing. So while it's a great campaign type to use, it's beyond the scope of this book. Contact WebSavvy if you would like more details.

When you use Smart Shopping campaigns, Google includes dynamic remarketing as part of them, assuming you have the right code installed on your site.

Merchant Promotions

By using Merchant Promotions, you allow searchers to see an additional line underneath your Google Shopping ad. You might use this for discounts, free gifts, or a deal on shipping costs.

To set it up, you will need to go to your Google Merchant Center account. The settings for this change all the time, so check the Google Help Center for more details. Figure 15–5 below shows you where these are located as of this printing. The main thing to remember is that your promotion must be able to be used by all shoppers and not a subset of shoppers—for instance, only first-time visitors.

FIGURE 15–5. Find Merchant Promotions in Your Merchant Center Account

Seller Ratings

If customers have rated or reviewed you and your store, you can display your star rating (out of five) as part of your ad. This works for both search and Shopping ads. You'll need to have at least 100 reviews in the past 12 months with an average rating of 3.5 or higher.

There are a number of third-party systems that integrate with Google to enable your ratings to show. Setup can be tricky, but this feature increases clickthrough rates. To see how to set this up, go to https://support.google.com/merchants/answer/190657.

Product Ratings

These are like seller ratings but for individual products. They are worth your time early on only if you have either very few products to manage or a high volume of sales.

Customer Reviews

This is a free service. If someone makes a purchase on your site, after checkout they can click to take a Google survey and rate their experience with you. This feeds into your seller and product ratings and displays a badge on your website. Read more about it at https://support.google.com/merchants/answer/7124319.

Shopping Actions

At the time of this writing, there's a beta program available in the U.S. and France that allows users to bypass retailer websites entirely and use Google as their shopping cart, adding products from multiple retailers and checking out just once. It's experimental but worth keeping an eye on. It will likely expand in the future.

YOUR QUICK ACTION SUMMARY

If you're an ecommerce site owner, Shopping campaigns are Google's gift to you. They let you use images to sell your products on Google's regular search pages.

- Speak with your webmaster about creating a data feed of your product inventory.
- Open a Google Merchant Center account and add in your data feed.
- Link your GMC account to your Google Ads account.
- Create a new Shopping campaign, starting with an All Products group, and then subdivide it into appropriate smaller groups.

Chapter 16

YouTube Advertising:
Billions of Eyeballs for Pennies

Tom Breeze, founder and CEO of Viewability,
a YouTube advertising agency

My good friend Fred got injured and had to back out of a marathon with just 14 weeks to go. He had already raised money for charity, so when he asked if I would run the marathon in his place, I said yes.

As soon as I committed, I went to Google and searched "How to run a marathon." I got some troubling results. Most websites said that you shouldn't even attempt a marathon without at least 25 weeks of training. But I had only 14 weeks left, and I had done zero training!

But I had said yes, and I could not back down. So I kept digging for further information.

I found out what shoes to buy, printed out several training plans, and started thinking about what to eat. I bought apps to track my running performance, and even bought some new running music.

I started my research on Google, but before long I was watching YouTube videos about running form and different types of exercises. I watched product review videos of all the latest tech devices to see what could help me train most efficiently.

To this day, I can still remember the videos I watched. That really is the power of video: People do not easily forget it. We can all remember the commercials we saw on TV as kids. You're probably remembering one right now, jingle included.

Video engages our senses. It's far more vivid than simple words or images. You get a story, music, and visuals in motion. It commands our attention. Viewers stick around longer.

And this effect is further enhanced with YouTube videos. Why?

First, YouTube is the home of online video. If people go to YouTube, it's because they want to watch a video. That's the whole premise of the platform. When people visit Facebook, they aren't necessarily looking for videos. But they are primed and ready for your video on YouTube.

And people go there with specific intent. In fact, there are four main reasons why someone might visit YouTube:

1. *People want to watch what they're into.* According to Google, 53 percent of online video viewers watch to be inspired or entertained. We all do this—we watch videos from people or brands we like to follow.

2. *People want to learn something.* We also go to YouTube to learn, explore, and research. There's virtually no topic on earth you can't find a YouTube video for. It's like having a Library of Congress at your fingertips.

3. *People want to learn how to do something.* Sometimes text simply won't do; you need to see how to do something—how to cook eggs, how to plant tomatoes, or how to run a marathon.

4. *People want to buy something.* YouTube is a great place to check reviews, learn about a product, and make buying decisions. Huge numbers of people watch "unboxing" videos, where people film themselves taking new products out of their packaging and showing the viewer what's included. It's the ultimate form of window-shopping!

When my wife and I found out we were expecting our second child, I went through many emotions (beyond the obvious one: sheer panic) and then went into another intensive bout of research. After watching several parents rave about a particular brand of double stroller, showing how easy it was to fold away, how light it was to carry, and what was included, I bought one immediately.

Now, you personally might not go to YouTube for that. That's fine. But other people do—lots of them. People watch nearly five billion videos on YouTube every single day. Your customers visit YouTube even if you don't.

As an advertiser, you can get your message in front of your customers right when they're looking for your help. I am going to show you how to do this—to master YouTube advertising so you can turn viewers into customers.

You may be asking yourself, "Does YouTube have a shelf life?" or "Have I already missed the boat?" The answer is no, you haven't. YouTube is not a social media fad or the cool new bar in town where everyone happens to be meeting temporarily. No, YouTube is like the library: it's used voraciously and is constantly expanding. In fact, as of this writing, 300 hours of video are being uploaded to YouTube every minute. YouTube gets more than 30 million visitors per day, and the "watch time"—the number of hours people spend watching videos on the site—is up 60 percent year over year. The average session duration is now more than 40 minutes. That's a long time to spend online!

With YouTube advertising, you're not competing to get on the front page of Google with your text ads or paying to appear on someone's news feed. Rather, it's about getting your engaging video ads on a rapidly expanding platform that offers hundreds of thousands of relevant videos people want to watch. So when you master YouTube advertising, you'll have a skill that will serve you for a lifetime.

Even though there are lots of brands and companies trying to advertise effectively on YouTube, very few seem to achieve success. That's because most advertisers treat YouTube like TV, using a single creative video ad designed for that medium, with no call to action and only the broadest targeting. Their goal—wrongly—is to "get more views" or raise brand awareness. If you have a huge budget to waste, that's a fantastic strategy, but if you want to see a good ROI and build a relationship with your prospects, I'd recommend a different approach.

WHAT WORKS ON YOUTUBE?

Think about your viewer. A YouTube user wants to be inspired or informed, to watch what they're into, or to know, do, or buy something. So they're already motivated, but it's not to see a TV ad or a sales message.

In our business, we preach "Aducation." The idea is simple but powerful: Create ads that are, in and of themselves, helpful and useful, so that even if viewers don't follow you any further online, at least they've had a positive, valuable experience with your brand. This strategy helps build rapport and foster a good relationship between the brand and the viewer, and it means you don't bombard (or worse, annoy) your viewers with a pushy sales message.

A basic tenet of Aducation is to focus on one core idea in each ad. Just one. Save everything else for another ad or for your remarketing efforts. You want to show your audience that you understand their needs and have a solution that is right for them.

The focus should always be to provide value to the viewer. Think about what your customer is doing as they're typing in a search query, and provide a useful experience to meet that need. This is where a lot of YouTube advertisers slip up. For example, when I was looking for marathon training plans, it would have been great to see ads for other related products—long-distance running shoes, run-tracker apps, or even hotels near the starting line. *But they weren't there!*

Timing is everything on YouTube, and you want to be in front of your shoppers with an ad that is right for them in the buying cycle (what we call the "Moment"). There are three types of shoppers online, and an effective YouTube ad will talk to each shopper as you would in real life (the "Message"). Through YouTube's incredibly specific targeting (the "Method"), we can meet our potential customers in the right moment with a relevant message and offer.

Before we discuss the three types of shoppers, let's talk about the Message and the Method.

THE MESSAGE

In terms of messaging, your aim is to be as true to real life as possible. Don't say or do anything in an ad that you wouldn't do if you were talking to that person in real life. For example, if you had a brick-and-mortar store and saw someone eyeing a pair of running shoes in the window, you might strike up a conversation with them, starting with, "Do you run?" You might ask if they're training for an event, how long they've been training, and what they're looking for in a shoe. You would then dig into your expertise and recommend a shoe based on their needs. This is healthy human interaction—and you can have this same normal, helpful interaction with shoppers online. Informed by Google's vast troves of data, you can show YouTube ads with a tailored message to each type of shopper by simply structuring your ads in custom ways.

Each ad should have three overall elements:

1. *Attention.* On YouTube, those first five seconds of a video are life or death. You have to grab the viewer from the start, with a video featuring something eye-catching, unexpected, or memorable—without succumbing to gimmicks, of course.

2. We had one client who promoted trading software, so we created an ad where the presenter bluntly told the viewer that if they were on YouTube to learn more about trading, STOP! Stop watching YouTube videos! That wasn't the right way

to learn how to trade the markets. (The ad was highly effective and ended up being copied many times over by other brands and industries.)

Once you have the viewer's attention, the next goal is to establish your credibility and expertise. You do this by introducing yourself, your company, or your brand and briefly describing what you do and what solutions and results you can deliver. Next, it's useful to give an early, soft call to action before the 30-second mark so you can convert leads before you start paying to show the pre-roll ad. Often we transition from the credibility segment to the soft call to action by quickly summarizing the substantive benefit to be gained in the video but allowing the viewer to click early to learn more.

3. *Advice.* This is the heart and soul of the ad, the meat behind Aducation. In this segment, we deliver value and useful content to the viewer such that the ad could stand alone as a substantive video. Here we want viewers to learn "what's in it for me" so they come away thinking, "Wow! That was worth watching. I want to learn more." We do this by sharing one core idea of content—whether it's an interesting fact, a handy tip, or a system of a few short steps that can be implemented immediately. If you can wrap this content in the context of a narrative story or case study, so much the better.

4. *Action.* After delivering great content and value to your viewers (for free), give them an incentive to click to continue their path toward purchasing from you. One effective technique is to follow the substantive advice section with a future-paced call to action where you invite them to imagine how their circumstances would be if they took the next step with you—for example, by unlocking the full substance that was discussed in the ad by joining an online webinar or getting a free trial or product. (Our clients have had great success with free book offers where the shopper only pays for shipping.)

Quick Tips

Here are a few short concepts to keep in mind as you navigate the world of YouTube:

- In tests at our agency, Viewability (https://www.viewability.co.uk/), we have found two minutes and 20 seconds is the optimal length for a YouTube ad. That's not to say longer or shorter videos won't work, but on average 140 seconds seems to be the sweet spot.

- Use the words "so you can" or "because" in your copy. They're useful tools for driving home the benefits of your product or service. Another excellent technique for instant trust building is the power of "but." Draw attention to a slight weakness of your product or service—which demonstrates honesty and creates trust with the viewer—only to negate it immediately with the stronger side of the argument. For example, you might say, "Yes, our restaurant is small, but that's why our diners report having such an amazingly intimate experience." It wouldn't work if you highlighted how small your restaurant is and then came back by pointing out how wonderful the lighting is. Your "but" must address the weakness head-on.

- In terms of production value, this is the time for a professional. You don't want your advertising to look amateurish—you want a clean, sharp visual aesthetic. Hire folks who know what they're doing with the camera, lighting, sound, and editing. And put your smartphone away—this is not the time for DIY.

THE METHOD

This is where the magic happens and where you can strategically and seamlessly appear before the right prospects at just the right time. YouTube ad campaigns are built on the Google Ads platform, so you'll be familiar with the many targeting options. However, there are some big differences between a YouTube ad campaign and a display or search campaign, so let's discuss the various ad types first and then look at the targeting options.

There are many ways of advertising on Google using video. With display campaigns, you can run video ads on the Display Network with nonskippable 15- or 20-second videos, Lightbox ads (interactive ads which can be expanded by clicking or hovering), or outstream ads (mobile-only ads that appear on partner sites and apps outside of YouTube). You can even run video ads in Gmail. You can run six-second bumper ads on YouTube. If you have a bigger budget, you can invest in YouTube Mastheads. For this chapter, we're going to zero in on the TrueView skippable in-stream and Discovery video ad formats. We've found these to be the best place to get started with video ads, and it's where we typically see the best results. Google's TrueView, especially, is built on the promise that you'll only pay when someone chooses to watch your ad. For advertisers, that's simply incredible.

Figure 16–1 on page 155 shows an example of a video ad format you're probably familiar with. Commonly known in other environments as a "pre-roll ad," Google Ads calls this an "in-stream video ad." You'll see these play before a video you were about to watch, and you can "skip the ad" after five seconds. (This is why the first five seconds of your video are so important.) With these ads, you only pay when someone watches more than 30 seconds of it, reaches the end of the video, or clicks through to visit your website. If someone watches for 29 seconds and then clicks the Skip Ad button, you don't pay a penny.

FIGURE 16–1. An In-Stream Video Ad

With the in-stream ad format, you get to select a bid strategy based on a maximum cost per view (CPV), target cost per acquisition (tCPA), "maximize conversions," or even target cost per 1,000 impressions (tCPM). My recommendation would be to start with either a maximum CPV or tCPA.

Figure 16–2 on page 156 shows you another format. These ads are Discovery video ads (formerly known as in-display video ads). They appear at the top of the search results page on YouTube. They also show up on the right-hand side when you're watching other videos. In this case, you pay when someone clicks to watch your video ad.

With the Discovery ad format, you can select a bid strategy based only on a maximum CPV.

TARGETING ON YOUTUBE

When running TrueView YouTube ads, you have access to all the usual targeting options. However, because we're focusing our efforts on YouTube.com as a website, there are a few special distinctions.

Placement targeting can work exceptionally well, as it lets you select the exact video URLs or channels you'd like to advertise on. This means you can choose to show your ads on any videos your potential customers are likely to be watching, including your competitors' videos (if they've allowed advertising). Online software solutions such as Adzoola allow you to grab hundreds of relevant placements for various keywords, which can help you build campaigns quickly.

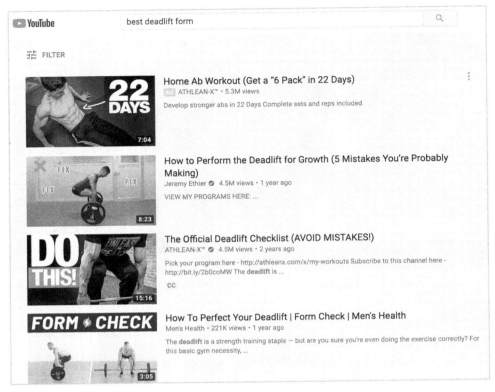

FIGURE 16–2. Discovery Video Ads

Keyword targeting on YouTube has its own unique wrinkles as well. Google now bases it on a user's search history, regardless of the specific query they've typed in on YouTube. For example, when I did my marathon training research on Google and then started looking at YouTube videos, Google would have referenced my search history and shown ads for running-related products or services—even if I was watching cat videos at the time!

All targeting options can work well when advertising on YouTube, but if you're just getting started, we recommend that you get a general handle on advertising with placements and keyword targeting and that you explore custom intent audiences, topics, and similar audiences before venturing into in-market, affinity, and custom affinity audiences (more about these in Chapter 18).

PUTTING IT ALL TOGETHER

You'll find that every type of unique visitor is just that—unique, with their own set of characteristics and searching traits. Let's meet them.

Window Shoppers

The Moment: These visitors are curious and have a strong inclination toward your product or service. They may not be actively searching for what you're offering, but your product or service is *related* to what they're searching for, which means they're likely to be interested.

The Message: Your ad should grab their attention, provide some advice or useful content, and then conclude with a call to action for a desirable offer relevant to their needs. You may not get the sale right then, but this type of ad helps you build a relationship with the shopper. For example, a hotel near the marathon's finish line could advertise a "marathon runner's weekend special" when I was searching for information about marathon training. Very effective.

The Method: Use in-stream or Discovery ads to target people using custom affinity audiences, similar audiences, and placements of videos or channels that your audience would be passionate about.

In-Store Shoppers

The Moment: These folks are actively looking for a product or service like yours. They're researching a problem or need, and because you have a useful solution for them, they're especially receptive to your message and offer.

The Message: Your ad should provide advice or useful content and conclude with a strong call to action. For example, when I was searching for "marathon training plans," a savvy personal trainer could run an in-stream ad sharing his top three tips for marathon training and then invite me to join his training program. Similarly, when I was searching for "best shoes for long-distance running," I would have paid extra attention to any ad showing me a specific brand of running shoe along with a call to action to purchase.

The Method: Use in-stream or Discovery ads and target with keywords and placements of relevant videos.

Checkout Shoppers

The Moment: These people are very close to making a purchasing decision. They're likely watching review or product-comparison videos. They may have seen your videos or visited your website already and be familiar with your brand.

The Message: Although you don't yet want to push a sales message on them, you can be more direct about the products or services you offer. With previous ads, you've provided useful advice and information; in this case, your message focuses more on the benefits and features of your product, followed by a strong call to action.

The Method: Use in-stream or Discovery ads and target with in-market audiences, keywords, placements of relevant videos, video remarketing (to people who have engaged with your videos before), and website remarketing.

Quick Tips

Keep these two tips in mind and you'll be rocking the YouTube world (and the Ads world) in no time.

1. *When creating your ad, think about what happens when visitors click to visit your website.* Design a landing page specifically to work with your YouTube ads—not just to be compliant with Google's policies, but also to ensure that there's an obvious and seamless flow of content from the video to the offer on your site. And it doesn't have to be elaborate: Because your viewers have just seen a video ad, they understand you and your product or service much more fully than if they had clicked over from a simple text or image ad. This means that your landing page doesn't need to do all the heavy lifting to make the sale. A simple, basic landing page that easily enables the viewer to opt in or buy is all you need.

2. *Track everything to optimize and scale correctly.* Watch for view-through conversions. If a user sees your in-stream ad and clicks through to your website (within the first 30 seconds) and then opts in or buys, triggering your conversion pixel, you'll see the conversion appear in the view-through conversion column in your account. With in-stream ads, it's considered a "view" when someone watches past 30 seconds; up until that point, it's only considered an impression. With the Discovery ad format, it counts as an impression when a user sees your video ad's thumbnail image. Should that person click, it will be counted as a view as soon as the video loads.

YOUR QUICK ACTION SUMMARY

Try a brainstorming exercise to build a "moment" in your ideal customers' life.

- *Paint a picture of these people.* Are they male or female? How old are they? Where do they live? What is their household income? Do they have children? Do they use a desktop, laptop, or mobile device to look at YouTube videos?
- *Imagine them in a scene that's part of their daily life.* For example, picture a husband in his early 30s, sitting next to his wife in bed and searching his iPhone for a light-

weight, tandem double buggy that will fit through the doorway of his London home.

■ *Now ask yourself some questions about his state of mind.* Why is he searching through those specific videos? What is he thinking or feeling? What does he need? What triggered him to start seeking out information in the first place? Where is he in the buying cycle? What is his biggest problem or frustration? How can you provide a solution to that? With the example of our London friend, we know that he and his wife probably have some disposable income to spend on a nice stroller. They want something they can use to take their two children around the city but that isn't so bulky they can't get it on public transportation or through their own front door.

■ *Next, focus on one core idea that you would share if you were to meet this person in real life.* What would you say? Craft your message around this core idea using the Aducation template: Attention, Advice, and Action. So again, with our friend in London, you'll get his attention by showing how your product is small, lightweight, and can be easily maneuvered around city streets. Present some tips on clever ways to take advantage of the buggy's clever design. Then call him to click and explore more or choose a version he might like best.

■ *Then think about your offer.* What will entice the viewer to click through and follow you to your website? What would be most valuable to them? If you're selling a stroller, a quick demo video may be sufficient. It all depends on what your ideal customer finds most useful in that moment.

■ *Finally, you'll want to choose the right campaign and targeting to ensure you get in front of your ideal customer when they need you.*

Voilà! You've built your first "moment." Continue to do this exercise for each moment in your ideal customer's life, focusing on the one target market you serve. Discuss and brainstorm your ideas with colleagues, friends, or family. Make it fun.

Once you've done all this, build your campaigns on YouTube, scale, repeat . . . and then celebrate!

Chapter 17

Gmail Campaigns

Gmail serves more than a billion users each month. There's a paid version and a free version. In the free version, users see ads inside their account, which typically look like unopened emails.

There's opportunity here that lots of advertisers overlook. Setting up Gmail ads is a bit more involved than regular display ads, but the limited competition means cheap clicks, and that makes it well worth the effort. In this chapter, we'll discuss how you can set up a Gmail campaign that pays off in the long run.

HOW TO SET UP A GMAIL CAMPAIGN

First you'll need to create a new Display Network campaign and choose Gmail from among the options, as shown in Figure 17–1 below.

FIGURE 17–1. Choosing a Gmail Display Campaign

There are two ways to create Gmail ads:

1. You can upload a single image ad. (The specifications for this change frequently, but you can consult the Google Ads Help Center for details.)
2. You can assemble various ad assets and create a responsive ad. (See Chapter 10 for more on this.) From there, Google will optimize your ad for you.

Either way, you'll need a few elements in place:

- a headline
- a description
- a business name
- a call-to-action button
- various images

For a Gmail campaign to work, you'll need two ads, not one. These will show in sequence:

1. A mini (collapsed) ad that shows at the top of the user's email account. When they click on this, it opens the second ad.
2. The main (expanded) ad.

The mini ad shows on all three device categories—desktop, tablet, and mobile. It includes a couple of lines of ad text. On mobile devices, it shows just a small image. You get charged at the point when the user clicks on the mini ad.

The purpose of the expanded ad is to get the user to click a *second* time to go to your landing page. (Don't worry; you won't be charged again.) The game is to get clicks on both ads.

One creative option for the expanded ad is to add a link to a YouTube video, which can be opened and played in the Gmail interface.

You can also combine your Gmail campaign with your Shopping feed and show Google Shopping ads directly inside a user's Gmail account.

How Much Should I Bid?

We've generally seen the best results in the range of 10 to 20 cents per click.

After you've gotten a bit of traction—100 or more clicks—you can usually lower these bids. Depending on the market you're in, you can get good volume for as little as two to five cents a click.

Targeting

Who do you target with a Gmail campaign, and how?

This is similar to regular display campaigns. You can target by using audiences (remarketing, in-market, etc.). You can also target by keyword. But note that Google no longer scans the content of users' emails to decide who to show ads to. (They faced massive privacy complaints over this: "Google is reading my emails!") In this case, keywords serve only as a general theme that suggests to Google where your ads might show.

You can also use Google's demographic targeting. If your product is aimed at older women, for example, you could target women aged 55 to 65 in the U.S. without any need for keywords or audiences.

Messaging

The more your Gmail ad looks like the subject line of a regular email, the better it will perform.

That said, try testing special offers using price or other promotional triggers. Typically, copy that evokes some kind of urgency or scarcity will do especially well within Gmail.

How to Measure Results

When you first see your numbers, it will look like your campaign is performing spectacularly. You may see a high volume of clicks and a high CTR.

But take it with a grain of salt: The clicks you see in your report are from the mini (collapsed) ad, not the expanded ad.

Of the people who click on your first ad, typically fewer than 20 percent will click on the second one. Be sure to turn on the additional column of metrics inside your campaign called "Gmail clicks through to website." You'll need to do some calculations yourself to work out how much you're paying for each visit to your website.

EXPERIMENT AWAY!

To get the best performance out of your Gmail campaigns, test different audiences and different types of targeting. We recommend one ad group for each targeting option.

You'll especially want to experiment with your expanded image. That one is the ad that gets people to your website.

YOUR QUICK ACTION SUMMARY

Get feedback from your prospects before spending huge sums of money on product and web development:

- Create a new Display Network campaign and choose Gmail from among the options.
- Have your elements ready to go (headline, description, business name, call-to-action button, images).
- Create your two ads: your mini ad and your main ad.
- Turn on the additional column of metrics inside your campaign called "Gmail clicks through to website" and watch as your numbers come in.

Chapter 18

Targeting Audiences

Have you ever run a TV or radio ad, or seen the inside of a Facebook campaign? If so, then audience targeting is nothing new. You're taking a message and aiming it at a group of people based on their common traits and interests.

We've seen how to target your search campaigns using keywords. We've shown you the different audiences you can target with your display and video campaigns. We've explored how targeting your Shopping campaigns is automatic, based on your data feed.

Now Google has taken the power of audience targeting to a new level, allowing you to combine it with your search keywords and Shopping feeds for even better results.

In this chapter, we'll look at your advanced targeting options, including ways to layer various audiences on top of your existing search and Shopping campaigns.

WHY USE AUDIENCE TARGETING?

If your search and Shopping campaigns are working just fine, you might be wondering why you should complicate things with more targeting options.

Let's say you sell washing machines. There's a whole population of people on Google's various sites looking for washing machines this week. They search for certain terms; they visit certain pages; they click on certain ads; they watch certain videos.

Google's AI looks at their behavior and says, "Ah. These users are *in the market* to buy washing machines."

The Google system keeps an ongoing dynamic list of these people. This list is called an "in-market audience." In this case, it's an audience made up of people looking to buy washing machines.

Now, let's also say you've been bidding on some variation of the search term "washing machine." Consider the in-market audience above. Any of the people in that audience who see *your* washing machine ad and click through to your website should be far more likely to buy from you.

Audience targeting lets you test this idea.

WHAT ARE MY TARGETING OPTIONS?

You have two audience settings available: Targeting and Observation.

Let's talk about the observation audience first. By layering an audience on top of your regular search campaign, Google will let you "observe" how that subset of people behaves on your site.

So imagine you discover that those in-market people we mentioned above—the ones who've been looking for washing machines and who see and click on your ad—buy at a rate 1.5 times higher than all the other people who are searching and clicking through to you. An observation audience lets you figure this out.

Aha! Now you know that you can continue showing ads to all people searching for your keywords, but—just for people in Google's in-market audience—you should bid more (say, $1.50 per click instead of $1), and have your ads show to them at higher positions and more often.

The Setup

We recommend you start with an observation audience (we'll explain targeting audiences in a minute). Here's how you set this up.

Head to a specific ad group (inside one specific campaign) that you'll test this on. You're going to choose an audience and add it to that individual ad group.

On the left-hand side of your Google Ads interface, click on Audiences.

A blue + or a pencil icon will show up. Click on it.

Near the top of the resulting page, it will give you the option of which campaign or ad group you want to add an audience to.

Choose the ad group, and Google will then give you a choice of either Targeting or Observation (see Figure 18–1 below). Pick Observation for now and set the bid adjustment to 0 percent.

Once you've made your choice, you can search for an audience you want to add to that ad group or pick from the list of ideas.

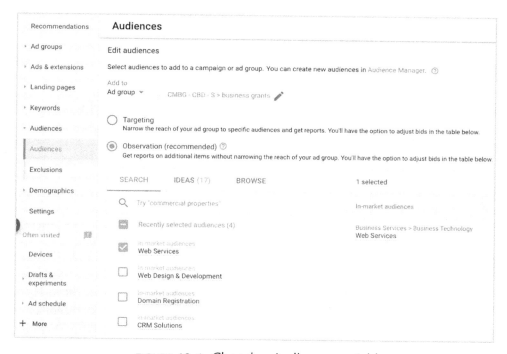

FIGURE 18–1. Choosing Audiences to Add

Targeting Audiences Are Great . . . with One Caveat

Now imagine you set up your "washing machines" ad group layered with an in-market audience, but this time you choose Targeting instead of Observation. Now Google will *only* show your ad to people who search for "washing machines" *and* who are in their in-market audience for washers as well. That's a better-targeted group of people, but a much smaller one.

With the Targeting setting, you're narrowing where your ads get shown and who they reach. You'll need to measure your return on ad spend in each case and decide which one results in better numbers for you.

AVAILABLE AUDIENCES

Since rolling out audience targeting for search and Shopping, Google has continued to make more audiences available. At the time of this writing, you can layer any of these onto your search campaigns:

- in-market audiences
- affinity audiences
- custom affinity audiences
- remarketing audiences
- similar audiences
- combined audiences
- customer lists

An exhaustive explanation of all these would be beyond the scope of this book. But we've included a few comments on them below.

Remarketing Audiences

These used to be called remarketing lists for search ads (RLSA). Google has since expanded beyond search and made these available for Shopping campaigns, too. They're quite useful. For example, you can create either an observation- or targeting-audience ad group that reaches people who 1) searched for "washing machines" *and* 2) have been to your site at least once in the past 14 days. Then if they behave differently (for example, they demonstrate that they're more likely to buy), you could increase the bid for that ad group.

You can also *exclude* various audiences from your campaign, such as recent buyers. This is useful if they're not likely to buy again any time soon and if showing them more ads would annoy them.

Demographics for Google Ads Search Campaigns

This feature allows you to layer demographic data over the top of your search and Shopping campaigns. With it, you can see how different segments of your audience perform, grouped by age, gender, and household income.

To set this up, go into your Google Ads account. From the page menu on the left, click Campaigns. Choose the campaign (and the ad group, if you like) where you want to add demographic targeting. Figure 18–2 below shows you how from there you can click Demographics and choose the specific groups you want to target.

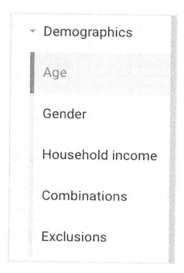

FIGURE 18–2. Demographic Targeting Options

Layering Audiences

As you get more advanced, you can combine multiple audiences for greater control and precision.

Note that not all the people in an audience will behave the same. That said, there are situations where this is a good strategy. Let's say you sell a product used almost exclusively by older women. In that case, it might be useful to exclude men from seeing your ad, or people under the age of 35. You can also layer in-market audiences over your campaign and even add some detailed demographics, such as homeownership status. The best part is that your keywords and data feed don't change when you do this.

ULTIMATE GUIDE TO GOOGLE ADS

YOUR QUICK ACTION SUMMARY

Get feedback from your prospects before spending huge sums of money on product and web development:

- Find a specific ad group in one specific campaign; you'll choose an audience and add it here.
- On the left-hand side of your Google Ads interface, click on Audiences.
- When given a choice of Targeting or Observation, pick Observation for now.
- Once you've made your choice, you can search for an audience you want to add to that ad group or pick from the list of ideas.

Chapter 19

Mastering Tracking

In Chapter 7, we introduced you to the basic concepts of tracking, the key to your success as a paid search professional. You can't optimize your account until you know what matters most to you, and the way to discover that is through tracking.

Your prospects can take a few major key actions with you: They can opt in, call you, or buy from you. We call these actions *macro conversions*, and naturally you'll want to track those. But getting a firm grasp on the possible *micro conversions* as well can set you apart even further as a skilled manager of paid search.

Thus far we've shown you how to track basic thank-you pages, where each conversion is worth more or less the same amount to you. In this chapter, we're going to show you how to track other types, values, and combinations of conversion actions. For ecommerce store owners, we'll show you how to use Google to track not only the number of sales your ads trigger but also your revenue and profit from each sale.

We'll divide all this activity into three main categories of conversions: phone calls, revenue, and assorted micro conversions. Let's look briefly at each one.

TRACKING PHONE CALLS

Data and experience will tell you that an incoming phone call is more valuable to your business than a form filled out on your website. The conversion rates for people who fill out an online form falls off precipitously within a few minutes of leaving your site—a trusted principle called RFM, which stands for recency, frequency, monetary. (See https://www.perrymarshall.com/Ads/rfm/ for a strategy you can use to put this knowledge to work.) In fact, phone calls are among the best leads any business can get. Somebody is there, ready to talk to you, and you don't have to chase them.

But there's an extra challenging step with these valuable phone calls—you'll want to tie each one back to the original search, keyword, and click that made it happen, so you know where you should adjust your bids.

We'll have more on phone tracking later in the chapter.

TRACKING REVENUE

If you're an ecommerce store owner, this is a plus. Most online retailers sell products in a range of prices, and if you can only track your total number of sales, that's not super useful. Tracking actual revenue is vital, and Google lets you do just that.

The key is to measure the revenue you've generated and compare it to the amount you spent on ads. We call this figure the *return on ad spend,* or ROAS (which you first read about in Chapter 3). It's your conversion value divided by your cost.

TRACKING MICRO CONVERSIONS

Some actions your prospect takes will be more valuable to you than others.

We've talked about the main macro conversions—completing a form, calling you on the phone, or making a purchase. But there are also a number of smaller micro conversions you can measure—early steps your prospect takes that indicate they're on the right path. Tracking these will allow you to adjust your bidding, targeting, and messaging to generate more revenue in the future. These micro conversions can include:

- clicking to view a specific page
- scrolling 80 percent of the way down a particularly important page
- downloading a PDF
- clicking to play a video
- signing into a free membership area
- downloading your app
- taking an important action inside your app
- requesting driving directions on Google Maps

UNDERSTANDING YOUR DATA

There are two sets of conversion numbers inside your Google Ads account.

The main macro conversions we discussed earlier are recorded in the Conversions column, as shown in Figure 19–1.

Conversions	Cost / conv.	Conv. rate
20,558.00	US$17.21	0.22%

FIGURE 19–1. Basic Conversions Data

Meanwhile, the data on your micro conversions is recorded in an All Conversions column. You can see this by clicking on the Columns icon, clicking again to expand Conversions, and selecting one or more of the All Conv. check boxes, as seen in Figure 19-2 on page 174.

Any time you set up a new conversion action, it will be included under Conversions by default. Figure 19-3 on page 174 shows how you can choose to list it under All Conversions instead by unchecking the box next to Include in Conversions in the Conversion Action settings.

Time Recorded

Historically, Google Ads has generated data differently from Google Analytics. With Google Ads, if your prospect clicks on Monday but doesn't purchase until Thursday, it

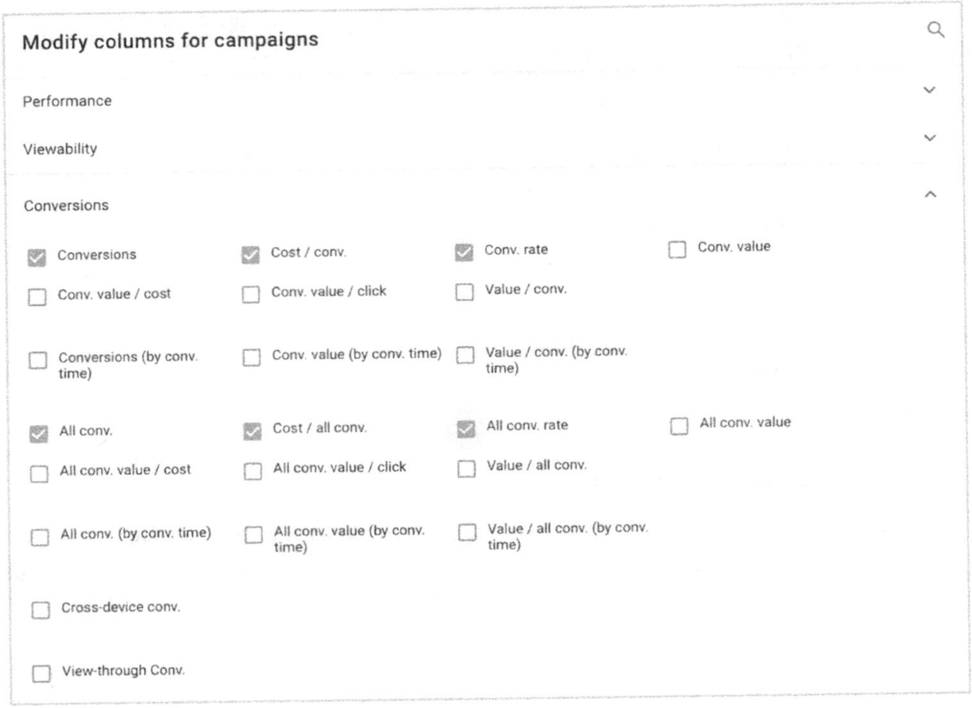

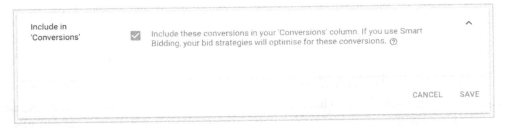

FIGURE 19-2. How to Modify Your Conversion Columns

FIGURE 19-3. Listing a New Conversion Action

is still recorded as a Monday conversion (i.e., it goes by the date of the click). But with Google Analytics, the goal is recorded as having taken place on Thursday (the date of purchase).

This has confused search marketers for more than a decade. So Google has now added a new column option showing you conversions By Conv. Time. This allows you to see conversions based on the date of the conversion rather than the date of the original click, thus aligning your Ads numbers with your Analytics numbers.

How Many Metrics Do You Need?

In each set of conversion data, there are various metrics you should know:

- *Conversions:* The total raw number of conversions you've received.
- *Cost per conversion:* How much you spent on average to generate each conversion.
- *Conversion rate:* How many conversions you averaged for every 100 clicks, expressed as a percentage.
- *Conversion value:* The total value of the conversions for the time period you're looking at.
- *Conversion value divided by cost:* Your ROAS, or return on ad spend.

Conversion value per click and *Value per conversion* are metrics we've found less useful. You can probably ignore them.

Conversion Counting Options

You can choose how Google counts your conversions. Choosing Every means Google will count every single conversion action after an ad is clicked. Choosing One means Google will only record one conversion per ad click.

If you're an ecommerce site, you'll likely select Every. If somebody purchases items on three different visits, you'll want to record that as three different sales, even if one click originally brought the person to your site.

Lead-generation sites will typically use the One option. For example, if a person clicks through to your site and downloads five different PDFs, you'll still want to count them as only one lead, not five separate conversions.

In the Tools & Settings drop-down icon at the upper right, under Measurement, click Conversions, as shown in Figure 19–4 on page 176. Click the name of the conversion action you want to edit and click Edit Settings. Then click Count and select One or Every.

Conversion Windows

One business might have a buying cycle of longer than 30 days, where a person clicks on day one and completes a purchase on day 49. Another business might be running a seven-day promotion, so it needs to see the clicks and conversions inside just that weeklong window. As you can see in Figure 19–5 on page 176, Google allows you to set the conversion window, which enables you to handle these kinds of scenarios in your conversion tracking.

In the Settings section, click Edit Settings and choose Conversion Window.

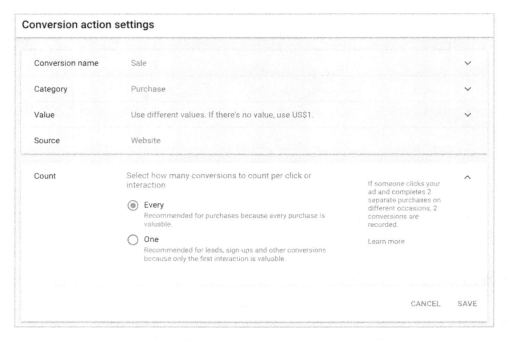

FIGURE 19–4. Choosing How to Count Conversions

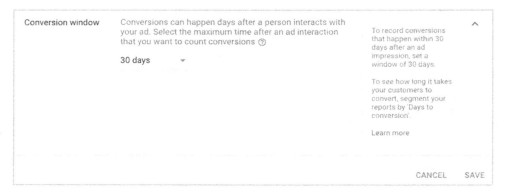

FIGURE 19–5. Setting Your Conversion Window

View-Through Conversions

Sometimes a person sees your ad and doesn't click on it, but later they come to your site and complete a conversion action. If you want to see when this type of view-through conversion happens and how often, you can add it as a column in your interface by clicking Columns > Modify Columns and finding the "View-Through Conversions" check box under the Conversions section.

Attribution Modeling

The last option when creating each new conversion is to choose an attribution model. This is a more advanced topic that we'll cover in Chapter 27, when we discuss Google Analytics.

THE PROS AND CONS OF PHONE CALL TRACKING

We mentioned earlier that inbound phone calls are a high-value conversion action. If you track which clicks resulted in which phone calls, you can better optimize your account.

But there's a trade-off. To track phone calls, you'll need to use new trackable numbers in your ads and on your website. Some business owners are reluctant to do this, as they believe it may confuse their prospects and negatively impact their branding. We're strong proponents of tracking phone calls—we believe it's more important to have correct data, so you can make sound decisions and save money.

Calls That Can Be Tracked

There are four ways to track inbound calls:

1. *Track calls that come straight from an ad.* This is the easiest option—you either add a call extension or use a call-only campaign. We covered these in Chapter 7.
2. *Track calls made from your website.* For any visitor who comes by way of a Google ad, the landing page dynamically inserts a phone number that can be tracked by the Google system. This is used most by advanced advertisers.
3. *Track when somebody clicks on your phone number from your mobile site.*
4. *Use a third-party tool such as CallRail.*

Creating Your Trackable Phone Number

You have two main choices for creating a trackable phone number. The easiest is to use Google's free service. There's no cost for creating the phone numbers, and there are no additional charges for time spent on the phone with your prospects. Best of all, Google will track the call back to the exact click that led to it.

There are many third-party systems that offer similar features. A downside of those is that you'll pay for the ongoing service and you'll pay per minute for phone calls.

Those services come with additional benefits, though. They can usually record all your calls, which is useful for training purposes. And they'll show missed calls, which is valuable if you're an agency that generates calls for clients and you need to demonstrate that your ad campaigns are triggering the volume of phone calls that you claim.

Setting Up Phone Call Tracking

Click the Tools & Settings drop-down in the upper right, and under Measurement click Conversions. Click the blue + button, and on the resulting page click Phone Calls, as shown in Figure 19–6 below.

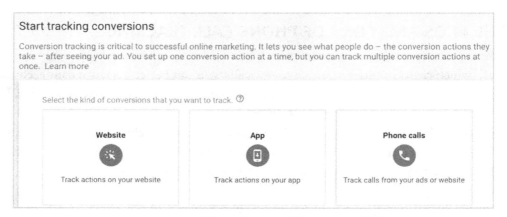

FIGURE 19–6. Tracking Phone Calls as Conversions

You can determine how long a call must last before it gets counted as a conversion. The default is 60 seconds, but you can adjust that if you like.

We recommend choosing the One setting (not Every) for measuring conversions, so that one person calling you three times would count as just one lead.

Remember to set a conversion value, an amount appropriate relative to the other conversion actions in your account.

Once you've created the conversion action for tracking phone calls, Google will give you some code to install on your site. You can have your web developer help you with this process.

ADVANCED CONVERSION TRACKING OPTIONS

The option to import conversions from your customer relationship management (CRM) platform is used by only a tiny fraction of search marketers. We'll comment briefly on it here. It may become more necessary in the future, as tracking with cookies is falling further out of favor and is blocked by an ever-growing number of browsers.

Each time a user clicks on a Google ad, Google generates what is known as the Google Click ID (GCLID), a unique string of letters and numbers, typically 80 to 100 characters in length, that Google uses to track conversions and other data.

When somebody lands on your website, you can capture the GCLID. (Ask your web developer how.) When they fill in a form and send data to your CRM, you can send the GCLID along with that data, typically in a hidden field.

This is useful if you want to count sales that happen at a later date, beyond the initial lead. For example, Mary fills in a form on your site, triggering a conversion action. Four weeks later, after multiple phone calls, she purchases a $9,000 service from you. You would love to be able to tell Google that Mary, as a lead, not only converted but was worth a four-figure sum to your business.

With GCLID, you can do just that. By regularly exporting data from your CRM and sending it back to Google with the GCLID of the original click and the dollar amount of the sale, you can record the value of Mary's original conversion. (Exactly how this is done will depend on your CRM and how frequently you pass data back to Google. Talk to your web developer to learn more.)

Preventing Duplicates

If you are an ecommerce site owner, you can deduplicate order numbers in Google's system. That way, if somebody refreshes a thank-you page, it won't trigger a new conversion action. To do this, you'll need to add some code to pull the unique order number into Google, along with some other conversion data. Your web developer can help with this, as the exact method may change based on the platform you use.

YOUR QUICK ACTION SUMMARY

This is an easy one: From the list of micro conversions earlier in this chapter, find one you're not yet tracking and add it as a new conversion type to at least one of your campaigns.

Chapter 20

Niche Domination, Part 1:
Chisel In Where the Chiseling Is Easy

We need to step away from the mechanics of Google Ads for a few minutes and talk about *strategy*. Pay close attention to these next two chapters.

My friend and mentor Dan Kennedy, founder of Magnetic Marketing, spent years on the speaking circuit. Once he found himself in a green room with General Norman Schwarzkopf, aka "Stormin' Norman." Schwarzkopf was celebrated in the 1990s for leading the military forces in Operation Desert Storm, which freed Kuwait from the Iraqi invasion.

Dan asked the general, "Norman, what was the secret to your success? How did you become such an awesome celebrity overnight?"

Schwarzkopf replied, "I only played games I could win. Desert Storm was a game we could win."

Contrast this with the later Iraq War that began in 2003, which in hindsight was a game *nobody* could win.

Famous marketers and marketing gurus sometimes appear to walk on water. But what we really do is find places where the water is denser than a human body and walk on *that*. We only *appear* to defy gravity!

Picking battles you can win is one of the most vital marketing skills you can learn. And in Google Ads, you can fight to worm your way in where the competition is fierce . . . or you can target niches where no one has decisively claimed the top spot, or the top player is weak or not paying attention. That's the best way to chisel in with minimum resistance. In this chapter, we'll show you how to use that technique to dominate your niche, no matter what it may be.

THREE SIGNS OF AN OVERLOOKED NICHE

Some may discount niches as "too small." But that's a strategic mistake when it comes to Google. After all, niches are where the dedicated audiences live. Here are three signs that a niche is overlooked:

1. *A good niche almost always has at least one advertiser.* If you find a keyword for which there are zero advertisers, odds are 95 percent that there is no money in that niche.

2. *There is a major unmet need in that market.* Sometimes this is very easy to tell. For example, people search Google for "lemon-scented hand soap," but almost none of the advertisers on Google specifically cater to it.

    Admittedly, the "lemon-scented hand soap" niche is small. But it is unclaimed. "Lemon-scented soap" is bigger and is probably better. In these niches, it will not be hard to write a winning ad and landing page and become a big fish in a little pond. You might only sell ten units a month, but it's a good start. It is much better than getting your head handed to you by trying to compete in the overcrowded "hand soap" market.

3. *There is a major unmet need in your market that is **not** readily obvious from keyword research.* Psychologist and marketing consultant Glenn Livingston has devised a very easy, elegant way to discover this unmet need. The following is adapted from Chapter 21 of *80/20 Sales and Marketing*.

THE 80/20 SURVEY TECHNIQUE FOR HYPER-RESPONSIVE INTELLIGENCE

Please pay close attention. This is one of the most important sections in this book! It will get you to the money in any niche faster than anything else I know. (You will also find an extension to this section in the online supplement for book buyers, available at www.perrymarshall.com/supplement.)

Ninety-nine percent of marketers have absolutely no idea how to use surveys. They think they're supposed to ask people what their most important need is and then just echo these needs back to them in priority order, kind of like a FAQ. But the problem with frequently *asked* questions is that they're also frequently *answered* questions.

Frequently Presented Needs Are Also Frequently Catered-To Needs

In other words, all a standard survey does for you is identify the price of entry benefits for a market. It doesn't give you any way to distinguish which needs represent the market gap or where you might position yourself with point-of-difference benefits.

Moreover, these surveys typically don't ask why respondents are frustrated, which really hamstrings the purpose of doing the survey in the first place.

For example, which is more powerful: to know that 40 percent of your prospects need a computer that boots up quickly, or to know they need to boot up fast because their pay is based on per-unit productivity? In the first case, you don't know how to cast the tone of your advertising, whereas in the second you know it's all about the frustrations of per-unit workers.

Here's a simple way to fix this problem. Ask them what their single most important question or need is (related to your topic), but also ask why they chose to look for a solution today and how difficult it was to find a good one. Then score it using the following protocol, which also takes into account each prospect's level of engagement.

THE 80/20 PROTOCOL

Send these three questions to your prospect and customer list; recruit people via forums such as Twitter, Facebook, and other social media on your bull's-eye keyword; or ask on your landing page that's getting Google traffic from your target keywords:

1. *The WHAT question*: "What's your single most important question about [keyword]?"

2. *The WHY question*: "Why would it make a difference in your life to get a good answer for this problem or find a solution for your need? (Details, please.)"

3. *The HOW DIFFICULT question*: "How difficult has it been for you to find a good answer for the above to date? (Not at all difficult, somewhat difficult, very difficult.)"

So what do you do with this information once you have it?

The quick and dirty summary: You throw it into a spreadsheet, discarding the "not at all" and "somewhat" difficults and keeping only the "very" difficults. Those are the people who really have an itch that they can't figure out how to scratch.

Then throw away the short answers and keep the long ones. What's left are your most persuadable, 5 to 10 percent who will actually give you money for a product that solves their problems. Their answers are literally a page out of their diary. And now you know exactly what problems your product has to solve.

There's a better approach, however, that's much more precise. I have devised a simple scoring system for your survey, which you can download at www.perrymarshall.com/supplement.

When you're done, sort your data by this score ("hyper-responsive score"), and look at the top 20 percent of responses. (If you have thousands of responses, look at the top 5 percent instead.) *These* are your most hyper-responsive prospects, and it's within their responses that you'll find the most motivating language, needs, and your point-of-difference benefit.

To listen to a full-length interview in which Glenn and I discuss depth-research techniques you can leverage in Google Ads, please visit www.LivingstonReport.com.

I cannot tell you how powerful this method is. I do Livingston 80/20 surveys on my customers at least once every few months and, unless I'm having a stupidity spasm, any time we go into a brand-new product category or market. In fact, I have been running a couple of these surveys continuously for years. One has amassed thousands of responses so far.

Trust the market—it will tell you what its unmet needs are. *If there really is an unmet need, you will not have trouble getting people to take the survey.* They will want to tell you what they're missing.

If you can't get people to take the survey, that's a strong sign there's no water in that swimming pool. Don't jump in it. Pick another market and go after that instead.

YOUR QUICK ACTION SUMMARY

Get feedback from your prospects before spending huge sums of money on product and web development:

- Send the three "what," "why," and "how difficult" questions to your prospects.
- Keep only the responses from people who indicated it was "very difficult" to find answers or help.
- Look at the top 20 percent of the longest responses to see what your most rabid prospects had to say.

Chapter 21

Niche Domination, Part 2:
Playing Games You Can Win

This chapter could help you make millions of dollars and add years to your life.

When I first met Ed Rush, a former Marine Corps pilot, he was casting about, trying to find his way in the world. He had recently left the secure, regimented world of the military, and the ever-shifting, bloodthirsty world of self-employment was perilous and scary.

He and his wife were surviving on bologna sandwiches and ramen. She was hoping he would figure something out before too long. He was hoping he wouldn't be a miserable failure.

He tried all kinds of things. He was fascinated with leadership. At one point, he sent me a CD of him giving a talk on leadership. I told him, "Ed, nice try, but leadership is way too competitive of a field, and you have way too few credentials to make that fly."

He did some soul searching and realized he was an expert on something few others knew: how to become a pilot in the Marines.

The odds are heavily stacked against anyone who wants to do that. Ed had deep inside knowledge, he'd had a very successful career, and—guess what? People were searching on that subject, and nobody selling information on that topic had the credibility he had. It was an under-exploited niche.

Ed told his customers: "I can't promise you'll get *in* if you take my course, but I can promise your chances will be much, much higher with my help than without it." He added a satisfaction guarantee, created a product, built a website, and started driving Google traffic.

That site went on to generate substantial income for Ed. He became *the* dominant player in the "Become a Marine Corps pilot" niche.

Ed's story is a perfect example of how you succeed with Google Ads: You find an underserved niche where you have a strong unique selling proposition (USP), and you address that unmet need with your greatest strength.

Many people would say, "Yeah, but in my market there's already an Ed Rush, and he's number one. He's probably raking it in. Meanwhile, I'm sitting here at number 20, or whatever the last position is. How do I make this work?"

You *don't* try to be a bigger, badder version of Ed and go head to head with him. That strategy is almost always doomed to fail.

Unfortunately, that is what most Google advertisers do. They think, "All I need is better ads, a better landing page, and a better offer, and then I can beat Ed and become number one instead." Well, technically that's true, but there is almost always some additional element you will have a tremendously difficult time with. For example, if Ed already has overwhelming social proof, such as 100 glowing testimonials, and you only have five, the next 95 testimonials are going to take a l-o-o-o-n-g time to get. And by then he'll have 200.

The way you chisel your way in is to find a sub-niche that Ed doesn't serve, such as "How to get accepted as a Marine Corps pilot if you are in the Air Force, Army, or Navy."

Now, maybe the process is absolutely identical, or maybe there are no differences at all. Maybe your chances are exactly the same whether you're white or Black. However, I doubt it's exactly the same. Even if it is, *if customers who are searching perceive it's different for a Black pilot, then there's a market.*

Obviously, you'd almost certainly have to be Black to pull this off. But this is a perfect example of identifying an underserved sub-niche. If Ed is already the number-one Marine

Corps pilot training guy, it's going to be very hard for you to replace him as number one. But if nobody is the number-one Black Marine Corps pilot training guy, it's very *easy* for you to claim that spot.

This is how you chisel your way into Google Ads!

Notice that what I just went over doesn't really have all that much to do with Google Ads per se. It has a lot to do with keywords and market research, as I'll describe in a minute, but it has more to do with your USP and your offer.

And really it goes deeper than that. Stick with me, because I'm going to explain one of the most powerful concepts in this book.

THE "WORKING STIFF TO $400 MILLION" NICHE DOMINATION STRATEGY

Richard Koch wrote the million-copy-selling classic book *The 80/20 Principle*. When I read it, very early in my Google Ads career, it set my mind on fire and altered the way I saw everything. Suddenly, I understood that there are tiny levers everywhere that can swing open huge doors.

Eventually, I wrote my book *80/20 Sales and Marketing*. Richard and I had become friends, and he wrote the foreword to the book. He was already *the* 80/20 guy, and I had little chance of displacing him. However, I used the same strategy I just described for Marine Corps pilot: I decided to become the 80/20 guy for sales and marketing. That was a much easier battle to win—I just carved off a smaller unclaimed niche, like settlers in the 1800s claiming their free 160 acres of land in Nebraska.

Richard Koch has a fascinating story. He started out in corporate consulting, doing stints at Boston Consulting Group (BCG) and Bain & Company. Though his time at those companies was frustrating and not outrageously successful (he quit BCG before they could throw him out), he absorbed a tremendous amount of knowledge and insight from BCG's founder, Bruce Henderson, as well as from Bill Bain.

He left and formed another consulting firm, L.E.K. Consulting, with two ex-Bain colleagues. L.E.K. succeeded because Richard combined the wisdom and experience he had gained at Bain and BCG with a completely new niche and business model—and smart partners.

L.E.K. prospered, and Richard sold his stake in the company a few years later for $6 million, which was reduced to $4 million after taxes.

At that point, he became a consulting private equity investor, using his vast experience and acumen to precisely define:

- What kind of companies to invest in
- Which niches to pursue

- Growth strategy for those companies
- When you should get in
- When you should get out

In other words, the same things you should be deliberate about as you maneuver in Google Ads.

Richard began taking equity positions in small companies. Over the years, he's applied the 80/20 principle and focused his efforts on 19 select firms. Not 190. Just 19.

Half the companies Richard has invested in have gone on to be tremendously successful, selling for many times what they were originally worth. Nearly half his investments have grown five to 50 times their size from when he bought in. He has grown his net worth from $4 million in 1990 to more than $400 million as of 2020.

Richard's asset base has grown an *average* of 20 percent per year for more than two decades. If you don't believe me, get out your calculator and do the math. $4 million to $400 million in 26 years. The 80/20 formula applies broadly:

- Warren Buffett became the world's richest man for a time on 20.3 percent per year.
- Peter Lynch of the Fidelity Magellan Fund made just 29 percent annual returns.
- And forget his famous $1 billion day—George Soros' Quantum Fund averaged just 30 percent annually.

How can Richard consistently beat the market by double digits year after year? How does he attain results within spitting distance of the world's richest billionaires?

He's not a mutual fund manager, a corporate analyst, a mathematician, or a "spreadsheet junkie." He doesn't have an array of computer monitors with charts and market data blaring at him every day.

When a venture capitalist (VC) invests in ten companies, they expect seven to go belly up, two to do OK, and one to explode to ten times its original worth. Even the best are lucky to bat 10 percent.

Yet Richard has invested in only 19 companies and hit serious pay dirt on eight. That's far too many to ascribe to luck.

So how is it possible that Richard Koch bats .500 when most venture capital firms are delighted to get a hit one out of every ten times they're at bat? The icing on the cake is that Richard spends, at most, one to two hours per day working on his business.

The answer is that Richard picks his winners based on three factors that he calls the Star Principle:

1. Your niche is growing 10 percent per year or more.
2. Your company is number one in its niche.

3. If you are not number one, create a sub-niche and appoint yourself number one.

Opportunities that match these criteria are worth your time. You will get an exponential return on your time and money with Star Principle companies.

I don't know if Marine Corps recruiting is growing 10 percent per year, but everything else Ed Rush did matched the Star Principle criteria. *That is why he was successful building a lucrative business with Google Ads traffic.*

On the other hand, if you do not have a strong USP, if you are far from number one in your niche, if you go into a niche with lots of competition and little to differentiate you from everyone else, or if you go into a niche that is shrinking (CD manufacturing, for example), then all the Google Ads techniques in the world cannot save you.

That's because even if 95 percent of Google advertisers do a lousy job, which is usually the case, the 5 percent who know what they're doing will still beat you.

I've created a more in-depth tool where you can evaluate any product or market you're in or are thinking of going into. The tool scores your business on a scale from 1 to 200, with 100 being the threshold for Star Business status.

Go to www.StarPrinciple.com and get your score.

The tool is free and doesn't require registration. Answer 12 quick questions and get your score in 60 seconds. If you wish, you can sign up for a report that explains the tool and your score in detail.

SUCCESS THROUGH ELIMINATION

Every major success I've had in business has matched up to the Star Principle criteria fairly well. A quick Star Principle test is now one of the first things I do when evaluating an opportunity or client business.

As entrepreneurs, we thrive on action, excitement, and adventure. Many of us become adrenaline and activity addicts. Most of us habitually say yes to everything. But the best thing you can do to ensure future success is say NO to far more opportunities, markets, and even keywords than you say yes to.

We go into even greater depth on the "success through elimination" principle in the online supplement for book buyers, at www.perrymarshall.com/supplement.

YOUR QUICK ACTION SUMMARY

To get the ball rolling, head over to www.StarPrinciple.com and find out your business's Star Score.

Chapter 22

"Deep 80/20":
It's Not What You Think . . . And I Can't Tell You How Profitable It Is!

What I'm about to share is so incredibly important that it would be criminal not to devote a whole chapter to it. It's critical. Master this chapter, and you'll work less, make more, be more focused, and feel less guilty about everything.

The 80/20 Rule, aka the Pareto Principle, says:

- Eighty percent of what you get comes from 20 percent of what you do: small effort, big reward.

- Twenty percent of what you get comes from the other 80 percent that you do: big effort, small reward.

Most marketers have heard about the 80/20 Rule. Most *think* they know what it is. But most people who "know" about it do not actually understand it. I was just like everybody else. I *thought* I understood the 80/20 Rule, but I was completely wrong.

A true, in-depth understanding of the 80/20 Rule is one of the most powerful marketing skills you can master. "Deep 80/20" is right up there with getting website traffic, writing ads, developing USPs, and building lists. But here's the important point:

All good marketers understand traffic, copywriting, USPs, and list building. But far less than 1 percent of marketers understand Deep 80/20. Read this chapter carefully, because it will reveal all kinds of places where you are leaving money on the table.

Deep 80/20 is one of the main reasons you are reading *this* book right now and not someone else's. Back in 2003, Google Ads was brand-new, and nobody fully understood how to make it work. It was a strange beast. Deep 80/20 was how I figured out Ads in the first place. It still is.

I experienced a huge epiphany reading Richard Koch's classic book, *The 80/20 Principle*. Suddenly, I saw layers and layers, where before I'd only seen the surface. Eventually, I used these insights to write *80/20 Sales and Marketing*. Today, I'm going to give you a quick, chapter-sized sample of Deep 80/20. Pay close attention. This chapter will teach you the highest-leverage skill that currently exists in marketing.

BACK WHEN I THOUGHT I UNDERSTOOD 80/20 . . .

I first heard about 80/20 when I was working as a sales manager. I printed out a sales report from QuickBooks and went through it with my calculator. Sure enough: 80 percent of our sales came from the top 20 percent of our customers, and the other 80 percent of our customers generated the remaining 20 percent of sales.

One of our customers, Dimitri, liked to call me all the time and nitpick about our software, even though he didn't buy much. Dimitri was near the top of my time-suck list and near the bottom of my money list. That 80/20 exercise made me realize he was chewing up time he didn't deserve. But it stopped there. I didn't think much else about it and moved on.

A few years later, when I read Richard's book, a torrent of insights flooded my brain. I'm going to share them with you now—and show you how to specifically apply the 80/20 Rule to Google Ads, so you waste way less time, get more done, sell more products, and make more money.

80/20 APPLIES TO JUST ABOUT EVERYTHING YOU CAN MEASURE IN A BUSINESS

Sources of incoming phone calls, sizes of commissions for salespeople, number of customers, physical location of customers, popularity of products, and the quantity of each type of product defect can all benefit from applying the 80/20 Rule. And, yes, Ads issues, too: keywords, impressions, ads, conversions, and visits to web pages. Just about every metric in this book obeys 80/20.

This means four-fifths of everything is trivial, and only one-fifth really matters. This can be a huge timesaver. But that's only the tip of the iceberg.

80/20 ISN'T JUST DIVIDED INTO TWO GROUPS

It's actually a predictable *power law* that you can put on a graph, as seen in Figure 22–1 below. The 80/20 Rule means that if you have a column of data, and you know just one

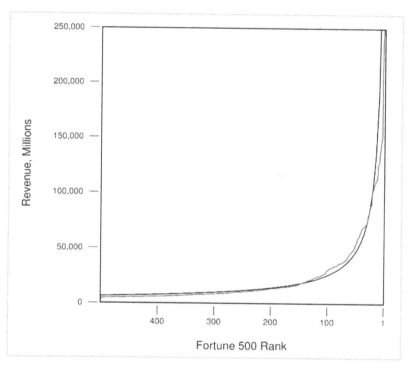

FIGURE 22–1. 80/20 Rule vs. Actual Data

or two things, like the number of items and the total, you can predict with scary accuracy how they're all going to stack up. I'll show you.

Let's say you read the following online: "Southwest Airlines, the 167th largest company in the U.S., with revenues of $15.7 billion . . ." Guess what? You already know enough to size up the entire Fortune 500.

This is tremendously useful and *very* powerful for marketers. You might be leaving a million dollars a year on the table without even knowing it! Now, in less than five minutes, you've exposed holes in your product line or pricing strategy. I created a tool called the 80/20 Curve (https://www.8020curve.com/) that accurately predicts where you're missing opportunities.

THERE'S AN 80/20 INSIDE EVERY 80/20!

The 80/20 Rule still applies to what's left after you peel away the bottom 80 percent. Not only does 80 percent of your money come from 20 percent of your customers, but 80 percent of that 80 percent comes from 20 percent of the top 20 percent.

That means 4 percent of your customers create 64 percent of your income. That's $80/20^2$. And it's still true of the top 4 percent: 0.8 percent of your customers deliver 51 percent of your income. That's $80/20^3$. It keeps going until you run out of people.

This means you can extract huge amounts of money from tiny groups of people, keywords, ads, or web pages. This is because 80/20 is an infinite repeating pattern. It's "fractal"—on a micro or macro scale, it's the same pattern again and again. There is *always* an inequality. Most people underestimate how great it is.

YOU CAN OVERLAY MULTIPLE 80/20S AND DOUBLE YOUR MOJO

Not only do you get 50 percent of your business from 1 percent of your customers, but you may also get 25 percent of your profits from just one of your 250 products. You could easily make 10 percent more profit by pampering five big customers and fattening the margins on that one product.

The information age offers you more things to fix, optimize, and pay attention to than you could possibly attend to in a lifetime. That's why 80/20 has never been more important.

Google Ads, Google Analytics, and more flood you with reams of data 24 hours a day. If you pay attention to the wrong thing, you could waste your entire life polishing turds. The 80/20 Rule isn't just a rule of thumb in business—it's a law of nature. So let's look at how it works specifically in Google Ads.

As you saw in the earlier examples, the numbers "80" and "20" are not carved in stone. Sometimes it's 70/30, sometimes 60/40, 90/10, or 99/1. Keyword lists run very consistently at 95/5. Take a look at Figure 22-2.

Keyword	Clicks	Percent of Ad Group
[how to write a book]	4,317	60.3%
how to write a book	1,452	20.3%
"how to write a book"	679	9.5%
"how to write a childrens book"	142	2.0%
how to write a children's book	112	1.6%
how to write a good book	92	1.3%
free how to write a book	61	0.9%
learn how to write a book	41	0.6%
how to write a fantasy book	30	0.4%
how to write a book proposal	26	0.4%
how to write a non-fiction book	24	0.3%
how to write a childrens book	23	0.3%
how to write a fiction book	22	0.3%
how to write a self help book	20	0.3%
tips on how to write a book	20	0.3%
how to write a book in 14 days	13	0.2%
how to write a nonfiction book	12	0.2%
how to write a chapter book	12	0.2%
how to write and publish a book	10	0.1%
how to write a picture book	9	0.1%
how to write a text book	9	0.1%
how to write a business book	9	0.1%
instructions on how to write a book	8	0.1%
how to write a murder mystery book	8	0.1%
how to write a book about my life	6	0.1%

FIGURE 22-2. Clicks as the Percentage of an Ad Group

This ad group has 25 keywords, but more than 80 percent of the traffic comes from just two of them. Notice that the top three keywords are just match type variations on "how to write a book."

80/20 IS WHY "PEEL AND STICK" IS SO POWERFUL!

The 95/5 keyword pattern is universal. Peel and stick is simply recognizing that since 5 percent of your keywords generate 95 percent of your traffic, you can optimize the other 5 percent by peeling them out and sticking each one into its own unique ad group. You get 95 percent of the optimization by doing 5 percent of the work!

Peel and stick is the single most important Ads skill you can learn next to split testing. That's because it allows you to happily ignore up to 95 percent of the stuff in your ad campaigns!

This is true at the campaign level as well as at the keyword level. One of my Google accounts has 41 campaigns and 995 million impressions. The number-one campaign has 617 million impressions. One campaign generates two-thirds of the exposure. That top campaign has 28 ad groups, and 80 percent of the traffic comes from the top 11 groups.

The account in total has 3.1 million clicks and 2,857 ads (yes, we've tested a TON of ads!). The number-one ad has 303,000 clicks. One ad out of 2,857 generated 10 percent of the traffic. Five ads have gotten more than 100,000 clicks apiece.

You could say the purpose of my 2,000-plus ads was simply to arrive at a dozen killer Google ads—the supreme winners that generated half the traffic—and you would be right.

The 80/20 Rule also describes:

- Clicks your ads get in each of the 11 ad positions on Google search (the top three premium spots get 80 percent of the traffic)
- Traffic from placements on the Display Network
- Conversions from placements on the Display Network (top conversion sources will be different from top traffic sources)
- Visitors by city or state or country
- Conversions by city or state or country (again, top conversion sources will be different from top traffic sources)
- Clicks on the various ad formats and sizes
- Traffic to each page on your website
- Sales for each page on your website
- How many page views you get from the people who click on your site
- How much time your visitors spend on your site

- How much money your buyers spend with you
- How many times your buyers buy
- How frequently your buyers buy
- How long customers stay loyal to you

The 80/20 pattern is truly everywhere. It radically changes how you manage your campaigns and your business. It means that most impressions, clicks, ads, keywords, ad groups, web pages, prospects, and customers *simply do not matter very much.*

It also means that a *few* impressions, clicks, ads, keywords, ad groups, web pages, and customers determine almost everything! The trick is determining which is which.

When you start, your job is to throw just enough spaghetti against the wall to see where it is *starting* to stick, and then immediately channel your efforts into improving what is working. This is why it's so important to build your business on what people actually do and want, so you're not trying to steer a parked car.

PERFECTIONISM CAN GET IN YOUR WAY!

People who are good at Google Ads usually have a perfectionist streak. Perfectionists *like* the idea of coming up with the best possible ad, doing split tests, putting up the best possible landing page, etc. You're constantly improving, and your job is never done. You know you can always make it better, and that's exciting.

But perfectionism has a dark side. If you don't ignore most of what goes on in your Google campaigns, you'll never have time to focus on the few things that are actually working. This is true in all aspects of marketing. Yes, I know you have a 1,000-page website and you'd love to give the whole thing a face-lift. But in real life, 75 percent of your business is generated by just three of those pages, and no matter what you do to the least-visited 800 pages on your site, it won't make a bit of difference. You have to set hard limits on your perfectionism so you don't waste time perfecting the wrong things.

The real power of 80/20 comes when you make it three-dimensional. Your ads are showing on 15,000 placement sites, but 50 percent of your traffic comes from 10 of them. You have 20 landing pages, but 75 percent of your leads come from one of them. You have 86 ads, but 20 percent of your sales comes from one of them.

So you copy your best ads, and you do peel and stick for each of those placement sites. You also copy your best landing pages and make unique pages just for them.

Then you optimize. The ideal ad and landing page for each site will be different, so you start split-testing ads and A/B landing pages. It's not unrealistic to expect that even if you did a good job testing before, this new level of refinement could double your sales.

Those 10 placements were sending you 50 percent of your traffic, and since you doubled your conversions, now your whole business has grown 50 percent. And you did it with ten minor changes.

You can also peel and stick geographical locations—*but only do it for the highest-converting cities.* If San Francisco is a great city for you because it has 1 percent of the U.S. population but brings in 10 percent of your sales, then create a campaign just for San Francisco. You might use unique ads and color schemes.

But San Francisco gets way less traffic than the entire country, so you can't test as many things. So you do your color scheme tests just on 250 x 300 pixel banners (which usually get a lot of traffic). Whatever works on those, you apply to all the other banner sizes. This saves you a ton of money in design fees, and you'll still make good decisions 80 percent of the time.

Visually, it looks like what you see in Figure 22–3 below.

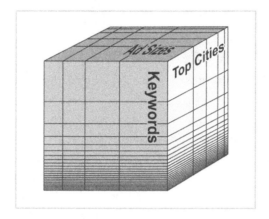

FIGURE 22–3. Visual of 80/20 Geotargeting

An inevitable consequence of 80/20 is that you sometimes feel like all your eggs are in one basket. And yes, there will always be a few baskets with a lot of eggs. Andrew Carnegie said, "Put all your eggs in one basket, and then watch that basket."

The biggest "too many eggs in one basket" mistake people make is *only* advertising on Google. I wish I had a dime for every customer who was going great guns and then got his ads disapproved or his account banned. Yes, do Google, but do Facebook ads, too. Do direct mail. Do LinkedIn ads.

THE MYTH OF THE LONG TAIL

Chris Anderson, then editor in chief of *Wired* magazine, wrote a book in 2006 called *The Long Tail: Why the Future of Business Is Selling Less of More.* He explained that the internet had made it possible for books that sell only ten copies a year to stay in print forever, whereas in the old bookstore model, obscure titles wouldn't have a prayer.

Those ten copies a year, on a graph, are the "long tail"—the millions of items that receive little attention but sell a few copies steadily for a long time.

Anderson makes a valid point, and it's why so many tiny groups and niches now have a voice on the internet. The phrase *long tail* is very useful because it's simply the left side of the 80/20 curve.

But you *must* be careful about the long tail. The received wisdom is that you can get lots of traffic from "long tail keywords" such as "how to write a murder mystery book."

Frankly, that's wrong. The phrase "how to write a murder mystery book" got eight clicks in two years. Yes, you should try to be a big fish in a little pond. But no fish can survive in a puddle. This keyword phrase is not worth anybody's serious time or attention, and while it may add a tiny amount of incremental revenue, it's trivial in the grand scheme of things.

On the other hand, if you can dominate just *one* high-traffic, high-conversion keyword, you can generate leads and sales for years. If you can improve one keyword's ad by 10 percent, you might increase revenue by $100,000 per year.

There is a right way and a wrong way to approach "long tail." The wrong way is to just dump thousands of keywords into your campaign. The right way is to deliberately choose to be a big fish in a little pond and become the king of an overlooked but viable niche.

There are thousands and thousands of such niches. The indicator you're looking for is not that there aren't advertisers and bidders in the space; rather, it's that nobody in the niche has a really great USP and the customers are itching for something more.

The common belief about the long tail is simply wrong. Yes, the internet has made it possible to sell ten copies per year of some obscure book written in 1913, but it's even more possible for hitherto unknown writers and reporters to achieve worldwide fame, as Malcolm Gladwell did with his 2000 book *The Tipping Point*.

Winners win big on the internet. My hope for you is that you'll be the big kahuna in your market, the number-one player, the alpha dog. And when you are, it'll be because you ignored 80 percent and got 1 percent exactly, precisely right.

SOME 80/20 RULES OF THUMB

I strongly recommend you pick up a copy of my book *80/20 Sales and Marketing* because it will take you much further on this journey. Meanwhile, here are some handy 80/20 rules:

- One-fifth of the people will spend four times as much money as the rest of them. If you have 100 customers who bought a $100 product from you, you can be sure that 20 of them would have bought a $400 product, and may still if given the right offer. Four of them would willingly buy a $1,600 product. 80/20 virtually guarantees this will be true.

- One percent of the work you did last year earned 50 percent of your money. The only people who normally see this with perfect clarity are salespeople who work on straight commission, but it's true for pretty much everybody.

- "Average" is seldom important in Google Ads. Your average keyword, ad, or customer barely matters at all, but a few of your keywords, a few of your ads, and a few of your customers matter a lot.

- The top 20 percent of factors—the people and things that make the most difference—usually send signals ahead of time. If you ask a survey question, a casual buyer will often answer with a sentence fragment. A hot buyer will talk to you on the phone for 45 minutes.

Archimedes said, "Give me a a place to stand and I will move the world." With Ads, you have a lever, a place to stand. With a great product and a USP, you have a place to stand. Just know that 80 percent of your levers will get you nowhere and 20 percent will make you rich.

You can purchase 80/20 Sales and Marketing *at www.perrymarshall.com/8020.*

Chapter 23

How Email Transforms Those Expensive Clicks into Long-Term, Profitable Customers

No discussion about Google Ads would be complete if I didn't show you how to turn that expensive, split-second click into a long-term relationship. When someone clicks on your ad, Google charges you 50 cents, regardless of what happens next. If they leave your website after five seconds, they are gone, and you probably won't get them back without paying for *another* click.

Fifty cents for five seconds of someone's attention—dang, that's $360 an hour! It's kind of depressing if you look at it that way. On the other hand, if that person gives you their email address, you can communicate with them on a regular basis for little or no cost going forward. Then 50 cents starts to look pretty cheap for a promising lead.

If you're trying to sell a $1,000 product, which is easier to get from your prospects: a $1,000 order or an email address?

The more complex your sales process, the more important it is to break it up into bite-size steps. In this chapter, we'll show you how email marketing can boost your Google Ads strategy to the next level.

HOW TO PUT PERSONALITY AND PIZZAZZ INTO YOUR EMAIL MARKETING

In an era when much of the American manufacturing industry was downsizing, cutting management, laying off employees right and left, and moving its operations to India and China, B+B SmartWorx in Ottawa, Illinois, set growth records. It had to hire more staff to handle its growing number of incoming catalog orders and mounting list of willing buyers.

Most people would never think to utter the phrase "infectious personality" and "electronics manufacturing company" in the same breath, but B+B managed both. It refused to surrender to the dull, corporate geek stereotype. Instead, the company had fun with it. B+B regularly courted its customers' inboxes with witty, lively messages poking fun at the stale image of the cubicle-farm engineer. Marketing director Mike Fahrion graced customers with his regular "Mike's Politically Incorrect Newsletter" rant column.

One techie's girlfriend wrote B+B to thank it for turning the engineer stereotype on its head:

> Hey Mike,
>
> This is the hapless girlfriend who shares an email account with a techie who subscribes to your newsletter.
>
> The amount of dry, poopy emails that we get in our inbox is criminal, and it's pathetic that the other electronic types are perpetrating the geek image that's out there by sending those incredibly boring messages.
>
> I mean, come on! "All you've ever wanted to learn about C++, Extensive Layer Management Plug-In for Mental Ray Pipeline"? BRUTAL!
>
> Thank you for the sense of humor in your newsletters.
>
> Mike, I think you need to start a "How to Write a Cheese-Free Newsletter" course. I can think of many companies that need your help!
>
> Signed,
>
> Disgruntled Dish

> ### Build a Business Around Your Uniqueness
>
> Use email correctly, and your customers will stick around three times longer. It's the most personal online medium there is. With it, you can sell to your customers again and again by building trust and creating an entire business around your unique personality.

Does B+B owe all its stellar growth in a stagnant industry to its email? No, but it's a vital ingredient of its carefully thought-out marketing strategy.

Mike understands this, which is why he originally hired Perry to ghostwrite his "Politically Incorrect Newsletter."

Whether you're B+B SmartWorx or Martha Stewart, capturing a person's email address turns a one-time click into an opportunity to build a long-term relationship.

Buying Google traffic is only the first of many important steps in your marketing process. If we had to credit our own success to just one thing, it would be our use of email and autoresponders.

POWER IN THE PERSONAL: SIX KEYS TO EMAIL MARKETING SUCCESS

Most run-of-the-mill advertisers have little respect for the personal nature of email. They don't realize how easy it is to turn off otherwise receptive prospects to their message just by violating that.

You need to write to each person as an individual. Unless the person you're writing to is part of a group where they personally know each of the other members, the last thing you want to do is write as though you're talking to a crowd.

Your email is you, a human being, talking to your customer, another human being. Let's explore some ways you can do that.

1. A "From" Field That Shows You're a Real Person

If you want the actual text of your email messages to emphasize that they're coming from a person, that same principle should apply to other details in your email as well, such as your "from" field. Consider the different impressions these "from" lines create:

- Bill Kastl
- William Kastl
- William D. Kastl
- Nakatomi Corporation

- William D. Kastl, Nakatomi Corporation
- Nakatomi Sales Department
- Bill Kastl, Nakatomi Sales

You want to be warm and personal without looking like spam. This is a challenge because spammers are themselves always trying to make their messages look like they're from some forgotten friend. The key is to say something that is so specific to readers' interests that they know no spammer would ever come up with it.

Pick a "from" field that your customers will understand, and stick with it.

2. A Provocative Subject Line

The most important thing about email is that its success or failure is all about *context*. Email subject lines work not because they follow standard copywriting formulas but because they tap into what specific people are interested in at a particular time.

If I showed you generic examples of email subject lines, they would sound exactly like spam to you.

So let's take examples from a specific context that *you* understand: Google Ads. Here are the subject lines of some of the emails I've sent out to my Google Ads customer list:

- When Google Is NOT the Best Way to Get a Customer
- Are Google Employees Spying on You?
- Google's "Don't Be Evil" and All That
- 5 Insidious Lies About Selling on the Web
- Fistfight at the Board of Directors Meeting

These subject lines do not assault the recipient with cheesy-sounding promos, but they do hint very strongly at a story inside the email. They provoke curiosity rather than scaring people off.

3. Everybody Loves a Good Story

B+B SmartWorx sells industrial communication hardware via catalog and the web—a "boring" tech business if there ever were one. But when Perry wrote its monthly newsletter, he turned that image on its head and interrupted a dreary day of engineering with wry humor.

The method? Storytelling.

Subject: ZIGBEE AND THE GEEKS' REVENGE

Leslye was the girl who made my heart go pitter-patter in junior high school.

I was always sure to take the long way to social studies, down the stairs to the first floor, past her locker, then back up to second. Just checkin' up.

I was not the boy who made her heart go pitter-patter. She liked Sam, and maybe Rodney, too.

She wasn't interested in me. And she never discovered that I liked her. It was my little secret.

Now maybe you didn't run the sound system in junior high like I did. Maybe you ran the film projector instead. Maybe you programmed Apple II computers in BASIC and belonged to chess club.

Still, you and I were geeks, and the pretty girls took no notice of us.

But it's a new age now, and we smart guys rule the world. We're the people who really know what's going on. All the pretty boys and their material girls have viruses on their computers and they can't function without us. They're at our mercy.

And the latest Geek Revenge these days is . . .

ZigBee.

ZigBee is sort of like wireless instant messaging for sensors and smart devices. You drop ZigBee nodes wherever you want, no cables necessary, and the more nodes you have, the more communication paths there are and the more reliable your system is . . .

This was a little wonky. It certainly didn't surrender to the old stereotype that engineers were dull, lifeless geeks who only understand ones and zeros. No. It *celebrated* it. It turned it into the central message. It played with the concept and had no end of fun with it.

More important, though, while it celebrated the engineer stereotype, at the same time it smashed it to pieces.

Engineers make buying decisions based on emotion just like the rest of us. Storytelling works when marketing to them, no differently from people in any other profession. Plus, everyone has suffered the heartache of unrequited love at some point.

Every time B+B sent out an email blast, it got emails from customers saying, "Your newsletter is the only one I read every time it comes" and "I always look forward to getting emails from you guys."

Why We Chose Engineers as an Example for Email Marketing

Most people stubbornly insist you can't use storytelling and humor to sell to "logical" people like engineers and scientists. They also think that B2B marketing has to be dreadfully serious.

This campaign shoots holes in those beliefs because we're doing both at the same time here—using emotional, human-touch email marketing to sell B2B products to engineers and scientists.

Does this work in other markets? You bet. Bryan Todd sold more books on learning Chinese and ignited more feedback and fan mail through this one message than anything else he sent out:

Subject: WOMEN WHO HOLD HANDS; MEN WHO HUG

William kept brushing against me as we walked down the street.

Now, I'm a guy like he is—and I'm straight, too—and I found this a little unnerving. This was back during my first month living in mainland China, William was my new friend, and he had some habits that were awfully strange.

And when we'd go out walking somewhere, he always rubbed his shoulders up against me. I kept thinking I was crowding him, so I'd move to the right. Then he'd move right too, get closer, and rub up against me again.

Sooner or later, I figured out that this was just his way of being friendly. No, not "friendly," just friendly—you know, normal, nice-guy friendly.

It's that classic issue of personal space.

Every culture has different rules. My Chinese guy friends rubbed shoulders with each other, and with me, as they walked down the street.

Americans don't do that unless they're in a relationship.

Younger women in China hold hands. Sometimes regardless of age. Arm in arm, hand in hand, they saunter together down the street.

Ah, but do they HUG you?

None of my friends ever did.

At least, not until I was with a couple of guys being visited by a lady pal of theirs from Shanghai . . .

> ### Why We Chose Engineers as an Example for Email Marketing, continued
>
> This email was part of Bryan's regular, timed email autoresponder series and didn't even explicitly promote his book. But it got a *reaction* from people. Still does. It turns the spotlight on a sensitive yet eminently funny subject.
>
> It also paints Bryan as completely human. Not a peddler, not a salesman, not a pushy marketer, but a regular guy whose experiences we can all share. Even if we've never been to China, we've all felt the awkwardness of misunderstanding someone else's intentions.
>
> Most important, this approach *trains* people to read your emails by convincing them that you've always got something interesting to say.

4. People Can't Forget You When They Hear from You Often

Get an autoresponder series going, and you can win your customers' hearts for life:

- We like five-day sequences: one email per day for five straight days. Five is a good number. Other prime numbers like three and seven are good, too.
- After that five-day sequence is done, keep in touch at a slower rate. In our online course "The Nine Great Lies of Sales & Marketing" (available at https://www.perrymarshall.com/9-lies/), my messages arrive every day for nine straight days. Then they continue as one message every few days after that and taper off for more than two years afterward. (You read that right: two years.)
- Your unsubscribe rate should be between 3 and 10 percent. If it's more than that, your message isn't matching your market. (If it's less, you may not be edgy enough.)
- Want to squash refunds and returns? After people buy from you, send them a series of messages that show them how to use your product more effectively and share features they might have missed.
- When people complain that they've missed a day or two from you, it's a sign that your content is good and that the spam filters are doing their job.

5. If You Violate the Expectation of Relevance, You Damage Your List

Let's say you're a chiropractor and you've just launched a new herbal remedy. It's a fantastic product, and you want to tell your customers about it. What should you do? Should you blast your entire list with it?

Odds are you could maximize your sales total for that day by doing so. But you'll pay a price. All the people on your list who aren't interested in herbal stuff will now be *less responsive* to everything else you do—even if they don't unsubscribe. You've just taught them that you like to send out emails about stuff they're not interested in.

And that means they're much less likely to read your next email.

It's a nasty mistake to treat everyone on your list the same unless they really are. If you have a back pain newsletter, it's likely only a few people on that list would ever be interested in a knee pain newsletter.

Typical marketers treat everyone the same, so when they get a back pain subscriber, they'll also send knee pain stuff, neck pain stuff, herbal stuff, environmental stuff, whatever.

The smart marketer will not. The smart marketer will have different sub-lists for each topic.

So if you're the chiropractor, you build an herbal sub-list and then sell the herbal remedies just to those folks. That way, you maximize the value of every single list you have.

In email—and, by extension, direct mail and other forms of communication—that means that some of your prospects and customers don't ever want to hear from you (the bottom 5 to 10 percent). They, of course, don't matter. They can unsubscribe. But for the people who do matter:

- Some of them (maybe 50 percent) would like to hear from you no more than a few times a year.
- Some of them (20 percent) would like to get your three-, five-, or seven-day auto-responder sequence for a few days, and then only hear from you if something important happens.
- Some (5 to 10 percent) would like to get all your newsletters, and if you have email lists for six different problems or products, they'll want to be on every single one.
- Some (1 to 2 percent) would like to hear from you every day.
- A tiny handful (less than 1 percent) would literally read ten emails from you every day, if you were willing to send them.

6. The Human Touch Sells

Don't hide behind your email. Use it to express more of yourself. You're not a faceless corporation; you're a person. Show that side of you, and people will remember you. And buy. And tell others about you.

Express a personality that people can instantly recognize. This is free branding. When you introduce new products or make changes in your marketing program or message, you can attach those to a name—your name or another person your business is known for—and now your name itself has even more meaning and credibility.

A MEDIUM THAT WILL NEVER GO AWAY

When you communicate with your customers through multiple media rather than just one, it greatly solidifies your power in the marketplace.

There's benefits for you in adding off-line marketing to your arsenal. Communicating with your customers via direct mail takes you out of the ephemeral, fly-by-night online world and connects them to you by an entirely new medium that is harder to break into but potentially more rewarding and enduring.

You can bank on the fact that the person in the blue-gray uniform who comes to your house every day is going to *continue* coming to your house every day pretty much as long as the earth keeps rotating on its axis (or as long as politicians depend on them to deliver their campaign mailings).

A customer who finds you off-line and goes to you online is usually more valuable than a customer who knows you only online. In the same way, a customer who knows you both online and through physical mailings and products is going to be a much more valuable customer than one who only knows you online.

OPT-INS: MORE THAN JUST AN EMAIL ADDRESS?

Most opt-in pages only ask for a name and email address, but is that really all the information you want? Many, if not most, businesses should also collect physical addresses and fax numbers. Asking for this information, or even requiring it, makes your database much more valuable.

It also gives you a useful communication medium besides just email. What if you accidentally get on a spam blacklist, your email service goes belly up, or email suddenly gets a lot more expensive? It's a mistake to rely solely on email to communicate with your customers.

THEY CAN KNOCK OFF YOUR PRODUCT, BUT THEY CAN'T KNOCK OFF *YOU*

Anybody can have a TV talk show, but there was only one Oprah. Anybody can rant about the Democrats, but there was only one Rush Limbaugh. Products can be replicated and ideas can be stolen, but personalities cannot be duplicated.

Use email to express your personality, and you'll have a unique bond with your customers that nobody can take from you.

YOUR QUICK ACTION SUMMARY

Very simply, create a five-day series about you or your services that visitors to your page or site can opt in for. Use personality and storytelling to engage your readers. Once you've done that and it's collecting optins, add additional messages past the five days with diminishing frequency.

Chapter 24

Getting More Advanced:
Tips and Tricks to Improve Your Success

There are a few additional elements and tools that you'll want to know about to make your campaigns successful. This chapter is about those. We'll cover your Quality Score, impression share, experiments, labels, and more.

QUALITY SCORE EXPLAINED

Can you think of any aspect of your business where making more money results in third-party suppliers charging you less? We're not talking about vendors giving you bulk discounts. We literally mean that the more profit you make, the more your provider slashes your final bill.

That just doesn't happen, right? It's always the opposite:

- When your business earns more, you pay more taxes.
- When you ship more orders, your shipping invoice is larger.
- When your TV commercial produces sales and you want to increase your airtime, the network charges you more.

But there is one exception—Google Ads rewards success. *The better your ads perform, the cheaper they get.*

How is this possible?

The answer is your Quality Score. Paid search expert Craig Danuloff calls the Quality Score system a "bozo filter." It weeds out the "accidental bozos" who write bad ads because they don't know how to be relevant as well as the "intentional bozos" who are trying to game the system.

As long as you're not a bozo, the system is heavily weighted in your favor. Think of it as a preferred customer program (what Australians like to call "mate's rates").

If there's any downside at all, it's that Google's exact Quality Score algorithm is confidential—much like their main search engine algorithm. To create a level playing field for advertisers, they're willing to share general principles and a few details here and there. But they keep specifics to themselves, and they regularly tweak the system.

Why Improve Your Quality Score?

Google wants to show more "good" ads. If your account is in good standing with them, you'll get more impressions and your ads will show more often.

If Google regards you as a good advertiser (i.e., one that provides a good experience to their users), you'll be rewarded with cheaper clicks. But if you don't play by Google's rules, the cost of your clicks will increase over time.

What's Your Quality Score?

To find your Quality Score, log in to your Google Ads account and choose an ad group to view. Click the Columns icon, then Modify Columns, and then under the Quality Score section choose the Quality Score option, as shown in Figure 24–1 on page 215.

Once that column is displayed, you'll see a score between one and ten for each of your keywords.

Note that you as the Google Ads advertiser only get to see one Quality Score number for each keyword. However, behind the curtain Google is calculating many different Quality Scores in real time, which vary depending not only on how you construct your campaigns but also on what they know about the person searching. For instance, your

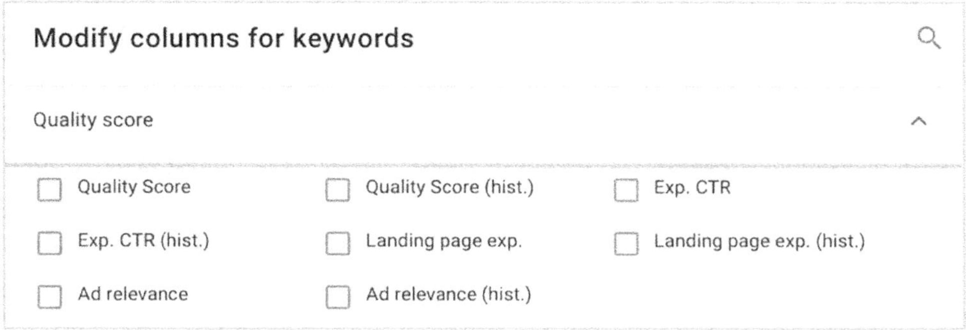

Modify columns for keywords

Quality score

☐ Quality Score	☐ Quality Score (hist.)	☐ Exp. CTR
☐ Exp. CTR (hist.)	☐ Landing page exp.	☐ Landing page exp. (hist.)
☐ Ad relevance	☐ Ad relevance (hist.)	

FIGURE 24–1. Options for Showing Quality Score

ad may have one Quality Score for a searcher from the UK on an iPhone and another for a searcher from Australia on a laptop.

Although you can find a Quality Score number for each of the keywords in your Google Ads account, consider it a general guide. At best, it will help you figure out which of your keywords and ad groups could use a little work and which are best left alone. Figure 24–2 below shows you what this looks like.

Again, remember this is a guideline, not a precise set-in-stone number. It's an average score for each keyword, with a much more complicated calculation happening invisibly behind the scenes.

Now that you know your Quality Score for each keyword, what should you do about it? Here are some guidelines:

- *9–10 Excellent.* Don't change anything. You're right on point and are probably paying the lowest possible price for your clicks.

Keyword	Cost	Conversions	Cost / conv.	Conv. rate	Quality Score
	A$46,313.68	10,429.45	A$4.44	3.66%	9/10
	A$720.47	500.05	A$1.44	5.36%	10/10
	A$8,312.27	324.21	A$25.60	4.37%	9/10
	A$7,285.44	302.66	A$24.01	4.59%	9/10
	A$2,437.23	120.39	A$20.20	4.15%	10/10
	A$2,417.10	116.47	A$20.74	4.06%	10/10

FIGURE 24–2. A Quality Score Report

- *7–8 Very Good.* You're doing fine. You could potentially push your score a bit higher, and it might be worth checking whether you're missing anything obvious (such as cramming this keyword along with too many others into a single ad group). But don't spend huge amounts of time trying to improve it.

- *5–6 Average.* These are the keywords that could benefit from a little additional TLC.

- *3–4 Poor.* This is a warning sign. Your ads for this keyword aren't showing very often, and when they do you're probably paying well above average for each click. If the keyword in question has the potential to generate high volumes of traffic, then fixing its Quality Score should be your priority.

- *1–2 Terrible.* At this level, Google is barely showing your ads for this keyword and is charging you a fortune per click. Take action immediately!

- *"–"* This means Google doesn't have enough data yet to assign a Quality Score. Come back and check again once that keyword has more impressions.

What Factors Go into Your Quality Score?

You could compare your Quality Score to monthly mortgage payments that vary depending on how you look after your house. Mow the lawn and take out the trash, and your payment goes down.

But does Google prefer your house to be red or white?

That's where things get tricky. Maybe you paint your house red this month, and then next month, your mortgage payment goes down even further. But was it because you painted your house, or was there some other cause?

Plenty of Google Ads experts have experimented and drawn helpful conclusions about how Google rates its advertisers. And at the very least, Google has been upfront about the *most important factors* in its Quality Score.

You can visit https://support.google.com/google-ads/answer/7050591 for the most current explanation, but below is our summary of the key items, along with our assessment of the ones we feel are the most significant.

Expected Clickthrough Rate

This should be a priority for every PPC marketer. Of all the things Google cares about, CTR is always at the top of the list. According to Frederick Vallaeys, CEO of PPC software maker Optmyzr, your CTR (compared with your direct competitors) contributes two-thirds or more of your Quality Score.

The logic is simple: If users click on Ad 1 more often than Ad 2, Google assumes that Ad 1 is more relevant and interesting. But they don't look at the CTR of each ad in isolation; they also take into account the CTR that other advertisers obtained for the same keywords you're bidding on, the position on the page on which your ad was shown, and the overall CTR you're receiving for *all* your ads across *all* your ad groups.

You're graded on the curve, in other words.

Landing Page Experience

Some site owners try to create a unique landing page for every ad. That certainly makes for relevant landing pages, but it's very time-consuming, probably expensive, and may make tracking your conversions unnecessarily complex. The truth is that the relevance of your landing page is only moderately important compared with the CTR of your ad.

Review Chapter 11 on landing pages, where we cover the five factors to consider when you want to improve your landing page experience.

Keyword-to-Ad Relevance

This is about the relationship between the search query, your keyword, the text in your ad, and the text on your landing page.

Every ad group needs to center tightly on a keyword theme and contain a small number of keywords. You can certainly dump all your keywords into just one or two ad groups, but your CTRs will suffer.

For example, if I search for "chiropractor," I'm not likely to click on your ad unless it has "chiropractor" in the headline. If I type in "sciatica" and your ad says "sciatica relief," I'm far more likely to click on your ad than if it only says "back pain relief."

The only way to account for all these factors is to have separate ad groups for each of these types of keywords. In this example, you should have one ad group for variations on "chiropractor," one on the theme of "sciatica," and one about "back pain relief."

Geographic Performance

Google keeps track of *where* people are clicking on your ad. If, for instance, users in New York are clicking on your back pain ad more often than users in Philadelphia, your ad will be given a different Quality Score for these two areas. (Note: You won't see this reflected in any of your Google Ads reports; it happens behind the scenes.)

Targeted Devices

Google keeps track of how well your ad performs on each type of device (desktop vs. mobile vs. tablet), and they'll assign you a different Quality Score accordingly.

Quality Score on the Display Network

If you're using CPM bidding, Google will only consider the various landing page quality factors as listed above.

If, however, you are using CPC bidding, Google will also factor in the historical CTR of your ads.

Three Myths About Quality Score

There are three big common misconceptions about Quality Score.

Myth #1: *Match type matters.* Google only considers the exact match of any keyword in your account when calculating Quality Score.

Myth #2: *Low CTR on the Display Network hurts your Quality Score.* It doesn't. Google understands that Display Network ads get lower CTRs and takes this into account. Quality Scores for Google Search and the Display Network are calculated separately.

Myth #3: *Ads must show in high positions to get high Quality Scores.* Google is gracious enough to account for the positions that your ad shows in. More important than your CTR is your CTR *compared with other advertisers* when their ad shows in the same position on the page.

IMPRESSION SHARE

Once you bid on a keyword, your ad will automatically be shown every time somebody makes a related search, right?

Your ad may sometimes be in a low position on the page, but it'll always show up somewhere, right?

Wrong.

Google almost never shows *any* advertiser's ads 100 percent of the time for a given keyword. There are several reasons for this, with the most important being that Google wants to test other advertisers' ads to see how they perform. Plus, Google makes more money showing 20 ads 50 percent of the time than showing seven ads 100 percent of the time. Google controls whose ads they show and how often. The percentage of the time they show your ads for any given keyword is called *impression share* (IS), also known as *coverage.*

There are things you can do to increase your impression share and ensure that more people see your ads more often. Google provides reporting data that shows your precise impression share and even hints at what you may need to do to improve it.

Imagine you have a profitable ad group, but you discover that your impression share is only 20 to 30 percent. With a few key fixes, your ads could be seen *three to five times as often as they are,* and your profit would multiply by a similar factor. There's a huge opportunity to increase your bottom line, simply by improving this number.

How to Find Your Impression Share Numbers

To turn on this particular metric inside your Google Ads account, go to Modify Columns and select Competitive Metrics. Then add the following three columns to your stats, as you can see in Figure 24–3 below: Search Impr. Share, Search Lost IS (Budget), and Search Lost IS (Rank).

You can view this data at the campaign, ad group, and keyword level. However, Search Lost IS (Budget) only shows at the campaign level, so we suggest starting there.

Your impression share number will be a percentage that indicates how close you are to being seen 100 percent of the time. So if your impression share is 50 percent, this means you're only being seen half of the time you could be. In this case, if you're receiving 1,000 impressions a day on a particular keyword, a 50 percent score means there are up to 1,000 *additional* impressions available to you on any given day—provided you can make the right improvements to your campaign.

"Search Lost IS (Budget)" is simple to understand and fix. Let's say your daily budget is $10, but there are actually $100 worth of available clicks every day. Your impression share in this case will never exceed 10 percent, and the reports will probably tell you that your impression share *lost* due to your budget is 90 percent.

"Search Lost IS (Rank)" is a bit more complex and involves a number of elements we'll look at more closely in a moment. In brief, if Google doesn't feel that your campaigns are of a high enough quality, they'll limit your impression share even further.

"Search Top IS" is the percentage of time your ads were shown anywhere above the organic search results.

"Search Abs. Top IS" shows your absolute top impression rate—that is, the percentage of time your ads were shown in the very top position above the organic search results.

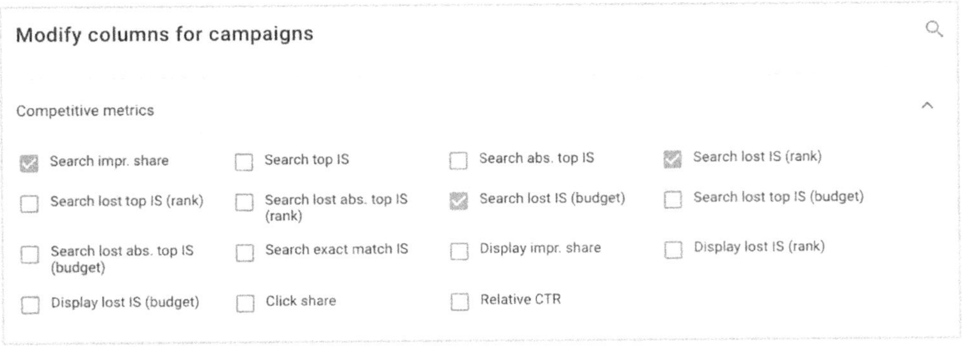

FIGURE 24–3. Choosing Impression Share Metrics to Display

How to Improve Your Impression Share

Impression share is a fantastically simple way of seeing how often your ads are showing, but it's also a quick way to measure how Google perceives the quality of your campaign and the potential to increase your profits.

There are two reasons Google might limit your impressions (apart from their need to test the inventory of other advertisers):

1. *Your daily budget is too low.* This is simple to diagnose and fix. It's possible to double or even triple the impressions on a profitable account simply by increasing the daily budget. Naturally you will need to exercise some caution. How profitable are your campaigns? What can your marketing budget sustain? Answer those questions, and you can raise your budget and impression share accordingly.

2. *Your Ad Rank is too low.* You can improve this by giving attention to three things:
   - *Ad extensions.* If you're not using them, jump right in and try some sitelinks, callout extensions, and call extensions.
   - *Quality Score.* If the quality of your ads and keywords is poor, your impression share will suffer. If you're showing a Quality Score of five or below, work on improving it.
   - *Maximum bid.* If you need to bump this up to improve your Ad Rank, do so incrementally. Review your maximum bid every day if need be, and don't raise it more than you can afford or sustain. It's better to have a low impression share in a profitable campaign than to have a high impression share and lose money!

You Can See Your Competitors' Impression Share, Too

You can spy on your competitors using third-party software applications, but you can also do it within your Google Ads account. You can see their impression share for individual keywords or even entire groups of keywords.

There's a cool feature called Auction Insights, which you'll find under the Keywords tab on the left. Pick out a few relatively high-volume keywords that you want to research, check the box next to them, and then (as shown in Figure 24–4 on page 221) choose Auction Insights.

This will load a report showing your impression share for those keywords, as well as for a few of your competitors. An example of this report is in Figure 24–5 on page 221. You can also run this report at the ad group or campaign level.

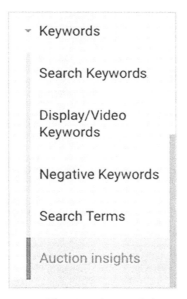

FIGURE 24–4. The Auction Insights Option

Auction insights

Custom 1 - 29 Feb 2020

Display URL domain	Impression share	Overlap rate	Position above rate	Top of page rate	Abs. Top of page rate	Outranking share
You	79.50%	—	—	83.82%	61.41%	—
	28.20%	34.12%	15.49%	58.68%	10.22%	75.30%
	27.35%	33.28%	11.09%	66.73%	7.28%	76.57%
	22.16%	26.61%	20.01%	71.33%	15.77%	75.27%
	16.27%	18.81%	12.85%	51.10%	4.19%	77.58%
	13.94%	17.22%	5.31%	54.73%	2.44%	78.77%

FIGURE 24–5. The Auction Insights Report

DRAFTS AND EXPERIMENTS

The great genius aspect of PPC is how quickly it lets you test, fail, retest, and succeed with your advertising.

Frankly, every situation in life is a kind of test, where you're guessing what you think will happen, running real-world experiments, and finding out if you're right. How will this person react if I do such-and-such? What happens if I say this? What happens if I invest time and money to try that?

Sadly, for all too many people, every small failure—in social settings, athletics, business ventures, or anything else—feels like death.

Life doesn't have to feel that way. If something you earnestly try doesn't succeed, you cut your losses and move on to the next test. As goes the famous quote by Thomas Edison: "Results! Why, man, I have gotten lots of results! I know several thousand things that won't work!"

Everything you do inside a Google Ads account is a little science experiment. Job One for you or the person running your Google Ads account is to be continually testing. In fact, the primary reason for having an Ads account is to experiment so you can learn what messages and offers do and do not work with your audience. (The quality traffic to your website is merely the side benefit.)

Google Ads drafts and experiments let you test changes to your account on a small amount of traffic without having to subject entire campaigns—or your entire account—to undue risk.

Why Use Experiments?

Think of experiments as a kind of quarantine—an isolated laboratory where the tests you run can't wreck you if they fail. The big benefit is being able to effectively limit the new idea to impact only a small portion of your traffic.

Imagine that you're considering testing a new bidding model on one of your major campaigns. That could cost you a significant amount of money, so it carries risk. But what if you could try out the idea on just a small portion of your campaign? The risk would be far less, and if it proved profitable, you could easily expand it to the rest of your campaign. (If it didn't work, you could simply end the experiment, with little to no harm done.)

And Google makes it easy to see the results of your experiments. No time-consuming double handling of data; no exporting Excel to create pivot tables; none of that.

How to Set Up Your Experiment

Always start with a hypothesis—the idea you're going to test. In other words, *if I do X, I expect Y to happen, which will mean Z for my business.*

A real-life example would look like this:

If I switch to the Target CPA bidding model and set my target at $55, I expect to get more conversions, or a lower cost per conversion, or perhaps both, which means more profit.

Because you don't know if this hypothesis will turn out to be true, you test it. To do this:

- Pick the campaign you want to test, and write out a clear if-then hypothesis.
- Create a draft copy of your test campaign and give it a name.
- Make the changes you want to test inside the draft campaign.
- Click "Apply" to turn the draft campaign into an experiment.
- Choose what percentage of your traffic you want to direct to the experiment. To be statistically relevant, you should aim for an absolute minimum of 30 conversions in a month with each new experiment campaign. That means that if your current campaign is getting 150 conversions per month, to ensure that your experiment produces at least 30 conversions, you'll want to allocate 20 percent of your traffic to the new test campaign (150 x .20 = 30).
- Set an end date for the test.

Types of Experiments

There are several different kinds of tests you can run. Take the time to test-drive some of the experiments that can help you maximize your results.

Test a New Bid Strategy

This is the most common type of experiment.

Google's Smart Bidding algorithms can work surprisingly well, but the system isn't perfect. Before you change the bidding setting on your most important campaigns, you'll want to test the impact of that change first. Running an experiment is a great way to do this while limiting your risk.

Test the Performance of a New Landing Page Design

Let's say your web designer has created a new landing page. In the past, if you wanted to run an A/B split test to see how the new page performed, you had two options: 1) use a tool like VWO, Optimizely, or Google Optimize to do the split testing, or 2) duplicate your Google ads, point the destination URL in the new ads to your new page, and let Google rotate the traffic. That often got messy.

Now it's simpler. Create your draft campaign, set the new landing page URL as the destination for your ads, and apply that to whatever portion of your traffic you choose—10 percent, 25 percent, or more. You can now see the results of your new landing page on that percentage of your traffic and compare it to your old landing page to see which performs better.

Test a New Campaign Structure

If you inherited an existing campaign from a client, you can use experiments to test the effects of your new ad group setup against the old one. You can test the impact of creating new ads or adding in new keywords.

Measure Your Results

Let your experiment run for at least two weeks. User behavior can vary significantly over weekdays as compared to weekends. If your early results are poor, you can turn off the experiment and go back to your original campaign setup.

Google makes it easy to see how statistically significant your results are. Each metric has a little icon next to it with one, two, or three arrows pointing up or down. The more arrows you have, the more statistically relevant your experiment is.

Roll It Out

If you're convinced you've had a successful test, experiments make it easier to roll out your draft as a new replacement campaign. Just hit the Apply button and then choose Update Your Original Campaign. Or, if you prefer, you can choose Convert to a New Campaign. This will pause the original campaign and run the new experimental campaign in its place.

SEGMENTING YOUR DATA

There are a few key ways to slice up your data so that you know what exactly is happening in your campaigns. Figure 24–6 below shows how Google divides up the following common data segments for you.

- *Time.* Segmenting your data by time can show you which day of the week or hour of the day your ads perform best. It also lets you see trends over time.
- *Click Type.* This shows the type of click made by the user—typically, a click on an ad, a call, or an extension. You can tell how well your extensions are working, or how many phone calls you're generating.

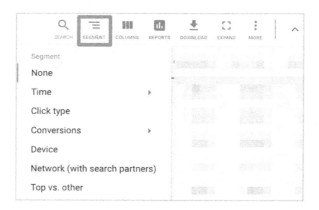

- *Device.* There are a number of different types of devices, the three most common being desktop computers, mobiles, and tablets. With the growth of YouTube ads, Google has added TVs to this list as well. No doubt more devices will be added in the future. With this you know when one or more of the device types is paying off for you . . . or costing you unnecessarily.
- *Network.* Your performance numbers on Google Search, the Display Network, and the search partner network can vary wildly. Segmenting your data by network will give you insights into how each network performs. (Note that we never recommend mixing search and display traffic within the same campaign.)
- *Top vs. Other.* This often overlooked but highly useful report shows the performance of your ads when they show above or below the organic search results. If your ads show in the "other" segment too often, try increasing your bids.

FILTERS

Let's say you want to see just the campaigns with "USA" in their name. Or you only want to see keywords with a Quality Score of three or lower. Filters allow you to do just that (see Figure 24–7).

To set this up, click on Add Filter, found between your performance graph and the data table.

If you plan to use a filter more than once, you can save it and quickly reapply it in the future.

One useful filter lets you zero in on entities (campaigns, groups, ads, keywords) with a particular label. Of course, to do that you'll need to understand how to use labels.

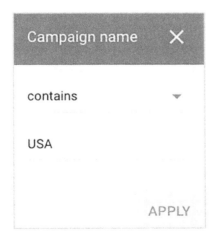

FIGURE 24–7. One of Many Ways to Filter Your Campaigns

LABELS

Labels are a useful way to help organize your Ads account. They're like tags you can quickly and easily add to various entities in your account. A label can help you remember why you made a particular change, quickly filter data, and even automate certain tasks.

For example, you could take two campaigns and label one as "Regular" and the other as "Black Friday Sale." With those labels in place, you can apply a rule to automatically pause one campaign and enable the other at a precise point in time, even in the middle of the night. (We'll talk more about rules when we discuss automation in Chapter 26.)

You can also use labels to flag something as a "to-do" item. This is great for agencies where more than one person is working on an account.

In late 2019, Google started rolling out an even more advanced version of labels called custom dimensions, which allows for a more structured and less ad hoc approach to labeling things in your account.

RECOMMENDATIONS TAB

There's a host of important features in the Ads interface that Google thinks are being underused, so they created the Recommendations page to encourage search professionals to make more use of these features.

But be cautious. These features are aimed at optimizing Google's revenue, not necessarily yours or your client's. Explore their recommendations, but take each one with a healthy dose of salt.

YOUR QUICK ACTION SUMMARY

- See what your Quality Score numbers are, and do triage in any key places that might be severely hurting you.
- Find out your impression share on your top 5 percent highest-traffic keywords.
- Try out Google experiments, starting with a new bid strategy as your first test.
- Look at your campaigns using the six types of segments we listed, and see if you can glean any special insights into your traffic.

Chapter 25

Mastering Optimization

Google Ads is a competitive auction process. But the auction isn't your primary concern—or even the other bidders competing alongside you. How you optimize your account will determine your profitability and your success in the game.

The setup you start out with won't be the one that finally delivers the results you want. Your campaigns will be in a constant state of change.

In previous chapters, we looked at how to plan, research, and build various campaign types. In this chapter, we'll explore changes you can make to improve their performance.

WHY DOES OPTIMIZATION MATTER?

Did you know that when people first started searching on mobile devices years ago, it triggered a whole new set of search queries that had never been seen before on Google? This happened again in recent years when people started doing voice searches.

The principle of trying to enter the conversation inside your customer's head will never go away. But markets change, and what people search and click on changes as well. What worked in your market a year ago might not work now. Never mind staying ahead. That's certainly your goal, but every advertiser needs to constantly optimize just to *keep up*.

When you optimize, you use data, not guesswork, to guide your decision making. And that means you save money. Online advertising is the only medium we know of where the better you get, the more your costs go down. (Certainly compared with the prices your competitors are paying.) With better clickthrough rates, you pay less per click.

WHAT CHANGES SHOULD YOU MAKE?

First, you need to decide what metric matters most to you.

For most businesses, the key metric is profit. But maybe you're aiming for the greatest volume of conversions, or the lowest possible cost per lead, or the highest return on ad spend. Some advertisers are solely interested in more reach, so they maximize the number of impressions their ads receive. At WebSavvy, profit is the metric we focus on.

Regardless, with your key metric in mind, aim for "more good, less bad." Then make whatever changes to your bidding, targeting, or messaging will improve your key metric.

WHEN SHOULD YOU MAKE CHANGES?

This is a common question. The answer depends on the size of your account. You should manage an account with a spend of $500 per month very differently from one with a budget of $500,000 per month.

We'll give you four basic time scales and a set of tasks for each scale.

Hourly and Daily

It's not possible to keep up with the volume of data inside a Google Ads account every minute—and that would be a poor use of your valuable time anyway.

The smaller your monthly or daily spend, the less likely it is you'll be logging in to check on it every day. You're looking for trends, and one day isn't enough time to spot a trend.

However, 24 hours *is* enough time for a major bug to erupt in your account, such as ads that suddenly stop serving or tracking that's broken. When those things happen, you could lose a lot of money very quickly. We recommend you check every day for this type of problem when your account or campaign is new, to get a sense of where things might go wrong. But before long, you'll want to set up your account to alert you automatically to major issues like this, using rules, scripts, and third-party tools. We'll walk you through how to do that in the next chapter.

Some questions you can ask every day, at least initially, are:

- What's happening here that I wasn't expecting? Any sudden surge in spending? Any sudden drop-off in activity?
- Is anything broken?

Weekly

Every week you'll be making changes to your bids, targeting, and messaging. You'll watch to see early trends forming.

Depending on the size of your account, you may not have the time or resources to go digging through every campaign and ad group. Observe the 80/20 Rule, and always start by examining the campaigns where you're spending the most money.

Questions you can ask every week include:

- What numbers here are starting to trend higher? Which ones are trending lower?
- Do I see any new trends among the various campaign types we're running? Among our ad groups? Among any of our individual keywords or audiences we're targeting?
- I've made changes in recent weeks. How have my ads performed differently since those changes?

Monthly

Each month you'll take a step back to look at your account from a higher perspective. You want to think of new strategies or experiments you can apply and look for longer-term trends.

Some questions you can ask each month are:

- How are each of my campaign types performing? Are there new campaign types I could be using?
- We did a new promotion recently. How did that do?
- What new experiments can we run? What new betas can we test?

Quarterly

Finally, on a quarterly basis, you'll take an even higher-level look at your account and think about your overall advertising strategy and how Google fits in your business. Some questions you can ask every quarter include:

- What assumptions are we making about our customers, our market, and our products or services? Are those assumptions still valid?
- What are we tracking? Are our conversion values correct? What else could we be tracking?
- What other marketing channels could we be using?
- Have our business objectives changed? Is our marketing still aligned with those objectives?
- What big changes are coming to the business? To our marketing and sales? To our website?

If you're an agency, we highly recommend that you do a quarterly business review just like this with each of your major clients.

For the shorter time frames, there are a number of tasks and inquiries you can automate, especially hourly tasks and alerts for issues and malfunctions. On the other end, quarterly tasks are very human-centered and strategic, so no machine can do those for you. Weekly tasks sit in the middle and may require a mix of the human touch and automation.

Automation is the subject of the next chapter.

YOUR QUICK ACTION SUMMARY

Get yourself into a good rhythm of evaluating and optimizing your campaigns.

- Choose the metric most important to you: profit, conversions, cost per lead, return on ad spend.
- When your campaign or account is new, check daily for major fires or mishaps.
- Check in each week to make changes to your bids, targeting, and messaging.
- Each month, think of new strategies or experiments you can apply. Look for longer-term trends.
- Do a quarterly evaluation of your campaigns to see how well your Google advertising is helping you reach your larger goals.

Chapter 26

Automate the Grunt Work and Manage Campaigns with Ease

One of the first giant 80/20 leaps you'll take in your business comes when you delegate or even outsource the low-dollar repetitive tasks you've been wasting hours on every week. When you get the low-value work off your plate, you can focus on the high-leverage, high-value stuff that's the real reason you got into business in the first place.

There's a good chance you've thought at some point during the workday, "If I could just automate this . . ." And we'll bet that if you haven't had that thought about your Google Ads account, you will soon. This is equally true of creative tasks (such as ad writing and keyword research) and data-driven tasks like reporting. There's tremendous value in having key data handed to you in an easy-to-use format rather than having to search for it, dig it up, clean it off, polish it, and interpret it.

That's where automation comes in.

Automation is the future of Google Ads. Any PPC agency that *doesn't* use it will soon be dead and buried. No exaggeration.

On a more practical level, it's a great way to keep your team happy, even if you're not an agency. By automating the grunt work, you can all spend less time on mundane tasks like bid management and more time on strategy and customer relationships—the stuff of business that really makes a difference.

HOW TO SET UP AUTOMATED RULES

Google has given you an incredibly useful tool set called "rules" that is a great way to get your feet wet with automation. A rule is like a note or reminder you can set up that says, "Hey, Google, if you ever see such-and-such happening with any of my ads or campaigns, please take the following action." And Google will do just that.

A single rule will run just once per day. But you can have lots of rules in a campaign. Examples are nearly endless:

- You can set up an ad to begin running on a certain date that your offer or promotion starts and then pause when the offer expires. This is useful if you're running a holiday promotion or a short-term sale.
- You can tell Google to increase your bids on certain days when you know you can get better-quality traffic, or decrease your bids on days when there's less worthwhile activity.
- If a campaign has been spending too much money, you can wind down the budget toward the end of the month.
- If a keyword is performing poorly, you can reduce its bid or pause it.
- You can send yourself an email to notify you that a rule was just run, or that you hit a certain percentage of your daily budget, or that there's an error you need to go fix.

Since any one rule will run just once per day, beware of a catastrophic error that could do damage before Google catches it. Make sure you understand the changes you're requesting before you hand over the reins to the Google machine, and keep a close eye on any new rules you put in place.

To set up a rule, click Tools & Settings at the top of the page, and under Bulk Actions select Rules. Under the Automated Rules tab, click the big blue + button and (as Figure 26–1 on page 233 shows) you'll see a nice long list of rule categories.

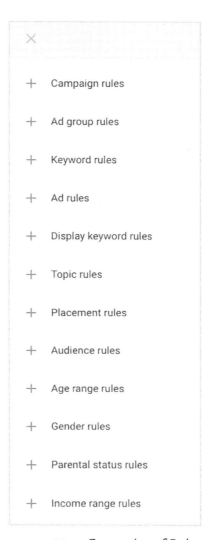

FIGURE 26–1. Categories of Rules

Once you've mastered rules and want to try something even more powerful, you can move on to Google Ads scripts.

WHAT ARE SCRIPTS?

Scripts are pieces of code or mini programs that run inside your Google Ads account and let you manage certain aspects of your account automatically. Similar to rules, they can make changes to your account or send you an email alert when certain conditions happen inside your account, but they have much greater power and flexibility than rules.

Scripts can automatically make changes in your account—for example, you can use a script to add a label to a keyword, ad group, campaign, or ad. They can also help you identify problems sooner. Should something go wrong in your account, you can set up a script to email you, such as: "Note: Impressions have dropped by 50 percent week-over-week on this ad group." Or they can help you find broken links (404 pages) quickly in an account that you might be sending a lot of traffic through.

Scripts let you do highly customized reporting. Let's say you've got a Google spreadsheet set up with an established template—a dashboard, charts, and so on. The right script can push your Google Ads data into that spreadsheet and populate it according to your template. You can even push tables of data into emails. That way, your reporting comes to you automatically with little to no effort.

You can get seriously creative with your scripts. You can use anything with an API (application programming interface) as a source of data that your script can refer to. For example, you can pull in data on the current weather in a particular city. If there's a sudden snowstorm, you can adjust your ads automatically to promote your specialty snow shovels.

You could have an inventory feed so that your ads automatically pause when a product is out of stock or down to the last one or two units. You can set it so that prices and availability change automatically in your ads based on the data in your feed.

Automated rules are a useful tool, but scripts are more powerful. One of the limitations of rules is that they can only run once per day. Scripts, however, can be scheduled to run up to once an hour.

You can run scripts at the Google Ads manager account level, rather than individual accounts. You are limited to 50 accounts at a time, but this is powerful if you're managing a lot of accounts and need to automate functions and alerts.

Scripts involve code, but you don't need to be a coder! If you can cut and paste, then getting started is quick and easy.

HOW TO SET UP A SCRIPT

Click on the Tools & Settings icon at the top of your page, and under Bulk Actions choose Scripts.

Click on the big blue + sign, and you'll be taken to a code window, where the first three lines of code have been written for you. Assuming you're more of a Google Ads person than a coder, we'll find some existing code that you can cut and paste.

Click the Documentation blue link on the upper right, and select Examples to find a stack of scripts ready for you to use immediately.

The Samples section of this page is useful, but they require some work to be functional in a script. If you don't know any code, start with the Solutions section, as all the code you need is written here for you.

We recommend choosing a script that won't make changes to your account to start. Try picking one from the Reports section. Copy the code. In the code window, remove the three default lines of code and paste in your new reporting script.

Give a name to your script where you see Unnamed Script. You'll need to authorize it, as it will be making changes to your account. (This is Google providing a layer of safety.)

Next, hit the blue Preview link on the lower right. Always preview your script before you save it and schedule it to run.

Once you have the script in your account, you can either click the Run button or the +Create schedule link. Scheduling options include hourly, daily, weekly, monthly, one time, or none. (For example, you could schedule the script to run just once at 1 A.M. on August 18 or every day at 4 P.M.)

USEFUL AND SIMPLE SCRIPTS (FREEBIES!)

We mentioned above that you should start with a few scripts that won't change anything in your account but simply report on the data they've found.

Here's a good example of such a script. Set it up, and it will send you an email every day that not only tells you the impression score of your account but also sends you a chart so that you can see what's happening in the account at a glance.

This URL will take you to a text file of the script. Check out the ones available here http://goo.gl/4nkVfx. Go there, copy the code, and paste it into the code window of your Google Ads script editor (remember to delete the three default lines of code that are already there!). Change the email address at the top to indicate where you would like your daily notifications sent. Name the script and authorize it. Preview it, save it, and schedule it to run daily.

You can find loads of script examples to copy on Google's developer site for both single accounts and manager accounts. Check them out here: https://developers.google.com/google-ads/scripts.

The link checker script—which you can use at the Google Ads manager account level—checks for any broken links on your site. (You don't want to waste money on ads going to "Page not found" 404 error pages.) That's a useful tool you'll find here: https://developers.google.com/google-ads/scripts/docs/solutions/link-checker.

Scroll down to Google's setup instructions and find the link checker template (a Google spreadsheet) that you'll need to store the output from this script. Make a copy of the sheet and give it a name of your own. Once you have that, go to the address bar in your browser, select and copy the URL, go back into Google Ads, and paste the URL into the fifth line of code where it says "SPREADSHEET_URL =". (This deletes the placeholder code that's currently there.)

Paste in Google's code. Then name the script and authorize, preview, save, and schedule it.

Another great place to find scripts is Search Engine Land (https://searchengineland.com).

GOOGLE ADS EDITOR

Google Ads Editor is a free tool provided by Google that you can use to make bulk changes to your accounts. This used to be an invaluable tool that every Google Ads professional needed to master, but Google has gradually moved most of the Editor's functionality directly into the regular Ads interface. Certain bulk actions may take a bit more time in the interface, but it saves having to learn a separate new tool.

That said, there are two main use cases where you might prefer the Editor:

1. *When you need to make ad group, campaign, and account changes on a large scale.* With the Editor, you can select a group of campaigns and work on all the ad groups, keywords, and ad extensions together within that subset of campaigns. You can work on multiple accounts at once. You can do bulk copying and pasting. For example, if you need to copy an entire campaign (or even multiple campaigns) from one account to another, this feature is a massive timesaver.
2. *When you want to use custom rules.* The Editor comes with roughly 30 rules out of the box that can be customized to your liking. You can set up rules to look for typos or misspellings, to ensure that you're using the correct bidding strategy, to find ad groups that are missing ads or keywords, and much more.

An important note if you have accounts with multiple managers: Be sure that every time you use the Editor you refresh your data so you can see all the most recent changes.

Third-Party Tools

Of the wide range of third-party tools available to you that are worth exploring, we can highly recommend three.

Optmyzr (https://www.optmyzr.com/) and Opteo (https://opteo.com/) are both powerful tools designed for a wide range of Google Ads professionals, from beginner to expert. They help you build new campaigns and optimize existing ones. Each has its benefits and quirks, so experiment to find which one suits you best.

PPC Samurai (https://ppcsamurai.com/) is for expert users. It offers a visual interface and incredible power, but you'll need to know what you want it to do. Opteo and Optmyzr guide you through the optimization process with a number of prompts and suggestions, whereas PPC Samurai starts with a blank canvas, so you can build the automations yourself.

TROUBLESHOOTING YOUR AD CAMPAIGNS

It's impossible to come up with an exhaustive list of everything that could go wrong in a Google Ads account. But let's look at a common issue for beginners: What if your ads aren't showing? Here's a troubleshooting checklist that will help.

Start with the Ad Preview Tool. Click on the Tools & Settings icon at the top of the page, and under Planning select Ad Preview and Diagnosis. Enter a search term and a keyword you're bidding on, and the tool will tell you if your ad is showing for that term. If it's not, see if one of the following issues is the reason:

- *Ad approval.* Check that your ad has been approved. It may still be under review. If it's been disapproved because you violated one of Google's policies, you'll need to contact them to find a solution.
- *Billing.* In order for your ads to run, you'll need to ensure that your billing details are up to date. For example, if your credit card has expired, your ads won't run.
- *Location.* Make sure that the geographic targeting of your campaign reflects where you want to show your ads.
- *Budget.* If your budget is too low, your ads may not show. One of the fastest ways to improve an account that's already working is simply to increase campaign budgets.
- *Keywords.* Check that the keyword match types you're using are not too restrictive. Also check that your keywords are not marked as "low search volume." If there aren't enough people searching for the keywords you've chosen, Google won't show your ads. Check that you don't have a conflicting negative keyword that is blocking your ad, and make sure your keyword Quality Score is high enough.
- *Bids.* If you're not seeing your ad on a particular device, check that the device bid adjustments are set appropriately and that the base bids for your keywords are high enough. You can use Google's Keyword Planner to get a sense of the typical CPC for each keyword.
- *Enable everything.* Check that your campaign, ad group, keyword, and ad are all set to "enabled" and that nothing is paused.

- *Audience.* If you're using audience targeting, check that it's set to Observation and not to Targeting. Check the size of your audience; if it's too small, it can't be used as a targeting criterion.
- *Ad schedule.* If you're not seeing your ad, and everything else is set up correctly, it might be because you or someone else inadvertently set an ad schedule. Double-check the times of the day your ads are set to turn on and off, and check the time zone setting of the account as well.

YOUR QUICK ACTION SUMMARY

Google's automation tools are a terrific playground for experimentation.

- Start by setting up a few simple email alerts that will catch any big changes or errors in your ad campaigns.
- Play around with a few scripts. Take the examples we provided and try them out on one or two accounts.
- Check out the free scripts available from Google and from sites like Search Engine Land and Optmyzr. You can simply copy and paste them, so they're worth exploring, testing, and using.
- Use the Editor any time you need to 1) make a bulk change involving multiple ads, ad groups, or campaigns; or 2) work on multiple accounts.

Chapter 27

Google Analytics:
Know Exactly Where Your Visitors Come From and Where They're Going

A year after I escaped my "Dilbert" cube and started my consulting firm, I got an ecommerce client who had a large website and sent out a million catalogs a year. When we began working together, they didn't track much of anything. I smacked my hand down on the conference room table and said, "Well, that's going to stop right now." I was confident (even a little cocky), so we rolled up our sleeves and went to work. Consider this chapter your personal hand-smacking moment. We're going to introduce you to the analytics tools you need to succeed in your Google Ads efforts.

A MILLION-DOLLAR AD TRACKING DISCOVERY FROM MY FIRST BIG CLIENT

As I said, this company mailed out a million catalogs a year to a list made up of current and former customers and names rented from 16 different trade magazines. The impact of the catalog mailings was obvious: Like clockwork, sales spiked two weeks after the catalogs went out, as did visits to the website.

But which of those 16 rented mailing lists were actually working, and which ones were a waste of money? How much of the website traffic came from the catalog? What percentage of online sales came from PPC traffic, and what percentage came from organic free listings? And how about blasts to the email list?

At this time, I was solidly grounded in direct-marketing techniques, so I expected it to be easy.

Boy, was I wrong.

It might have been easy to track sales generated by the catalog if we used different part numbers in the catalog than we used on the website. But that would cause endless confusion in tracking inventory. We could track different mailing lists if we printed different versions of the catalog with different part numbers in each version, but that would make things even worse.

Some customers called on the phone; others ordered online. Sometimes the engineer specifying the product ordered it himself, and sometimes he sent the order over to purchasing. Sometimes the product got installed in Philadelphia where the customer ordered it, and other times it got shipped to an oil refinery in Houston.

In short, connecting the dots on every sale was essentially impossible. I quickly realized that despite my direct-marketing dogma about measuring absolutely everything, I had to focus on what *contributing factors* were influential in closing the sale.

The first thing we tested were the 16 rented mailing lists. We did this by mailing out postcards to portions of each list, offering a white paper. That was easy to measure, and we figured that the response to a white paper offer would reasonably approximate their likelihood to buy from a catalog.

You're probably not surprised by this point to find out that 80 percent of the responses came from four of those 16 lists. The other 12 were a waste of money. We immediately cut our catalog mailing volume in half—and lowered our costs significantly—with almost no loss of sales.

As we began to measure more and more contributing factors to each sale, we cut out more and more waste. The money they were spending on stuff that didn't work started going to things that did. In short, the company quadrupled its sales over the next ten years—despite being in a very slow-moving, declining industry.

Even if you don't mail out a million catalogs a year, don't do a lot of off-line marketing, and your customers don't hand their orders off to a purchasing agent in Houston, you still need to measure those contributing factors. Sure, in theory, people should see your Google ad, click on it, and buy, and everything should be trackable. But real life is almost always messier than that. That's why Google Analytics (GA) can be a big help. With GA, you almost always have at least a decent idea of what factors are influencing your customers to buy.

WHAT HAPPENS AFTER THE CLICK?

Google Ads is great at telling you which of your ads are getting clicks and even which of those clicks result in conversions. But what about the traffic you get from organic search or through your email campaigns? How do those sources convert? Are their conversions better than what you're getting from PPC?

Also, what about all the people who didn't convert? What did they do on your site? How long did they spend reading your pages? What videos did they watch? What outbound links did they click on?

And which of your pages need improving? Which pages are already working well? Google Ads can't answer those questions, but Google Analytics can.

Many people are intimidated by Google Analytics. Even the name sounds über-technical and daunting. But don't freak out. Plug GA into your reporting system, learn to watch and respond to it, and you *will* improve your PPC results and become a better marketer.

FIRST STEP: MACRO VS. MICRO CONVERSIONS

Let's say you're an ecommerce site owner and 1 percent of your visitors make a purchase.

You can study this 1 percent as much as you like in your Google Ads reporting—which keywords people searched on, which ads they clicked, where the users are located, what time of day they made their purchases, and so on—but none of that will tell you anything worthwhile about the other 99 percent.

You could be converting at 10 percent (a rate most online retailers would kill for), but that would still leave 90 percent of your traffic passing anonymously through your site, leaving you with no clue as to what, if anything, interested them.

This is where GA can help. The first step is to understand the difference between macro and micro conversions.

A *macro conversion* is the main action or actions you want your visitor to take. If you run an ecommerce site, you want them to make a purchase. If you run a lead-generation site, you want them to give you their contact details.

How to Dig Deeper into Analytics

This chapter is only a very basic introduction to Google Analytics. It's enough to get you started. If you want to fully master this area of marketing, we highly recommend Chris Mercer's MeasurementMarketing.io or Julian Juenemann's Measureschool (https://measureschool.com/).

Micro conversions, then, are everything else that represents a positive step *toward* that macro conversion, no matter how small. That could include taking a quiz, downloading a brochure, visiting your contact page, looking at one of your social media pages, or watching a video.

The more you know about which micro conversions people are completing—and about the people themselves—the better equipped you are to optimize your Google Ads campaigns. With that knowledge, you can shift more and more of your budget toward profitable keywords and demographics and away from the unprofitable ones.

What are all the possible actions on your site that you want visitors to do? Browse through your site and jot them down. Seriously—every last one.

Next set up these macro and micro conversions as "goals" in your GA account. Figure 27-1 below shows you how to do this. Go to the Admin tab inside your Analytics account, look under the View column for the Goals section, and create your goals there.

FIGURE 27-1. How to Create Your Goals

Google will walk you through the process. One of the steps will be to assign a value to each goal.

ASSIGNING VALUES TO YOUR GOALS

There's no scientific formula for how much value you should give to each conversion or goal. An easy way to determine value is to assign points to each conversion or goal. The goals that move people closer to converting get more points, and the conversion itself gets the most points. We recommend you start with the smallest micro conversion and assign it one point. Then work your way up through all the various goals you'd like to use.

If, for instance, you're an ecommerce site owner, clicking on one of your social media buttons might be worth one point. Interacting with your store locator could be five points, downloading a brochure could be ten points, and buying a $200 item could be 200 points.

Don't get hung up on trying to assign a dollar value for each action your visitor takes. That isn't the point of this exercise. The idea is simply to set a consistent scoring system so you can directly compare the different metrics on which GA reports.

With a crude points system in place, you can compare traffic sources. If the average visitor to your site via Google Ads performs five points' worth of micro conversions but visitors arriving via your email campaigns perform 20 points' worth, you can then dig deeper and figure out what's making the difference.

Maybe visitors from your email campaign are arriving at one landing page while your Google Ads visitors are going to another, and that's why there's a discrepancy. Comparing your micro conversions in this way tips you off to what is and isn't working.

You can compare many other things, too.

Even Better Analytics Data with Google's Campaign URL Builder

If you're running ads on networks other than Google Ads, use Google's Campaign URL Builder to properly tag your traffic. With this tool, Analytics can compile data and let you do comparisons.

For example, how does the quality of your paid Google traffic compare to your Facebook ads? Or how does either of these traffic sources compare to the direct media ads you bought? You can find the Campaign URL Builder at https://ga-dev-tools.appspot.com/campaign-url-builder/.

Which geographic areas give you visitors with the highest scores? Do visitors from Houston score higher on average than visitors from Chicago? If so, you might want to adjust your Google Ads campaign to bid higher and attract more Houston folks.

What about your ads on GDN? Does showing them on site A give you more conversion points than site B? Or are they both flops?

GA can help answer all these questions. Are you beginning to see the power that Analytics gives you to improve your Google Ads campaigns?

HOW TO GET GOOGLE ADS AND ANALYTICS TALKING TO EACH OTHER

It's possible to have a Google Ads account *and* an Analytics account without the two ever communicating, but that's not helpful. If they're going to work properly, you'll want to link them. Here's how:

1. Make sure you have admin privileges for both accounts and that both use the same login email address.
2. Go to your GA account and navigate to the Admin tab. Now find Property Settings in the middle column, and click on Google Ads Linking below it. Click New Link Group, and select your Google Ads account from the list shown.
3. Look under Account Settings in the left-hand column of the Admin tab and make sure you've checked the box (see Figure 27–2 below) next to Google Products & Services.
4. In Google Ads, while viewing all campaigns, click Settings in the menu on the left. From there, click the Account Settings tab at the top. Under Auto-Tagging (see

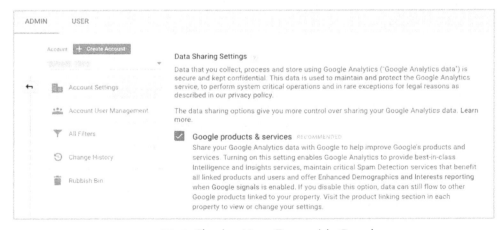

FIGURE 27–2. Sharing Your Data with Google

FIGURE 27–3. Enable Auto-Tagging

Figure 27–3 above), ensure that Tag the URL That People Click Through from My Ad is selected.

5. Finally, click on Tools & Settings at the top of the page, and under Setup click Linked Accounts, as shown in Figure 27–4 below. Look for the Google Analytics section. Click on Details, and make sure that your Google Ads account is linked to the correct Google Analytics view.

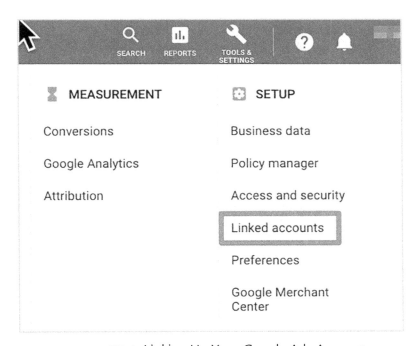

FIGURE 27–4. Linking Up Your Google Ads Account

Once you've completed this, you'll get more useful reports about your Google Ads traffic in GA. The two you'll be most interested in are:

- *Source/Medium report.* This is the report you'll need most frequently. At a high level, it shows how Google Ads (labeled as "google/cpc") is performing compared with other sources of traffic.
- *Google Ads–specific reports.* You'll find these under the Acquisition menu. (See Figure 27-5 below.) There's lots of valuable data here, so dig in and see what you can find.

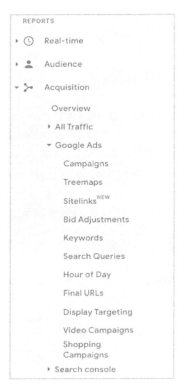

FIGURE 27–5. Options for Analytics Reports

ANALYTICS REMARKETING

We devoted Chapter 14 to remarketing, the single most cost-effective tool in your Google tool belt. The good news is that it works *even better* when you integrate it with Analytics—another good reason to link your accounts immediately.

Recall that with remarketing you build audience lists based on what actions people take on your site. Without integrating GA with your Google Ads account, your options are limited. For example, a business owner who specializes in coffee products might create a list just of people who visited pages under her site's/coffeemachines/directory.

But once you integrate GA, you can create scores of additional lists based on a myriad of other factors, including:

- The device a visitor used to access your site
- The length of each person's visit
- The amount of money a person spent
- The number of pages a person visited

You can even tie your remarketing lists to individual micro conversion goals: everyone who took your quiz, downloaded your brochure, watched a certain video, etc.

Revisit Chapter 14 on remarketing for a fuller discussion of this technique. For now, make sure you've carried out these two steps:

1. Update your privacy policy.
2. Go to the Admin section of GA, and under the Property column you'll find the Audience Definitions section. Click to expand it, and click on Audiences to find the option Add New Audience. (See Figure 27-6 below.)

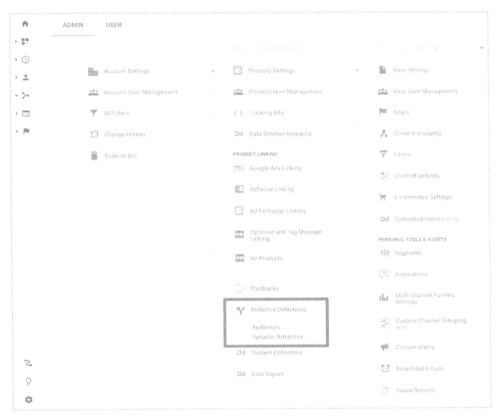

FIGURE 27-6. Defining Your Audience

ATTRIBUTION

This is a hot topic. Let's say your prospect hears about you on the radio. They do a Google search and click on your ad. Then they go back to Google to search on your brand name, click on your website link in the organic listings, and buy from you.

Which of these gets credit for the sale: your radio ad, your paid search campaign, or your organic listing?

Officially, Google will "attribute" the sale to the last click—in this case, your natural search listing. But real life is much more complicated. Every element in the process played its part. How significant was the radio ad? How much did the organic listings contribute?

Google has a tool to help answer this, called Multi-Channel Funnels. If you want to unlock the full power of Analytics, this is well worth investigating. Read about it at https://support.google.com/analytics/answer/1191180.

Unfortunately, there's no such thing as a perfect attribution model. Every model makes certain assumptions about which type of traffic is best. We can't tell you which model to use; we can only tell you to be sure you know what your model is telling you about the data. Here's a brief overview of the six attribution models Google uses:

1. *Last click.* This is the default model. Google Ads assigns 100 percent of the credit to the last ad that got the click. Google Analytics assigns credit to the last nondirect click in the customer's journey—in other words, it ignores direct traffic and backtracks to the last place the customer clicked through.
2. *First click.* This is the opposite of last click. In this case, the very first click you received from the customer gets 100 percent of the credit.
3. *Linear.* With this, every touch point in the customer journey gets equal credit for the conversion.
4. *Position-based.* This gives 40 percent of the credit to the first click, 40 percent to the last click, and the other clicks in the middle divide the remaining 20 percent equally among them.
5. *Time decay.* More recent clicks get more credit. That way, all clicks along the customer's path receive some credit, with higher weight given to the latest activity.
6. *Data-driven.* This is a machine-learning-based model, in which Google assigns a portion of the credit to each click along the way. One day this will be the default model, but for now it's available only to accounts with significant accumulated data from months or even years of activity across multiple campaigns and ad groups.

GOOGLE TAG MANAGER (GTM)

A timesaving way to install Google Analytics code on your website is by using Google Tag Manager. GTM eliminates the hassle of having to manually add or edit code on every page of your site. You'll need your web developer to help you set this up, but once it's done, you can easily manage or make future changes to the code yourself.

Think of GTM as an empty box (which Google calls a "container") on every page of your site. You can then add snippets of code (referred to as "tags") to the box so they're all organized in one place. For example, if you wanted to update your site's thank-you page, you wouldn't have to edit code on multiple pages. Instead, you make just one small change in GTM, which updates the coding on all your pages.

GA tags send information about activity on your site to Google—who visits which pages and how long they stay. You can add Google Ads conversion code and remarketing code into GTM as well. Plus, there are more advanced options, such as setting up events in Analytics or using GTM's Data Layer tool. Those are beyond the scope of this book, and so you'll want to have your web developer assist you with those. For more information, visit the Google Help Center at https://support.google.com/tagmanager/answer/6102821.

YOUR QUICK ACTION SUMMARY

Analytics is a gateway to learning more about your visitors and efficiently comparing your marketing efforts in real time.

- Make an exhaustive list of all the macro and micro conversions on your site—the actions, large and small, that visitors on your site can take.
- Create goals in Google Analytics for each macro and micro conversion.
- Assign a relative value to each goal.
- Link your Google Ads and GA accounts.
- Tweak your GA account to give you a greater range of remarketing options.
- Set up at least one remarketing audience.
- Ask your web developer to set up a GTM account, and add the GTM container to each page on your site.

Chapter 28

How to Hire the Right Google Ads Agency

One of my New Renaissance Club members, Bill Crawford, owned a basement waterproofing franchise in Chicago. Bill honed his Google Ads chops and found out (as is often the case) that even in a narrow niche like "basement waterproofing," in a limited geographical area like Chicago, you can attract a great deal of traffic if you build your campaigns properly.

His lead flow expanded dramatically in just three months, and his business went from struggling to prospering. Inevitably, he started talking about his success at franchisor meetings. Almost without trying, he picked up 16 clients—other franchisors around the country. He was able to easily replicate in other metro areas what he'd so painstakingly set up in his hometown. Suddenly, he had a devoted online following, and he had unwittingly become the world's number-one expert on Google Ads for basement waterproofing companies.

Many PPC experts, consultants, and agencies have sprung from similar circumstances. Hiring the right agency can be a huge boon for your business, too. But hiring the right agency is hard—a *lot* harder than finding a good accountant or attorney!

In this chapter, we'll walk you through 11 key qualifying questions you should ask before hiring any agency and suggest the best payment model for getting the results you need. We'll also show you how to sidestep the deadly pitfall of handing full ownership of your Google Ads account to someone else, while still getting the management help you need.

A WORD OF WARNING BEFORE YOU OUTSOURCE

This chapter is about how to identify a good agency. But before we begin, I want to once again emphasize the value and importance of mastering Google Ads yourself. If you have your hand on the throttle—buying the clicks, picking the keywords, writing the ads—you have your finger on the pulse of your marketing. You will gain deep insights and an intimacy with your customers that you cannot get anywhere else. Even though you view your customers only through columns of data, you are indirectly touching hundreds, thousands, or even tens of thousands of people.

There is no substitute for this. And there are few employees in any company more valuable than the person who buys the web traffic—especially when it's done right.

That's why you should only outsource your Google Ads campaigns with great care, and you must have full confidence in the person who manages them for you. Keep in mind that fewer than 10 percent of the Google Ads agencies in the world have even mastered most of what's in this book, let alone all of it. The other day, I met the founder of a $40 million company. He was chief shareholder and CEO, and he was still managing his own Google Ads because he hadn't found someone with the chops to do it properly.

Nevertheless, if you're handling your Google Ads well, your account will grow and your business will prosper right along with it. And as your business expands, every minute of your working day will become more valuable.

Eventually, you'll reach the point where your time is so highly prized that you can't afford to manage keywords and ads anymore. Optimizing your Google Ads campaigns is easily $100-per-hour or even $1,000-per-hour work, but you'll know you can find $10,000-per-hour work elsewhere.

At that point, it's time for someone else to take over the reins, so plan for that moment now. Decide you're going to hand your account off to capable people long before your PPC campaigns start to show signs of neglect.

Before we go on, though, let me make two things clear:

1. *Google Ads is not easy to outsource.* Typically, it's one of the hardest marketing jobs you can hand off to an outside person or firm. The money wasted by incompetent agencies around the world adds up to tens of billions of dollars of pure larceny.

2. *You should not outsource it too soon.* It's doubly hard to outsource if you don't thoroughly understand it yourself. Time spent learning Google Ads is *never* wasted. I can't tell you how many customers have said to me, "Perry, I learned Google Ads from you in 2005, and I've applied all the stuff I learned from you in all kinds of other situations that had nothing to do with Ads." Google Ads itself is the best direct-marketing education I know of. It's also a lucrative career for a consultant when the client understands the value of both Google Ads and the consultant's expertise.

Onward. You have two options for finding a manager for your Google account: 1) hire someone in-house or 2) hire an agency.

If you go in-house, they will have more intimate knowledge of your business, objectives, values, immediate plans, and so on.

Most people choose the in-house option to save money. But we believe this is a false economy. Any savings you get by hiring someone internally is easily dwarfed by the increase in profits that a quality agency can provide.

Google Ads–focused agencies give you a number of other benefits that internal employees will struggle to match:

- PPC is all they do, so these agencies have the time and motivation to keep up with Google's perpetual changes, improvements, and tweaks. In fact, this is probably the biggest argument for not doing it yourself.
- By managing multiple accounts, an agency can spot patterns and effective strategies that you might never notice working on your single account.
- Good agencies will have direct access to a Google representative—possibly more than one.
- Google often provides agencies with access to beta features before they're rolled out to the general public.

If you're ready to let a professional take the wheel of your Google account, nine times out of ten an agency is the smartest choice. But deciding to go the agency route doesn't mean your job is over. The difference between the best and worst agencies is a gap the size of the Grand Canyon. And bad agencies incinerate dollar bills at a frightening pace.

Next are some guidelines to help you make a confident choice.

WHAT PAYMENT MODEL SHOULD YOU FOLLOW?

Most PPC agencies will use one of the following three payment models.

1. Percentage of Spend

Expect them to charge something in the region of 10 to 20 percent of your total Google Ads spend. An agency may charge a bit more if your account is small, but anything above this range is dangerously close to overcharging.

Frankly, we're not fans of this payment model, since it gives the agency an obvious incentive to increase your ad spend. Yes, you want your business to grow, and you want to be able to spend more to attract the best customers. But a truly good agency should want to decrease your costs and increase your profits—not your spend.

2. Fixed Fee

This is simple, straightforward, and generally comfortable, since you always know where your agency stands. It's a good, reliable payment model.

3. Performance-Based

In this model, the agency offers to reduce your cost per action (CPA) to a fixed number, or perhaps to an agreed-upon percentage that's below your historical average. Then you pay them when they achieve it.

This sounds good in theory, and it can sometimes work. But tread carefully.

Let's say you have three keywords on your account, with CPAs of $5, $10, and $20, respectively. An agency might offer to reduce your average CPA to below $10. But how can they accomplish this?

An unscrupulous one would just shut down the $20 CPA keyword, even if that one brings in 80 percent of your leads and sales. Your average CPA has certainly dropped, but what has it done to your business?

A good agency is motivated to maximize your profits. You need to be certain that it has your best interests at heart if you go with this model.

You can also combine incentive models by, say, paying a retainer plus a percentage of ad spend and a percentage of sales.

11 QUESTIONS TO ASK BEFORE HIRING AN AGENCY

Some carry more weight than others, but none of these questions is trivial. See how many you can answer by researching the websites of the agencies on your shortlist. After that, speak to each agency directly to obtain answers to everything else.

1. Did the Person Who Is Going to Be Managing Your Google Ads Account Learn on Their Own Dime?

This is the acid test for account managers. Figuring out how to make a Google campaign profitable *using your own money* makes you get smart faster than anything else. Your mistakes are directly painful, and you never forget the lessons you learn. (Contrast this with an employee who is assured of a paycheck regardless of whether their traffic converts.)

If you plan to hire an agency (or employee or contractor) to manage your campaigns, *ask them to **prove** to you that they have built a successful, profitable campaign with their own money.* This is the gold standard.

The next best option is the contractor, employer, or agency who learned on someone else's dime but was incentivized by commissions to make the campaigns succeed. Again, make them prove to you that their campaigns hit pay dirt.

2. Is the Agency Really an Agency?

Find out if the company is really just a one-man band. You're looking for an agency with lots of resources, experience, and personnel. You don't want your Google Ads account to be neglected because its only manager has gone on vacation or come down with the flu.

Now, we do know a handful of expert colleagues who work solo. They know Google Ads inside and out and network closely with other experts in making strategic decisions. We trust them because we know them, and they have the respect of all the top people in the industry. They're an exception to this rule.

But beware of lone-ranger account managers who come with no credentials, no certification, and no backing of any kind.

3. What Services Does the Agency Offer?

The best answer is that they specialize in PPC and do little else. If they also offer search engine optimization (SEO), social media, web design, print fulfillment, and lots more, it's a red flag. Some companies will say that they offer PPC when it's really only a sideline or they outsource that service.

If you need knee surgery, you don't go to a general practitioner or a heart doctor. You get a specialist. PPC campaigns are no different. You're looking for stone-cold professionals who are obsessed with PPC. Your business deserves nothing less.

And never, ever just let your webmaster handle it or toss it to your IT guy.

4. How Did You Hear About the Agency?

The absolute best circumstances under which to hire an agency are:

1. A trusted colleague recommended the firm to you, or
2. You heard one of the agency's senior managers give a brilliant talk at an event.

If you hire one of these agencies, you should still be sure to always get references or case studies from previous or current customers.

If an agency contacts *you* out of the blue, by email or phone, what does it mean? Be cautious—they may be more focused on grabbing market share than on doing a high-quality job for you, the client. Many agencies are mills, where the salespeople are far more talented than the account managers.

5. Have They Worked with Anyone Else in Your Specific Market or Vertical Niche?

If not, it isn't a deal-breaker. But it's a good sign if they have prior experience in your sector. Every niche has its own idiosyncrasies.

6. How Do They Report Their Results?

The first answer you're looking for is: They'll connect your Google Ads and Analytics accounts and will always report your Google Ads results in the context of your other traffic data.

Beyond that, you need to know what kind of reporting cycle they have and the format in which they'll deliver it. They are there to provide what you need—weekly, monthly, quarterly, annually, and anything in between!

7. What Key Performance Indicators (KPIs) Do They Use?

Bad agencies talk about number of impressions, number of clicks, CTRs, or even the position of your ads. Good agencies talk about CPAs, volume of conversions and conversion tracking, lifetime value (LTV), and profit.

8. What Account Management System Do They Use?

It's not unusual for agencies to hold back specifics in the early stages of their discussions with you—that's fine. The important thing is to know that they have a system in place and they don't just manage their accounts on an ad hoc basis.

9. Who Exactly Will Be Working on Your Account?

Once the agency relationship begins, your account isn't managed by a computer or a company; it's managed by one or more highly trained PPC experts. Don't be afraid to

> ### How to Manage Campaigns Intelligently for Profit
>
> WebSavvy uses its own proprietary system for measuring its performance for every client, known as a SavvyNumber. By making a calculation based on all the main metrics, it provides clients with an assessment of the total profit their Google Ads account has achieved each month.
>
> Overall profit should always be the primary measure of any PPC agency's abilities.

ask for specifics about the people who will be working on your account. It's even better if you can meet them in person.

WebSavvy, for instance, manages each client's account using multiple specialists. The technical experts look after things like Excel pivot tables and Google Ads scripts, while the creative experts handle writing the ad copy and designing the Display Network ads.

10. Is the Agency Certified?

The agency should at least have Google Ads certification and belong to the Google Partners program. Don't be fooled into thinking that this automatically gives the agency legitimacy, though; certification only requires passing a couple of fairly easy exams, as well as maintaining a minimum monthly Google Ads spend of $10,000—which is a relatively low bar.

We've always said that if an agency doesn't have Google Ads certification, you're dealing with amateurs. However, this may change in the future. It's looking as though Google may force their automation onto agencies, and some agencies may resist and opt out of the Partner program as a result. Only time will tell.

11. What Does Your Gut Tell You?

Don't be horrified by this question. PPC isn't an exact science, and there's always a level of artistry that goes into the equation. Similarly, choosing an agency is a decision that can't be made solely through logic.

Continue to talk to agencies until you feel comfortable with your choice. The right agency will have good business sense, communicate well without using impenetrable jargon, understand the important elements of your business, and have an in-depth knowledge of the Google Ads machine.

If you have positive answers to the above questions and you don't feel an instinctive dread that the agency does not understand you or your business or what you're trying to achieve, you may have found your winner.

WHO WILL HAVE OWNERSHIP OF YOUR ACCOUNT?

We've left this question to the end to give it some extra emphasis.

No matter how professional and successful an agency appears to be, even if they tick all the boxes, *you* must *always* retain ownership of your Google Ads account. It's *your* business asset; you're simply granting the agency access to your property.

Completely relinquishing control of your Google Ads account to an agency is like giving full control of your bank account to your bookkeeper—utterly unwise and a recipe for disaster down the line.

For one thing, if your relationship with the agency breaks down, you must be free to turn your account over to a new firm. You could of course start a new account from scratch, but that's a massive headache, especially since your account history is a factor (albeit a minor one) in your Quality Score.

You may also consider selling your business at some stage, in which case your Google Ads account is a valuable asset to pass on to the new owner.

If you're completely new to Google Ads, make sure you open an account in your name and grant the agency access. Do not have the agency create its own account on your behalf. You want ownership rights to the account, should you ever choose to switch agencies or take management in-house.

If you're unsure what does and doesn't qualify as account ownership, consider the following:

- Can you access your account from http://google.com/Ads? If you can't, and the agency insists that you log in through its own custom interface, you probably only have partial access.
- Do you have admin-level control of your Ads account, including the ability to add and remove other people's access to your account? This is essential.
- Do you know your account customer ID (usually referred to as your CID)? This is a ten-digit number that looks something like 123-456-7890.
- Do you pay Google directly for your clicks, or do you pay through the agency? You should always pay Google if possible. When all is said and done, Google considers the person or business that pays for the clicks to be the owner of the account and the data it contains.

YOUR QUICK ACTION SUMMARY

Hiring an agency is a natural next step in your Google Ads management and the growth of your business. The right choice of firm can reduce your costs, cut your time commitment, and greatly improve your results.

- Create a shortlist of agencies based on trusted recommendations or your direct personal experience.
- Research the websites of those agencies to answer as many of the 11 key qualifying questions as you can.
- Speak to the agencies directly to get answers to any remaining unanswered questions.
- Be certain to maintain admin-level ownership of your Google Ads account.
- In the end, listen to your gut! Stay away from any agency if your deepest instincts suggest they're not trustworthy.

About the Authors

PERRY MARSHALL

Perry Marshall is one of the world's most expensive and sought-after business consultants. Clients prize his ability to integrate engineering, sales, art, and psychology.

He launched two movements in modern marketing. His Google Ads books laid the foundation for the $100 billion PPC industry, and techniques he pioneered are standard best practices today. More recently, he's turned "80/20" into a verb. 80/20 is no longer a statistic about your business—it's an action you take for your business. 80/20 is the central lever for every great strategy. His book *80/20 Sales and Marketing* is required reading in many growing companies, and his books are used in several business schools.

His other works include the bestselling *Ultimate Guide to Facebook Advertising* (Entrepreneur Press, 4th ed., 2020), *Evolution 2.0: Breaking the Deadlock Between Darwin and Design* (BenBella Books, 2015), and *Industrial Ethernet* (ISA, 3rd ed., 2016).

BRYAN TODD

Bryan Todd is a writer, trainer, and management specialist in Lincoln, Nebraska. He's worked in Europe and Asia and has spent most of his career teaching—everything from foreign languages and world history to advanced testing methods for the internet. He has worked with clients in dozens of industries, from health care and book publishing to manufacturing and computer software.

MIKE RHODES

Mike Rhodes is a Google Ads evangelist. As a popular speaker, digital strategist, and CEO of WebSavvy and AgencySavvy, he loves nothing more than to dive into the Google machine, pull it apart, understand it completely, and then share that knowledge with the world.

He's been asked by Google to consult on how to improve Ads, worked directly on 1,000-plus Ads accounts, and taught thousands of business owners and marketing managers how to use its power to grow their business.

Mike founded WebSavvy in 2006 to offer a "done for you" service to those businesses that didn't want to learn how to do it themselves. His team manages tens of millions of dollars in ad spending and guarantees their results.

A devoted dad and husband, he lives in Melbourne, Australia, with his wife and two daughters.

Index

CPSIA information can be obtained
at www.ICGtesting.com
Printed in the USA
JSHW030757080921
18539JS00001BB/1